Angels Unawares

C. K. LATERN

ISBN 978-1-68517-271-8 (paperback)
ISBN 978-1-68517-272-5 (digital)

Christian Faith Publishing
832 Park Avenue
Meadville, PA 16335
www.christianfaithpublishing.com

Printed in the United States of America

PROLOGUE

There was a man in the land of Uz, whose name was Job; and that man was perfect and upright, and one that feared God, and eschewed evil.

And there were born unto him seven sons and three daughters.

His substance also was seven thousand sheep, and three thousand camels, and five hundred yoke of oxen, and five hundred she asses, and a very great household; so that this man was the greatest of all the men of the east.

And his sons went and feasted in their houses, every one his day; and sent and called for their three sisters to eat and to drink with them.

And it was so, when the days of their feasting were gone about, that Job sent and sanctified them, and rose up early in the morning, and offered burnt offerings according to the number of them all: for Job said, It may be that my sons have sinned, and cursed God in their hearts. Thus did Job continually.

Now there was a day when the sons of God came to present themselves before the Lord, and Satan came also among them.

And the Lord said unto Satan, Whence comest thou? Then Satan answered the Lord, and said, From going to and fro in the earth, and from walking up and down in it.

And the Lord said unto Satan, Hast thou considered my servant Job, that there is none like him in the earth, a perfect and an upright man, one that feareth God, and escheweth evil?

Then Satan answered the LORD, and said, Doth Job fear God for nought?

Hast not thou made an hedge about him, and about his house, and about all that he hath on every side? thou hast blessed the work of his hands, and his substance is increased in the land.

But put forth thine hand now, and touch all that he hath, and he will curse thee to thy face.

And the Lord said unto Satan, Behold, all that he hath is in thy power; only upon himself put not forth thine hand. So Satan went forth from the presence of the Lord.

And there was a day when his sons and his daughters were eating and drinking wine in their eldest brother's house:

And there came a messenger unto Job, and said, The oxen were plowing, and the asses feeding beside them:

And the Sabeans fell upon them, and took them away; yea, they have slain the servants with the edge of the sword; and I only am escaped alone to tell thee.

While he was yet speaking, there came also another, and said, The fire of God is fallen from heaven, and hath burned up the sheep, and the servants, and consumed them; and I only am escaped alone to tell thee.

While he was yet speaking, there came also another, and said, The Chaldeans made out three bands, and fell upon the camels, and have carried them away, yea, and slain the servants with the edge of the sword; and I only am escaped alone to tell thee.

While he was yet speaking, there came also another, and said, Thy sons and thy daughters were eating and drinking wine in their eldest brother's house:

And, behold, there came a great wind from the wilderness, and smote the four corners of the house, and it fell upon the young men, and they are dead; and I only am escaped alone to tell thee.

Then Job arose, and rent his mantle, and shaved his head, and fell down upon the ground, and worshipped,

And said, Naked came I out of my mother's womb, and naked shall I return thither: the Lord gave, and the Lord hath taken away; blessed be the name of the Lord.

In all this Job sinned not, nor charged God foolishly. Job 1:1-22 (KJV)

CHAPTER ONE

Guardians

SPRING

Little Stevie Thorn was playing in the sandbox with his toy cars, merrily making little sand mountains and valleys to drive them through. Mom and Dad had taken this Saturday morning to bring their three boys to the city park in Lakewood, and the sun was rising to its noonday high. Stevie's older brothers were swinging on the large city swing set with their mother. She challenged them to see who could kick the highest.

"I can go higher than you can," she teased.

"No, you can't!" shrieked Tommy as he pumped his little legs hard. Squeals of delight pealed from the two boys as they kicked higher and higher. It quickly became evident that Mom was losing the contest.

Stevie's father was sitting quietly alone at a nearby picnic table in the park's Kiwanis Pavilion. Sipping coffee from a plastic thermos cup, he lazily glanced through the morning paper.

The late spring day was promising to be a hot one, but a mild breeze off nearby Lake Erie helped to temper the bright sunlight. It almost seemed that one could see the grass grow. It was a perfect morning.

A young raccoon brazenly approached the park's playground from the parking lot at the west end of the property. It had a glazed-over look to its eyes, and a sickly white froth drooled from its furry jaw as it meandered across the parking lot towards the young family at play. Entering through an opening in the park's chain-link fence, it attacked a windblown leaf, tearing it to shreds.

The suffering animal charged anything that moved. A candy wrapper blew out of a trash can and was chased unsuccessfully. The confused raccoon then attacked and bit itself several times, working itself into a painful rage. Searching for its nonexistent attacker, a small squirrel caught its eye just to the edge of the picnic grounds. The chase was explosive but short as the squirrel easily outdistanced its pursuer. The diseased raccoon could hardly walk in a straight line, let alone run, and it fell several times with exhaustion.

The infuriated squirrel noisily cursed the raccoon from a safe perch high above on a large limb of a giant old oak tree, and it flicked its tail several times in protest.

From somewhere outside its fogged-enshrouded mind, the tormented raccoon heard the sing-song voice of a small child. It spied a small human doing something in the dirt not thirty feet away. With the rage of the disease coursing through its blood, the insane animal leaped to its feet and charged towards the toddler, just on the other side of the oak tree.

BZZZZZZZZZZZZZZT! Poof!

Without warning, a large translucent arm holding a shimmering longsword blazed out from within the large tree, neatly dissecting the raccoon in two. The dead animal simply fizzled out of existence, leaving the stench to dissipate into the air. No one saw a thing. One second it was there, then it wasn't. Fast. Clean. Unwitnessed.

The rustle of feathers seemed to catch in the wind as two winged Guardians slowly emerged from within the oak tree. Both beings carried edged weapons that occasionally caught the glint of the sun.

"I have orders," explained the larger of the two. "His time is not now. He is reserved for a higher purpose."

"But how does His Majesty know he will do it at the appointed time?" asked the smaller angel. "And why do these mortals agree to serve Him in that way?"

"No one knows," the larger Guardian replied. "We just know that sometimes they do. It's all part of His plan."

"Wook!" cried out Stevie with eyes opened wide. "Wook it!"

He pointed at the large oak tree.

"Wook! Wook at *dem!*"

The three-year-old ran up to the two angels, and it was quite apparent that he could see them. They rose from the ground to the branch where the squirrel had found sanctuary from the raccoon. The squirrel also started to chatter away at the floating pair.

"Seems as if we've been found out," said the fair-haired larger Guardian.

"I still don't understand how the animals and these little ones can sometimes see us," said his dark-skinned companion.

The boy's mother trotted over to reel in her wayward son.

"Oh, that's just a squirrel, honey. You've seen squirrels before. Let's go play with your cars. Vroom! Vroom! Vroom!"

Pulling him back to the sandbox, she helped him find his toys buried in the sand.

*****

Later that evening, she prepared Stevie for his bath. After he had been stripped naked and safely deposited into the tub, she gathered up his dirty clothes for the wash. The inexhaustible toddler was busy playing with one of his brother's winged action figures, flying it around, swooping it down into the soapy water, and back up again.

As usual, the young mother found an assortment of oddities in his pockets. He was always collecting little boy treasures, and he had been busy this morning on another one of his many treasure hunts. This time, it had been a bonanza of feathers. Blue jay and robin feathers were stuffed in his coverall's rear pockets, and his large front pocket was filled with black feathers from the local crow population. But the one feather that caught her eye was wide, white with a red tip, and over eleven inches long.

"That boy!" she muttered under her breath.

Holding up the winged red-tipped action figure for her to see, Stevie croaked out, "Wook, Mom! It's dem! It's dem! Wook it!"

*****

3

THE GATE – SEVENTEEN YEARS LATER

The foreboding hallway was cold and located in a veiled place far from Earth. Its ceiling towered overhead, and a diaphanous mist swirled about, partially obscuring the smooth stone floor. Thirty feet wide, it stretched immeasurably into the distance. The ceiling height rose to over forty feet, and its entranceway was shrouded dimly in darkness. As one traveled down the corridor, it slowly and progressively grew warmer and lighter, giving the impression of traveling through some long dark tunnel towards a burning light.

Seven massive doors divided the length of the hall into six equal sections. All except the two end doors were left open, and the final door was encased in a great white wall of glittering alabaster, forming a huge sealed gate at the end of the corridor. This gated portal was bathed in the scattered luster of soft light from an unseen source and was guarded by a towering giant dressed in ancient battle garb.

The giant's unshorn dark hair and beard matched his shaggy clothing. His powerfully built body was covered with a tunic of animal fur, and his upper arms sported large bands of polished brass. He wore simple sandals upon his feet, and rawhide windings ascended from his ankles to his knees. A belt of thick leather at his waist held a small dagger, but the main offensive weapon he possessed was a longsword sheathed in a scabbard slung on his wide back. A large shield sat on the floor propped against the wall. It, too, was covered in a thick layer of animal fur.

He also carried a shepherd's staff the size of a weaver's beam, but it was no ordinary herding staff. It contained a glistening razor-sharp edge fastened within its large crook.

The staff was a wicked-looking weapon that had seen many battles, and great gouges scarred the thick pole where it had blocked many an aggressor's deathblows.

The sentry's name was Aram. His wings were folded neatly behind him, and as he leaned his heavy arms upon the staff, it creaked noisily as it took his ponderous weight. Aram's last skirmish with the enemy won him this post, and it was here where he recovered from the wounds he received in that battle. He'd been given other duties since then, but every few years, he was reassigned back to this main sentry position where he could be close to the Throne, basking in its Shekinah Glory. It was a position to be desired by any angel.

*****

The unforgettable battle that won him this posting had been high above the northern border of Israel twenty years earlier, but it still seemed like only yesterday to Aram. The last-minute rally of a small band of Guardians kept a formidable demonic force from overrunning Aram's position, and the combatants had fought to a draw that day, leaving a fragile and brittle peace in the region.

As commander of the sector's forces at that time, Aram's responsibility was to keep the lid on the regional powder keg, but the enemy was just as determined to bring about an explosive conflict leading to war between nations. Not trusting the planet's most important real estate to a lesser prince or chieftain, Lucifer had personally directed the assault upon Aram's position.

Although Aram and his troops were all warriors, they soon found themselves outmatched by a multitude of demonic infantry. But just before Aram's unit was completely overrun, the Archangel Miyka'el dispatched a relief column of a hundred angels led by a diminutive warrior named Da-Ved. The winged phalanx of angels plowed into the marauding demons and hacked their way to rescue Aram's troops.

It was during this battle that Aram and Da-Ved first met and became friends. Aram was engaged in brutal swordplay with two charging Blackguard fighters and was purposefully forced to the outer edges of the fray where he was ambushed by Gathen, the Great Beast of Persia.

Gathen was one of five truly monstrous devils that dared to stand against God on that infamous Day of Rebellion untold millennia earlier. Puny in comparison to Gathen's immense size and bulk, Aram soon found himself retreating under the relentless blows of the Beast and the other demons with him.

While parrying a blow from a charging brute, Da-Ved caught sight of Aram's desperate situation and streaked across the battle to assist him. Using a sling inspired by a young Hebrew boy from a more ancient day, Da-Ved hurled a blistering missile that found Gathen's wide forehead as its mark. The giant crumpled to the ground and imploded, rapidly shrinking in size until he was small enough to fall into the Abyss.

Lucifer was beside himself. With the loss of Gathen, his battle-field advantage quickly evaporated, forcing his troops to retreat to their original positions into Syria and Lebanon, and an uneasy peace soon settled over the land. Aram and Da-Ved did not go unnoticed by Lucifer.

*****

The huge door behind Aram opened, and a smaller entity entered the great hall. With the door open, Aram could hear cheering, earsplitting laughter, and joyous weeping. It was obvious that a grand celebration was taking place within the inner chamber.

"Here!" called out the entering angel. "The Lord Himself asked me to give this to you." And with that, he threw a goatskin-covered bag at Aram.

Aram dodged the airborne missile and caught it with one hand. With a second look, he recognized his diminutive tormentor and, caught off guard, dropped the sloshing bag.

"Da-Ved!" he cried.

Aram's tremendous size belied his great speed, and he caught up his small friend as if he were a rag doll holding him out at arm's length for a quick inspection.

"Uggh!"

Da-Ved found himself trapped in the paws of the enormous warrior. His own smaller shepherd's staff had fallen to the floor, and his arms were now pinned in the vicelike grip of the giant. His only other weapon was a sling casually draped around his neck.

A small shepherd's bag hung heavily from a knotted rope belt at his waist. He, too, was dressed in animal skins, but he also wore a small leather kepi upon his head. Dangling helplessly in the air, his five-foot-eight-inch frame hung a full four feet from the floor. He grinned back at his old friend and stopped his futile struggling.

Returning the smaller angel to his feet, Aram spoke, "My friend, it's been a long time. Too long."

Massaging and working out the numbness in his shoulders caused by Aram's crushing grip, Da-Ved said, "Yes, it's been years, hasn't it?"

"And what is this?" asked Aram, his attention once again drawn to the goatskin bag.

"Pure sparkling water from the River," Da-Ved said. "Just one of the many perks of duty here at the Throne."

Aram quickly snatched up the bag, pulled its stopper, and raised it to his lips. He drank deeply and with a sigh said, "I'd almost forgotten just how good it is."

He drank again, then offered the bag to Da-Ved who took it and drank.

The small angel wiped his mouth with the back of his hand and said, "I can't seem to get enough of this stuff."

After this I looked, and, behold, a door was opened in
heaven: and the first voice which I heard was as it were of
a trumpet talking with me; which said, Come up hither,
and I will shew thee things which must be hereafter.
And immediately I was in the spirit: and, behold, a
throne was set in heaven, and one sat on the throne.
And he that sat was to look upon like a jasper and a
sardine stone: and there was a rainbow round about
the throne, in sight like unto an emerald.
And round about the throne were four and twenty seats: and
upon the seats I saw four and twenty elders sitting, clothed in
white raiment; and they had on their heads crowns of gold.
And out of the throne proceeded lightnings and thunderings
and voices: and there were seven lamps of fire burning
before the throne, which are the seven Spirits of God.
And before the throne there was a sea of glass like unto
crystal: and in the midst of the throne, and round about the
throne, were four beasts full of eyes before and behind.
And the first beast was like a lion, and the second
beast like a calf, and the third beast had a face as a
man, and the fourth beast was like a flying eagle.
And the four beasts had each of them six wings about
him; and they were full of eyes within: and they rest
not day and night, saying, Holy, holy, holy, Lord God
Almighty, which was, and is, and is to come.
And when those beasts give glory and honour and thanks to
him that sat on the throne, who liveth for ever and ever,
The four and twenty elders fall down before him that sat
on the throne, and worship him that liveth for ever and
ever, and cast their crowns before the throne, saying,
Thou art worthy, O Lord, to receive glory and
honour and power: for thou hast created all things,
and for thy pleasure they are and were created.

—Revelation 4:1–11 (KJV)

CHAPTER TWO

The Throne

"So, Da-Ved, where've you been serving His Majesty the last few years?"

The small angel slapped the wooden stopper back into the bota. "I've been here at the Throne as a scribe. I know it doesn't sound like much in the greater scheme of things. It's not very close to the battlefield, but it's been an eye-opening experience. I've been privileged to witness the unfolding of many of His plans and have had a small glimpse of His overall wisdom and strategy."

"Sounds interesting, but isn't His strategy pretty straightforward? It's not all that complicated, is it?"

"Oh, I don't know. Sometimes, as angels, we presume more than we should. We like to think we perceive so much more in comparison to humanity's blind stumblings, but after seeing what I've seen, I know that we have no real conception of what His plans really encompass.

"As one of His scribes, I've recorded many victories...secret victories...monumental victories for people that Lucifer can't understand. He probably doesn't even know about them, for that matter. God's overall plan is truly of a mysterious and magnificent design. It's simply staggering in its scope.

"But Aram, how do you like it here? Does your present posting sit well with you? Or do you prefer the heat of a good battle?"

The huge sentry didn't answer right away but replied slowly and thoughtfully. "I'm not sure. This posting is only temporary, and I've only been here for a few months this time. I want to be out there standing against the Evil One at his every turn, but it's so peaceful here. I feel connected and fulfilled when I'm this close to the Throne. It's like being home. And to bask in His Glory is awesome. It's hard to put into words."

"I know what you mean. I feel it too. We all do when we're here."

Aram looked beyond Da-Ved toward the enormous closed doors. "What's going on in there? On the other side, I mean. I've heard the applause and cheering whenever mortals have passed through my post, but I've never seen why."

"You mean, after all these years, you've never been inside?"

"No. My service has been almost exclusively on Earth as part of the liberation force."

Da-Ved reached for the door's large handle. "Well then, let's have a look. He won't mind. In fact, I'm sure He's pleased you're so curious."

The small angel pulled hard on the heavy door, and as it grudgingly swung open, light and sound simultaneously enveloped them. The Throne Room was cavernous, circular in shape, and several hundred yards in diameter. Like spokes of a wheel joined at a hub, eleven other gated hallways just like Aram's also emptied into this huge chamber. Although the size of this room and its corridors were immense, they were also capable of expanding very rapidly. If need be—in the twinkling of an eye.

Over each of the twelve gates was a single large gemstone embedded into the wall. Each stone was inscribed with the name of one of the twelve tribes of Israel, and each entrance was bathed in the reflected color of its own colossal stone.

The doorway Aram was guarding was bathed in the reflected red light of a stone of sardius. Over the other eleven doors were stones of topaz, carbuncle, emerald, sapphire, diamond, ligure, agate, amethyst, beryl, onyx, and jasper respectively.

And just like Aram, eleven other armed warriors also guarded these hallowed portals.

God's Throne sat at the top of a great circular-shaped altar in the center of this massive amphitheater. The altar itself was fifty yards across and rose several stories above the courtyard floor. The chamber's arched ceiling stretched upward, forming an enormous dome.

If summoned, a mortal or fallen spirit could reach the altar by traversing through one of the twelve darkened corridors, through a guarded door, and down one hundred steps to the courtyard floor. The subject then crossed the royal courtyard where they would encounter the sacred furniture.

Evenly arrayed throughout the lower courtyard, these furnishings consisted of the genuine articles of worship copied and placed into the earthly tabernacle by Moses. Here resided the actual Brass Laver, the Table of Showbread, the Altar of Incense, and the Ark of the Covenant. They paled in comparison to the power and majesty of the One they only represented.

His Shekinah Glory no longer rested between the two, winged cherubim on the ark but was now manifested high on top of the altar at the very foot of His Throne.

A second set of steps emerged from this courtyard, ascending the altar towards His presence. Midway up this stone stairway, a wide landing opened which completely circumscribed the altar. Displayed on this landing sat two enormous scrolls resting on twin columns of polished white marble. An inscription was chiseled into the base of each column with the base of the column on the right engraved with the name Jachin and the column on the left engraved with the name Boaz.

The landing was cracked and splintered by the roots of a fruit-bearing tree which grew out of the rock from between the two scrolls. Between its gnarled and ancient roots flowed a spring of clear water which tumbled down the steps towards the courtyard. There, it created a deep pool overflowing into the headwaters of a sparkling stream, which then coursed directly across the crystalline floor to an immense opening at the Throne's outer wall. At this point, the stream fell over a rocky precipice to a great sea of crazed-crystal and flowed out of sight.

The mist created by this waterfall drifted upwards toward the ceiling, forming a dark boiling cloud high overhead. Out of this cloud growled deep subdued rumblings accompanied by bright flashes of lightning. Below this cloud hovered a shimmering rainbow set perfectly over the altar.

Upon reaching the summit of this altar, one encountered a large golden menorah surrounded by seven celestial trumpeters who each held a long ram's horn. The tips of this menorah were seven removable oil lamps filled with burning oil.

Four crystalline pillars rose elegantly from the altar arrayed to four main compass points. The many-faceted pillars refracted His Glory wildly in all directions, and at the top of each pillar sat a winged creature whose only purpose was to praise God continuously. Their appearances were like a lion, an ox, a man, and an eagle.

The regal lion sang hymns to the tribe of Judah and to the King who would someday reign. The beast of burden glorified the Messiah as a servant and sacrifice. Speaking praises to the fleshly tabernacle of God's Son, Yeshua, was the image of a man. And the stately eagle exalted God through praise to the Holy Spirit.

Although each creature sang a different song, their melodies and voices rose and fell together, harmonizing and complimenting each other as if singing the same song.

The Author of all that is, all that was, and all that will be occupied the center of this altar, and to His right stood His Son. Towering above the twelve entrance doors was a seven-tiered gallery completely encircling the huge chamber's interior wall. These galleries contained an immeasurable number of the Heavenly Host. As Aram and Da-Ved watched, a choir of a thousand seraphim resounded with a song exalting Ruth, the Gentile bride, and Boaz, her groom and kinsman redeemer. When they finished, another thousand seraphim sang a new melody glorifying the Passover Lamb and His redeeming love. As they sang, their wings burned with an unearthly fire.

When the second group finished, a third group of five thousand angels started a new song singing a tribute to Abraham, Isaac, and to the ram, Isaac's substitute. The light radiating from the precious stones over the doorways pulsated with the rhythm of these celestial choirs, and the stones themselves seemed to cry out with their musical vibrations.

The praise was a never-ending river of worship and adoration which flowed out of each song, telling and retelling a ceaseless and enduring story. Vast universal mysteries were being revealed here.

Winged messengers entered into the immense cavern from four great openings in the domed ceiling. At the top of the altar, these messengers received fresh instructions along with new assignments.

Everywhere was movement, music, and light, and the chamber seemed to vibrate with life itself.

Da-Ved put his hands together and yelled, "This is where I serve Him!"

Aram silently mouthed the words, "Awesome."

The small angel nudged Aram with his elbow and nodded in the direction of the altar. Descending the steps from God's presence was a young man who appeared to be about twenty years old. Waiting for him below were two Guardians.

A tall golden-haired warrior and his shorter dark-skinned companion stood facing each other beneath the ancient tree at the landing. They extended their wings fully, arching them forward, high over their heads. The scarlet tips came together to form a feathered arch for the young man to walk through, and they began to burn with an ethereal illumination as they touched.

As he descended through this fiery winged gateway, the gallery of angels broke into a roaring tribute to the youth. The two Guardians acknowledged the young man with wide grins and congratulatory pats on the back.

The young man momentarily stopped between them. His mouth opened wide in astonishment, and he blinked back warm tears.

Though he spoke, his words could not be heard because of the tumult. "I remember you!" he shouted. "You were there in the park...a long time ago."

The three embraced, and the youth disappeared under a canopy of red and white feathers.

Waiting for him below in the courtyard, a small crowd gathered, and he made his way down the marble steps to join them. As he approached, a young girl ran up and wrapped her arms around him.

"Oh, Steve, I'm so glad to see you!"

"Annie!" he cried as he hugged her and tussled her long blond hair.

Unable to contain her joy, she bounced continuously up and down on the balls of her feet.

An older couple approached with outstretched arms. He recognized them as family and took them into his arms as they smothered him with loving kisses and tears.

The little welcoming committee quickly surrounded him, and he hastily renewed many old friendships and became acquainted with the faces he didn't recognize.

The songs of praise intensified, reaching an overpowering crescendo of emotion and adulation for the young man who'd just arrived and for the Son. Heaven couldn't contain itself.

A deeply pitched and deafening victory cry reverberated from the gallery, and the gems over the doors rang out with harmonic vibrations. The timbers of the massive gates groaned resonantly as if in answer to the singing jewels.

Hundreds of angels launched into the air, carried aloft with the new songs to the Lamb. Each of the six-winged creatures at the top of the crystal pillars stood erect with wings fully extended to their entire thirty-foot spans. Triumphantly, they bellowed with deep angelic voices, "Holy! Holy! Holy! Lord God Almighty! Which was, and is, and is to come! He is the God from Everlasting to Everlasting! The Aleph and the Tav! The Alpha and the Omega! The Logos! The Word of Creation! He is the Great I Am! He is the Branch! He is the Great Servant Candle! He is the Lamb of God and the Lion of Judah! He is the Passover Lamb, the Unleavened Bread, and the First Fruits of all redeemed corruption who sleep! He who was accursed and hanged upon a tree was made a *curse* for them!

"He is the Kinsman Redeemer, Wonderful Counselor, the Almighty God, the Prince of Peace, Lord of Lords and King of Kings…the Messiah, Yeshua! All praise to His glorious and wonderful names!"

The four creatures' wings were covered on both sides with open blinking eyes. They'd just witnessed some fantastic deed and would bear testimony to it for all eternity.

The youth looked back to the altar to gaze once again upon the Son. Yeshua, now standing at the edge of the altar overlooking the reunion, laughed and waved to him. The young man waved back, tears now running down both his cheeks. The small crowd of saints escorted him from the courtyard along the river, towards the waterfall.

Pausing at a stairway leading down to the crystal sea, he turned back to the altar for a final look. There sat the Father bathed with a white light so brilliant it was difficult to perceive His actual appearance. His Son was nowhere to be seen, but in His place stood a small white lamb. The young man waved to the Lamb, and the joyful assembly of friends and family pushed him through the cool mist of the waterfall and forward to the stairs. There they descended into an enduring dimension of joy and peace.

Aram stood just inside the doorway, observing the spectacle. Finally, he leaned over to shout a question above the noise of the chamber, "What was that all about? Who were all those people?"

Da-Ved turned to Aram and shouted, "You just witnessed one of those mysterious victories I was telling you about!"

Leaning down, Aram held a hand to his ear. "Whaaat?"

Da-Ved shouted, "You just saw one of those victories I was telling you about!"

Shaking his head, Aram shouted, "What? What are you talking about? I didn't see any fight!"

Cupping his hands to his mouth, Da-Ved yelled, "It's a long story! Let's return to your station, and I'll tell you about it!"

They turned and walked back to Aram's post, shutting the massive door behind them. The sound faded as the heavy door closed.

"Now what's this all about?" Aram asked in a normal voice.

"The youth we just saw receiving such a spectacular reception is named Steven and is a hero for God's kingdom. Lucifer has set traps for all the humans, hoping to either trick them into believing in a false god or some other deceptive and beguiling belief system. Failing that, he has his methods of ruining reputations or ending lives early before they have any real chance of achieving some good work for His kingdom.

"And Steven is no different than any other mortal. Lucifer has had designs on him since he was a small child and made at least one clandestine attempt on his life that I know of. But His Majesty knows all of Lucifer's deceptions and placed a guard on Steven since his early childhood. By the way, I think you might be acquainted with his two Guardians. Ariy'el and Oreb?"

"Ariy'el and Oreb! I thought those two looked familiar. I haven't seen either one of them for ages. The boy must be pretty important to rate those two."

"Yes, he is. As are they all. Here, let me tell you Steven's story. Their instructions concerning him from his birth were to preserve his life for some future—"

"I know," Aram said. "I know. For a future time. For a time such as this."

"Yes, you're quite right," Da-Ved said. "A short time ago, Steven lost his life in an automobile accident. Our foes may have had a hand in this particular accident, I don't know for sure, but there are times when people make poor decisions and have to pay the deadly consequences for these decisions. And sometimes accidents just happen.

"Usually, God won't interfere with such catastrophic events because He gave humanity the gift of free will. That means people are free to have bad things happen to them as well as good things. And there are times it would appear that a mortal's life ends far too soon."

Aram pursed his lips, deep in thought. "Hmmm."

Da-Ved continued, "The prayers that His Majesty receives from the loved ones left behind after these unfortunate deaths wanting to know the *why* of an untimely demise truly breaks His heart. But He won't interfere with such tragedies just to amend a mistake or correct an injustice. If He did, the physical universe would soon find itself in chaos. Miracles circumvent the known physical laws, so He uses them only in extremely rare cases and for His purposes.

"Nevertheless, because of Steven's relationship with His Majesty and because of his friends' and family's unusually righteous prayers and faithfulness, He was willing to make a special exception in his case and was prepared to restore him to his earthly life. This is a very exceptional situation, but it does happen every once in a great while."

Scratching his head, Aram said, "But then why didn't the boy return to his former life if he had the chance?"

"Because before Steven was allowed to make his decision whether to return to his grieving family or to remain here with God, His Majesty explained to him just what would occur if he chose to forsake his life and all its priceless experiences."

Aram squinted, then asked, "Like what?"

Da-Ved leaned back against the great door, his wings splayed sideways against it. He crossed his arms and said, "Steven was made aware that he and others in his community have been specially groomed for some unusual task. The problem was that he and his friends had started to lose some of their fire for the things of God.

"Not because of anything they had done wrong, mind you, but they just started to get lost in the busyness of their lives. They were all pursuing marvelous goals with their education and careers as young people do. And they'd become separated and spiritually weakened by foolish quarrels that many human relationships go through. God planned to glean a rich harvest through this group, but He saw that they were starting to drift away from His will to the point where they would all live successful lives as individuals but would never realize the great victories He'd planned for them."

"Then why did the boy have to die?" Aram said. "Why would he choose death over life? I don't get it."

"It was just revealed to Steven how his early and apparently sense-less death would affect his community. His passing will cause such trauma to his friends. It will stop them in their temporal tracks and motivate them to take personal inventory of their lives. Eventually, they'll heal their hurting relationships and regain their fervor for God and His plans for their lives. This small band of friends will be like individual coals of fire being brought together to make a much larger and more intense fire. And a hot fire can spread, igniting other things. This group will do just that."

Aram leaned against the door, looking down at Da-Ved. "Just exactly how will that happen?" he asked.

"Oh, it'll take some time," Da-Ved said. "It won't be a quick transformation. Although Steven's friends will continue to pursue their own individual goals for the next few years, their homes will become the nurturing provinces needed for them to grow strong spiritually. From time to time, they'll come together to assist each other in finding their way back to Him. We have key people planted in the community to facilitate this growth also. No one has been left out. Nothing has been overlooked.

"Steve's sudden death will be the catalyst for this growth. Without it, there would be none, and his friends would slowly and eventually go their separate ways. His passing at this time will be like a stone tossed into a pool generating ever-expanding ripples across a pond."

"But what of Lucifer? Isn't he suspicious?"

"Ha! That's the best part! He foolishly believes he's won another trophy to sit with him at his final resting place. Don't you see the secret victory here, Aram? Steve's troublesome death is not meaningless. It's just that his friends and family won't know how meaningful it is until that day when they see His Majesty face-to-face.

"And besides, Steve had a choice. God was willing to allow him to return to his life, but he chose not to. Steven knows the pain and suffering his decision will inflict upon the people he loves, but he saw the greater good in the long run. But then, he *has* seen Him face-to-face."

Aram looked confused. "But who were all those people who met him below in the courtyard?"

"Ah, yes, good question," Da-Ved said. "Some were deceased family members and old friends. And some were people he never met but who'd made some positive influence on his life before they died."

Aram thought for a moment. "I think I…understand. It's like the humans see God as though they're looking through a darkly tinted glass, understanding situations, and circumstances only in part…but one day, they'll see Him face-to-face and—"

The heavy doors at the opposite end of the corridor creaked ever so slightly, and a faint breeze whispered upon Aram's face. Recognizing the telltale signs that the far end of the passageway had been breached, he instinctively unfurled his wings. Something had entered the corridor.

Put on the whole armour of God, that ye may be
able to stand against the wiles of the devil.
For we wrestle not against flesh and blood, but against
principalities, against powers, against the rulers of the darkness
of this world, against spiritual wickedness in high places.
Wherefore take unto you the whole armour of God, that ye may
be able to withstand in the evil day, and having done all, to stand.

—Ephesians 6:11–13 (KJV)

CHAPTER THREE

Principalities and Powers

Da-Ved looked to Aram. "You expecting anyone?"

Aram took a few steps and rose up, craning his neck for a better look. "No, there's no one scheduled that I know of."

Da-Ved joined him. "Then I suggest we prepare a proper welcome."

With that, Aram quietly withdrew his sword from its scabbard, and Da-Ved brought his staff to a ready position.

At first, nothing appeared to be amiss. Then a small spatial distortion near the third set of doors at the other end of the corridor manifested into a sixteen-inch shimmering blob of blackest ebony.

Solemn music from within the floating rift could be heard, and as the quivering distortion expanded, the volume of the music grew. A foul odor wafted through the opening along with the last words of a funeral hymn sung in mournful harmony.

> Hold Thou Thy cross before my closing eyes.
> Shine through the gloom and point me to the skies.
> Heaven's morning breaks, and earth's vain shadows
> flee; In life, in death, O Lord, abide with me![1]

A small blue orb darted from the rift and dashed about the immediate vicinity, bathing the walls of the corridor with blue light. The orb's blue luminescence then changed to an intense white light as it hovered overhead midway between floor and ceiling.

The drifting distortion grew to approximately four square feet in size, and out of it popped a small scaly creature the size of a large chicken. Birdlike, it had a large beak and foot-long wings covered with green feathers. It walked upright on long spindly legs.

Three claw-covered toes comprised the entity's feet with a four-inch wicked-looking spur facing rearward. Its legs were a shade of light-green, and a jaundiced yellow haze surrounded the creature as each step it took emitted small puffs of a yellow mist from the scales upon its legs. It smelled of brimstone.

Once it cleared the hole, the creature scouted the area. Returning to the hovering black void, it called out to it in a scratchy voice, "All is clear, my Lord! All clear!"

Instantly, the void expanded to a wavering cave-like opening, and the putrid odor of rotting meat poured out from it. One by one, five demonic warriors stepped through the floating portal.

The five beings were lanky and had the emaciated pale-blue appearance of inmates from some horrible gulag. Each wore head armor and breastplates of either brass or leather. The smallest warrior was just under seven feet in height, and his deep-set eye sockets revealed the dull eyes of existence without hope.

From each of their belts hung a gladius, the short sword of Rome's ancient legions. All carried a heavy shield and javelin.

The warriors' powerful wings were clipped, ensuring that retreat from battle would be impossible.

The tallest warrior pointed silently, and another stepped several yards out front, on point. The commander then signaled that all was clear, and two more creatures emerged from the quivering portal.

The first slithered from the floating fissure and, with a heavy thud, plopped out of the hole. The serpent entity was fifteen feet in length but had the upper torso of a winged man. It slithered about, cobra-like, with its upper torso held aloft. Its great bushy head towered eight feet above the floor. Six large rattles made up its long white tail which was held in check, quiet for now.

The spirit being's body was covered in beautiful scales, accommodating an array of colors, facets, and reflected light. Slung upon its back was a shield and a sword sheathed in a beautiful scabbard

22

overlaid with discarded serpent skin. The shield was large, six-sided, and reflected a large spectrum of light like a giant prism.

The demon deftly drew the long sword, filling the room with a ringing echo. The small birdlike goblin hopped away from the weapon's keen edge.

"Careful with that thing!" it crowed. The bodyguards snorted with brutish glee.

"Shhhh!" cautioned the serpent. "The Master is coming through." Its forked tongue flicked hungrily from its mouth.

Dull skittering noises could be heard approaching the quivering portal from somewhere deep within its inner recesses. A few seconds of silence ensued, then a large armored pincer thrust out of the hole followed by a second. Finally, a huge scorpion's head and body noisily clawed its way into the corridor. The giant amber-colored arachnid was as tall as a man and six feet in length, not counting tail and stinger. Its pincers and stinger were stained the color of dried blood, and bits of torn fabric and carrion hung from its right claw. The demon's eight legs made metallic-like clicking noises on the hard floor as it scurried about.

The scorpion screeched a warning, "He's coming! Keep back!"

The landing party moved away from the fissure. The orb had effectively night-blinded the small contingent of demons who could not see out into the semidarkness beyond its white luminescence. This transient blindness allowed the two angels to remain temporarily concealed.

Besides, the demonic entourage's attention was now riveted to the portal and the next traveler to pass through into the corridor.

Aram looked inquisitively at Da-Ved as if to ask, *What's up?*

Da-Ved whispered in a low voice. "T-h-e-y-'-r-e h-e-r-e-!" With an impish grin, he added, "I've always wanted to use that line."

Aram didn't laugh. Discerning the intruders for who they were, the large Guardian's grip tightened on his sword, and he stooped to pick up his shield.

He set his jaw in anger. "Unbelievable. No way," he whispered.

Sensing Aram's infuriated state, Da-Ved took the angered sentry by the arm. In a low voice, he cautioned, "They're in our domain now. Before we challenge them, let's see what they're up to."

Aram stiffened but nodded in agreement. Together, the angelic pair traversed the hallway quickly and took up positions, hovering high above the floor where they concealed themselves behind the third set of open doors. From here, they were able to keep a close vigil on the intruders without risking discovery.

The putrid odor emanating from the portal became much stronger, and a colossal six-toed foot stepped through the opening into the chamber. The quivering portal then expanded, quickly doubling in size.

A few moments later, a large head hastily poked through. With some difficulty, the entity navigated an enormous set of shoulders through the fissure and proceeded to pull its other leg into the corridor to stand erect to its full fifteen-foot height. There, in all his demonic glory shed of all that was once pure and holy, stood the fallen cherub, Lucifer.

His ruggedly handsome face was framed by shoulder-length blond hair, and his cruel eyes reflected the same piercing blue color of the flying orb. Fastened about his head was a metallic headband of purest silver, and from this headband, a triad of three golden curved horns thrust out and upward from his forehead.

Girdled about his chest was a breastplate of brass that contrasted regally against the coarse white robe he was wearing. Hanging from a golden necklace around his neck were the world's arcane occult symbols. Embedded in each symbol were crystals of differing colors and purities.

Tucked neatly behind him were his enormous translucent wings. Radiant with the blush of an all-enveloping aura, Lucifer's appearance was stunning.

"All is clear, Master! All is clear!" clucked the small goblin.

"Worry, you are a fool!" Lucifer cursed. "There is always a guard! Go and find them before I send you to the Pit myself!"

"Yes, yes, Ba'al Lucifer! At once! At once!" The small beast trotted off toward the outer edge of the orb's illumination near the open hallway door. The commander motioned to the sentinel on point to accompany the little demon.

The malevolent monarch was in a foul mood. "He won't get away with it this time! This time, I'm within my rights. The boy is mine!"

As its head bobbed back and forth with each deliberate step, the bird-creature trotted up to the door behind which Aram had concealed himself. It peered up the edge of the door, then quickly scampered to the other door concealing Da-Ved. It appeared to be searching for something and began to peck at the wood. Tilting its head to one side, it scanned the door with one eye and examined Aram's door again.

Sniffing twice, it cackled, "Master! I've found the guard! They're here! They're here!"

With that, Aram and Da-Ved descended from their hiding places. Da-Ved held his staff at the ready while Aram's sword cut a luminescent arc through the air, chasing the worrisome little goblin back towards his master.

"Ba'al Lucifer!" the small fiend cried out fearfully.

Eyeing Aram carefully, the demonic sentry on point readied his javelin and backed away slowly.

Spotting Aram and Da-Ved, Lucifer sneered, "Bah! There's only two of them."

Aram's eyes narrowed. "State your business here!"

Annoyed with the large sentry, Satan scowled, "And who am I addressing?"

"The Lord rebuke you," was Aram's only reply.

Lucifer and his small troupe winced, visibly pained by the retort. "We can at least converse civilly, can't we? I only wish to address the court."

Da-Ved challenged the Prince of Darkness. "I thought you weren't allowed around here anymore."

The warning rattles of the large viper-demon reverberated off the nearby walls. Aram vaulted into the air, and Da-Ved cartwheeled to the other side of the corridor taking a defensive position in front of the doorway.

The scorpion dropped its front legs low while arching its stinger high in the attack position.

"Huzzah!" As one, the five bodyguards brandished their javelins menacingly.

With the crack of a single thunderbolt, the door to the Throne at the distant end of the corridor opened and closed in an explosion of light.

Immediately, two additional angels appeared and took up positions behind Da-Ved and Aram. Their swords were drawn, and Da-Ved acknowledged them with a sideways glance.

"Trouble?" questioned Ariy'el.

Aram answered gruffly, "Nothing we can't handle."

The veins on Lucifer's neck distended. "Enough!" he whispered through gritted teeth.

"Thanatos! She'Ol! I do not want a confrontation here! We only came to talk."

The two princes lowered their weapons. The little imp, Worry, peered out from between Lucifer's feet with wide eyes.

Lucifer directed his attention back to Aram and Da-Ved to ask, "We've crossed swords somewhere before, I think?"

"Yes," Da-Ved said. "Golan Heights...twenty years ago."

Squinting, Lucifer replied, "Yes. I remember now. Yes, you two cost me much that day."

Turning to Aram, he said, "As I recall, I made you a little promise then, didn't I? Perhaps someday soon, you will give me the satisfaction of crossing blades again?"

Perceiving Aram's weight shifting to his left foot, Oreb quickly interposed himself between the two antagonists. Extending his wings as a barrier between them, he spoke to Lucifer in a loud whisper.

"His Majesty will allow your entrance to His Throne provided you conduct yourselves accordingly."

Lucifer's icy blue eyes bore a hole through Oreb. "Understand me, cockroach! I came here to reclaim my property. I will not be cheated again. I wish to prosecute my case in this accursed court, and I go where I want to when I want to. Now stand aside!"

"The Lord rebuke you."

The demonic entourage flinched again with Oreb's unmistakable reply. Casting his head back and throwing his arms overhead Lucifer cried out, "How I despise this place!"

"That's because while here, you are just like us with many of your angelic powers held in check," taunted Da-Ved. "You don't like being restrained to the many physical limitations that the humans experience. You're not so godlike while on Heaven's streets, are you?"

"Ho! Ho! When I return to rule my kingdom, I will remember you, little warrior. Now out of my way!"

With wings still fully extended, Oreb turned sideways, forcing Aram against the wall.

Lucifer stopped to look Aram in the eyes, saying, "Bah! I won't waste my time with you, Guardian," and he brushed past him as he continued his journey toward the well-lit door at the far end of the corridor. She'Ol, Thanatos, and Worry followed in his wake.

The five bodyguards clumsily caught up to the huge Cherub and proceeded to the front of the procession. The clamor of talons, claws, and armor-clad feet steadily waned as they made their way towards the distant gate. As if to watch over the quivering portal, the orb of luminescence remained dutifully behind.

At last, Oreb retired his wings and stepped away from Aram. "Don't concern yourself, Aram. The Lord desires Satan's presence in His court anyway."

Aram angrily sheathed his weapon. "I just don't like his arrogance. But I don't mind telling you it was good to see you and Ariy'el standing there behind us."

The four angels grinned and shook hands as one.

The massive door to the Throne opened and closed with a reverberating crash.

Satan had entered Heaven's sanctuary.

And the great dragon was thrown down, that ancient serpent, who is called the devil and Satan, the deceiver of the whole world—he was thrown down to the earth, and his angels were thrown down with him. [10]And I heard a loud voice in heaven, saying, "Now the salvation and the power and the kingdom of our God and the authority of his Christ have come, for the accuser of our brothers has been thrown down, who accuses them day and night before our God.

—Revelation 12: 9-10 (ESV)

CHAPTER FOUR

Satan in the Sanctuary

Heaven's gallery fell silent as the Prince of Darkness and his powers entered into their presence. It was a rare event whenever Lucifer penetrated this august assembly, and his impending claim made this truly a somber occasion.

Abandoning his entourage at the great door, Lucifer quickly descended the white stairway to the royal courtyard below. There he stopped and railed up towards the Throne, "I demand a hearing to determine an urgent legal matter!"

The Father inquired with a voice like brass, "Where do you come from?"

Ignoring His query, Lucifer reiterated, "I require your attention to a grievous injustice!"

Again, the question boomed down from the Throne, "Where did you come from?"

Lucifer took a few steps across the courtyard towards the ascending stairway to the Throne and vented his displeasure. "Questions! Always questions! You can never answer me directly, can you?"

The Father sat patiently, waiting for His answer. An awkward moment of silence followed.

Finally, Lucifer relented. "Very well then! You know where I'm coming from. I've just come from patrolling my dominion—Earth. We've just left the funeral of my latest conquest. Only upon my arrival at his memorial service, I discovered that the guest of honor was missing. I've been informed by my Blackguard that your son absconded with him at his demise. I want him back!"

The small white Lamb reappeared from behind the Father's Throne and nonchalantly walked to the edge of the altar where it could be seen by the unwelcome intruders.

Seeing fresh prey, Thanatos arched its tail, pumping a deadly drop of venom to the tip of its stinger where it hung like a fatal raindrop.

She'Ol rattled a warning across the great chamber, flooding it with a loud buzzing like that of a gigantic cloud of flying locust.

Even the little imp, Worry, puffed itself up and crowed, "Aha! A fine meal presents itself to us! And how delicious looking! Yum! Yum!"

Baring large pointed teeth, Worry hungrily scurried towards the small Lamb standing high above on the altar. Without invitation, Lucifer brazenly scaled the steps to the landing, suspending his ascent at the spot between the two great scrolls. Pointing his huge left wing and arm towards the altar, he mocked, "Lo...a weakling shows itself. Ho! Ho!"

Enjoying Lucifer's contemptuous disdain, his evil generals howled with glee. Their perverse bodyguards leaned comfortably upon their javelins.

"Don't he look pretty?

"Looks tasty to me."

"I'm getting hungry just looking at him."

"Ha! Ha! Ha!"

Aghast at the newcomers' irreverent courtroom behavior, the angelic choir became a sea of murmuring voices filling the chamber with a dull cacophonous hum. During this commotion, the alabaster doors to one of heaven's twelve thresholds quietly swung open as Aram and his three comrades entered. Summoned by the Son, the four angels took up positions within the entranceway. This vantage point allowed them to maintain the guard and still witness the celestial drama about to unfold.

By now, Lucifer had worked himself into a terrible fury and bellowed his complaint to He who sat upon the Throne. "I seek my prize, fairly won, I might add. I'm tired of your flimflamming son fleecing me of my property! Those fools on the planet make him out to be some sort of great champion. A redeemer they call him.

"A curse on him and all those who follow him! Redeemer? Bah! All he is a cheat and a liar. He takes their souls and leaves behind the empty husks like some cheap street hustler running a rigged pea-and-thimble game. I want it stopped, and I want the boy. Now!"

"I'm sorry, you'll have to take the matter up with My Son. I decided long ago to leave such matters to His discretion. But I will judge the *validity* of your claim."

Spinning around to face his unholy entourage, Lucifer roared with laughter. "So much the better. Bring him on. Where is he hiding? The other side of the universe, I'll wager."

His contemptuous entourage, enjoying the spectacle of their Prince's arrogance, continued with their mocking accusations.

"Coward!"

"Thief!"

"Swindler!"

Turning back to address the court, Lucifer noticed the Lamb had disappeared and that an enormous male Lion had taken its place. The hulking feline's black mane tumbled midway down its heavily muscled back, and an unearthly fire blazed within its eyes.

The Lion stood seven feet at the shoulder with its kingly head held towering above. For now, it just sat quietly upon its rear haunches, lazily flicking its long tail side to side in front of its massive front paws.

Dangling from a golden chain around its neck was a large six-pointed star. With a thick crown of woven briers perched upon its head, the predator arched its back and stretched out its front legs and heavy paws. The immense cat yawned, lazily extending its sharp black claws one by one from each feline digit. Awed with the sudden appearance of the Lion, the gallery fell silent again.

Visibly shaken, Lucifer's bodyguards slowly backed away from the stairway in front of them. As they did, they bumped clumsily into the four angelic sentries on guard duty behind them.

"What? You're not through already, are you?" inquired Aram with a heavy dose of sarcasm.

Chittering and hissing, Thanatos and She'Ol whirled about to face their insolent hecklers. The squad of Blackguard warriors raised their javelins menacingly.

Not wishing to cause a physical disturbance in the Father's presence the Guardians fell back. The Lion bellowed an authoritative warning from the altar.

With that single, earsplitting roar, the twelve stones embedded above the doors began to pulsate with a pure white light flooding the cavernous room with their overpowering radiation. Even the colorful hues of the shimmering rainbow overhead were temporarily washed out as the penetrating light filled the arena.

The two demonic generals became momentarily blinded, and their small platoon stumbled down the steps to the courtyard, overturning the foul-smelling little imp in the process.

Worry, finding himself temporarily blinded and flat on his back, screeched in terror. "*Oww!* I told you we shouldn't have come. We're outnumbered here. Let's get the lamb if that lion hasn't already eaten him and get out of here."

Taking a step backward at the sudden appearance of the huge predator, Lucifer quickly regained his composure. The fallen cherub lowered his wings and hands from his eyes as the intense light dissipated from the room along with the last fading echoes of the Lion's warning.

As they regained their eyesight, the interlopers stumbled down to the courtyard and then up the second set of steps towards the altar to gather nervously around their Chief Prince.

The Lion seemed to have evaporated into thin air, and something—or someone—now stood in its place. From where Lucifer and his retinue stood between the two great scrolls, the entity appeared directly in front of them at the very summit of the altar. The Father's Throne was located right behind it.

Light radiating from the Father backdropped the creature, but the radiance was so dazzling Lucifer could only make out a single dark silhouette. The shape was that of a man. It spoke, "I'm here."

With false bravado, Thanatos blustered, "Who's...ah...here?"

The figure moved away from the Throne to reveal the owner of the voice—the Son, Yeshua, the Messiah. He was wearing a robe of white linen and was girded about the breadth of his chest with a band of sparkling gold fabric.

Draped upon His shoulders was a blue and white tallit, the traditional prayer shawl worn by the faithful bachiyr—the chosen ones. The tzitzit tassels hanging from the two front corners of the shawl fell to the middle of his thigh, testifying to all Israelites as to His true identity. Attached to the rope belt at His waist dangled two large silver keys. Scars could be seen on His hands and upon his feet, He wore sandals of finely spun gold.

"I...AM...here. I've been here all along, not across the galaxy as your master suggests."

"Yes, I recognize your double-dealing voice!" Lucifer taunted as he ascended the stairs. "Where is my property?"

Yeshua laughed. "Who said he was *your* property? He's been in covenant with me since he was a little boy."

"But I—"

Yeshua cut him off with a wave of his hand. "Not today, Lucifer. I may have let you think that he belonged to you, but his relationship with me was never that strained. We always managed to mend our fences. Why do you think you were so unsuccessful over the years with all your devious little traps and snares to take him? My covering hand was upon him since he was quite young."

Lucifer rapidly charged up the stairs to the top of the altar. "I know that, you grave robber! But then...why then did you remove your shield if he hadn't fallen out of favor with you? It was so easy to just sit around, waiting for some mishap to occur once his guard abandoned him."

Standing next to Aram, Ariy'el turned a bright shade of red. "He wasn't abandoned!" he shouted across the arena. "We were there every step of the way with him. It was just his appointed time. Why do you think all you got was another husk? We were with him for twenty years, and it was my great pleasure to personally escort him to His Majesty's Throne before you even knew he was gone."

"Why would you do that?" asked She'Ol. "Why protect him all his miserable life, only to drop the guard after twenty years? Admit it, you messed up, and we took him! We have a claim on him now, so hand him over!"

Thanatos chimed in, his voice dripping with contempt. "So the great Master Planner, the Grand Architect of the Universe has made a mistake after all! You're not so perfect, are you? Ha! Ha! I can't wait to tell the rest of my troops."

Lucifer went straight to the heart of the matter. "Your son made a terrible mistake when he decided to come against me and my legions. This little error of his demonstrates we are every bit as capable as he is in running this kingdom.

"Now, we have a valid claim on this boy. We stalked him for years. We waited patiently for the perfect moment. We saw the guard momentarily inattentive, and we took advantage of the situation. Come now. Answer me straight. What is the boy's defense? He has none! Hand my prize over so we can be on our way. I have other engagements to keep this day.

"And by the way, your son is also a thief as well as a cheat. Many years ago, he stole a couple of other items from my two generals on his little visit below. I'll just take those two keys he has there while you're fetching me the boy."

The generals howled with delight. Their master had invaded the very Throne of heaven, challenged the Father and His sovereignty, and pleaded a victorious case against the renowned Wonderful Counselor. Thanatos' deadly stinger dripped again with exquisite anticipation.

The Father turned to His Son and said, "He does make a persuasive point about the boy. I find Lucifer has a solid claim on this one. What have you to say on the youth's behalf?"

"As counselor for the defense and as his intercessor, we believe we have an open and shut case, Your Honor. He is guilty, but his penalty has already been paid. We plead for the mercy and grace of this court. Abba, he has repented and he pleads—the Blood."

Turning to face the boy's accuser, the Father glared at the Prince of Darkness with utter contempt. "You're wasting my time, Lucifer. Case dismissed."

"But you can't—"

"I said you have no case."

The color drained from Lucifer's face, and he asked in a husky voice, "Ah, what about the keys?"

The Father bent over and stared directly into the Cherub's icy blue eyes. "They're yours…if you can take them. Now get out. Guard! Escort our guests to the outside."

This disastrous turn of events had an obvious effect on Lucifer's henchmen. Sensing it was long past time to depart, they quietly made their way back down the steps, returning to the courtyard. From there, they retreated up the steps to the doorway through which they first entered.

But Lucifer was furious and would have none of it. Never one to lose gracefully, he brazenly taunted the Throne.

"So! This is how you play the game! You're both so pathetic! You ignore or forget the facts of the case. You plea bargain. You reduce the charges. Your witnesses lie.

And the judge and defense councilor are related! How do I stand a chance of winning in this accursed court? No wonder those fools worship you. You always twist the outcome in their favor.

"Just remove your protection and favor for a few days and let me have them. They'll be cursing your name and the day they were born. Give me complete authority on that planet, and I'll show you real power. I'll show creation a real god, one she can worship proudly!"

Lucifer had made his way down to the lower courtyard when the Father called out after him.

"Return to the bar, Councilor!"

The fallen Cherub stopped next to the Ark of the Covenant, his back to the Throne, and face flushed with anger. He slowly turned and grudgingly climbed back up the steps towards the Ancient of Days. Without pausing at mid-landing, he stormed boldly to the very top of the altar to stand insolently in front of the Father.

The Father asked, "This is how you address this court and assembly? Let me lay out the facts for you as they truly are and not how you erroneously perceive them."

Counting on His fingers, the Father stated, "One! This is not a game nor will it ever be a game. This is *My* reality, and this reality will last for eternity.

"Two! In this case and all the other cases you have brought before this court, I have not ignored any of the so-called facts, allowed any plea bargaining, nor reduced any of the charges. You have prosecuted nothing but capital cases here and have always been allowed to present all your evidence fairly.

"Three! As for My personal relationship with the defense counselor, I would point out to you that the law is the law. I cannot allow any prejudice I may have toward the councilor or his defendants to change the law's dictates nor the consequences of its violation and remain a fair and just judge. Sin always demands payment. And as you know…there is no remission of sins without the shedding of blood. I will not defile My Throne.

"Four! Although transgressions have been committed by the defendant and he is most assuredly guilty in this case, you have once again overlooked a critical detail. The debt has already been paid and the defendant justified. A defendant cannot be executed when he is, in fact, already dead. He died with My Son and was raised with My Son when he accepted the covenant. He is no longer a defendant but has become a new creature and is now righteous in My sight.

"And five! Do I have to remind you that we've already had this conversation centuries ago? You challenged Me with this same hogwash once before."

Lucifer stood arrogantly in silence with his wings held aloft. His eyes were cold and furrowed into small slits. A contemptuous sneer spread across his face.

Shaking his head with disdain, the Father continued, "Remove My protection and favor indeed! *Hellooo?* Does the name Job ring a bell? You put that man and his family through great suffering, and yet he never once cursed Me or My Throne. The only questionable thing he did was to wonder why I allowed the cruel circumstances to happen to him in the first place. After I reminded him of just who I was and who he was, he even repented of that.

"So…I believe you owe Me. At your request, I allowed you to have your way with Job for quite some time, and you dumped unlimited misery on him in a test of his faith and My grace. Because of your arrogance and groundless accusations against Me today, I believe I'll demand a bit of satisfaction Myself. I would like to conduct a little experiment of My own."

"An experiment?" Lucifer asked. "What kind of experiment? You're not going to send your son down to my world again, are you?"

"No! No, nothing like that. My plans for repossessing the planet are set to a future timetable. However, I would like to take a more direct interaction with mankind than I've had lately. But I will, as you put it, be impartial. Neither I nor My Son will have a personal hand in the affair."

Lucifer screwed up his face and spat out mockingly, "What are your terms, O great god of the universe?"

"Terms! Terms? Now you want terms? What terms did you allow Me with Job? I let you do anything to him that you wanted to short of killing him, which probably would have been more merciful after all the evil you vented upon him.

"Very well. You want terms? Here are My terms. I'm going to send a messenger to a community on Earth to pour out a blessing. This messenger will only be there for a short time. He will be in disguise and will not be allowed to reveal his identity to anyone. You may observe, but you may not interfere with him or his mission. I will allow you one item of input into this matter. You may select the messenger from My Host. That shouldn't be too hard for you. After all, you once were the highest of all my Cherubim and should know all the angels by name."

A wicked grin spread upon Lucifer's face, and he cagily stroked his chin. "And…just…what are you attempting to accomplish with this little experiment?"

The Father covered his mouth with His hand, hiding His amusement at Lucifer's lame attempt at controlling the situation.

"Nothing would give Me more pleasure than to pour out a blessing upon all humanity, but knowing their current spiritual state, the results would be short-lived. You once attempted to show that a righteous man, in covenant with Me, would turn away from that covenant if I did not provide perfect and complete blessings on everything that touched his life. Job proved you wrong.

"Now I want to demonstrate to this assembly and to all of Creation the flip side of that premise. I will not entertain on that future Day of Judgment any misconceptions that things might have been different for the human race if only certain circumstances had been made more suitable for them.

"There are many on that tiny planet seeking a man-made utopia. A few so-called social engineers claim that if the physical, social, political, and religious environments could be nurtured and cultivated scientifically, they could build a paradise on earth. Many of them would dare to attempt to build the kingdom with their own hands, not Mine. In essence, they are declaring that they don't need Me."

Lucifer cocked his head. "But why a blessing? What's its purpose?"

The Father's face softened. "This blessing will demonstrate that although I can still covenant with men on an individual basis and make a personal difference in their lives, humanity as a whole will not allow My blessings to have a life-changing effect on them en masse. As long as they remain in a fallen state, they'll simply refuse to believe in anything they cannot experience with one of their five senses.

"Evil dwells continually in their hearts, and it will make no difference if they have acquired a perfect environment or not. It may be difficult for them to make correct choices in their lives, but I still hold them responsible for the freedom I have given them.

"For a person to attempt to clean up the sin of their heart on their own is like trying to clean up a mess with a filthy rag. It can't be done. This blessing will show them that they still need a personal Redeemer in order to approach Me, and that the Redeemer is My Son.

"Besides, I was not pleased with the cruelty of the trials and tribulations you rained down upon My man, Job. He will be delighted to watch you squirm with the loss of a few of your disciples to My kingdom."

Gritting his teeth, Lucifer protested with mounting hostility, "What if I don't agree to your terms or your little test? What then?"

The Father stood. "In case you're still deluded as to your power and authority, I would like to point out that I AM sovereign here and I AM the one sitting on the throne, not you. I would have turned you into a piece of crisp swine flesh long ago if I could have done it without judging mankind with similar and equal punishment. My Son has provided the way to do that now, so don't push your luck."

The fallen Cherub rubbed his hands together, a defiant sneer upon his face. "Go on! Have your little test! You will only prove that the humans are fully capable of improving their plight under the right conditions. They will build that utopia you detest, and you will provide me the means of your own undoing.

"Ha! Ha! I, of course, will provide the needed leadership. Two men from the political and religious arenas have already been groomed by me to show the fools below a new lie. A blessing indeed. I love the idea. I only wish I had thought of—"

Shaking his head, the Father said, "Not at this time, Lucifer. This blessing will be only a small demonstration. I will allow you your big chance at world leadership in due time. But for now, you will watch...and wait."

"When will you start your puny demonstration? I suppose you've been preparing for this visitation for some time now. It's just like you to stack the deck again. Am I not allowed to prepare even the slightest defense?"

The Almighty leaned forward, His eyes radiating with wondrous glory. Lucifer raised a hand to shield his eyes and looked away.

"Just so all will know the truth, I have only decided in these past few moments with you to do this thing. It is true, though, that there are godly men and women below whom have been on their knees for years petitioning My Spirit for revival in their congregations and families. I have selected one of these communities to receive the blessing. Now you may make your selection of My messenger."

Lucifer stroked the bridge of his nose deep in thought. "First, be generous and answer me a question or two. How will you enforce your no interference zone?"

"Lucifer, you are exasperating! All right. If you insist. I will direct Miyka'el to dispatch a legion of angels to set up a buffer zone around the community. The strength of this angelic force combined with the prayers of the local saints will make this shield impenetrable by your forces. Trust me. Don't even think about it."

"I would like to select two of your Host to be assigned to this mission," Satan said in an effort to manipulate the conditions of the test. "I care not which one is selected to carry the blessing. I only wish to meet them far from this place and somewhere in my dominion."

Shaking His head, the Father said, "You truly are slippery as an eel, you serpent. You would again dare to change the terms of My quest?"

The cunning Cherub's arrogant demeanor faded, becoming less belligerent, and he altered his voice deceitfully. "'Tis only a small change, sire. And you still retain the final selection of the actual messenger."

The Father quickly agreed. "Very well, it's done. Whom do you want?"

Smiling with a knowing grin, Lucifer quickly said, "Da-Ved and Aram. They are old friends of mine, and we just might run across each other down there. Now, which one will you select as your messenger?"

Looking over to Da-Ved and Aram, the Father smiled. "That, my crafty foe, will be up to them to decide. Da-Ved! Aram!" He called out to them. "Escort this vermin out of here and then return. I have an old friend I want you to visit."

"Bah! Don't bother! I know the way out!" With that, Satan extended his wings, and with one downward swoop, he bolted through the dark thundercloud hovering overhead. As he exited through an angelic portal, he screamed a final insult, "My kingdom...*Come!*"

Aram pushed on the large door to the outer corridor and graciously held it open for the remaining uninvited guests. They stood dumbly, gawking at the empty portal where their master had just departed. Stunned at their sudden abandonment in heaven's lair, they needed a little prodding.

"Hey!" Aram scowled at the group. "Your master's gone. If you know what's good for you, you'll take the hint and leave too."

"Says you!" the irascible imp pecked at Aram's feet with a vengeance.

Aram gritted his teeth, lifted a large foot, and brought it down hard upon the little goblin.

WHOMP!

The thing made a popping noise and a foul-smelling cloud puffed out from under the large Guardian's foot. Raising his leg, a hundred tiny replicas of the pesky goblin scrambled about running through the open door into the corridor. As these Lilliputian creatures raced down the corridor, they reassembled once again into the foul spirit who wasted no time scurrying down the long hallway. It screeched in hellish fury as it returned to the hovering fissure.

Just before returning to the outer corridor, Thanatos and She'Ol turned to take one last look at the Throne. In utter amazement, they saw that the Son had disappeared and that the Lion and the Lamb had both returned to the Altar. The Lion lay stretched out upon its belly with its two front legs extending out in front of it. The Lamb was sleeping peacefully between its powerful front paws.

She'Ol glanced at Thanatos and spoke in a low tone. "Uh-oh. That reminds me of something but I can't remember exactly what."

"You're always having nightmares," grumbled Thanatos. "Let's get out of here while we still can. Squad, move out!"

Retreating through the gate, Lucifer's entourage headed toward the dark end of the corridor and the temporary portal leading back to the planet.

Back to their home.

Arise, shine; for thy light is come, and the
glory of the LORD is risen upon thee.
For, behold, the darkness shall cover the earth, and
gross darkness the people: but the LORD shall arise
upon thee, and his glory shall be seen upon thee.

—Isaiah 60:1, 2 (KJV)

CHAPTER FIVE

The Blessing

Oreb and Ariy'el assisted Aram and Da-Ved, escorting their unwelcome guests back to the fissure with considerable enthusiasm.

"Move along there, you!" Oreb said, prodding a Blackguard who had dared to look back at the great door.

As they approached the drifting black void, they discovered that Worry had not waited for the others to return but had already departed the corridor.

Without fanfare or the slightest hesitation, She'Ol, Thanatos, and their grisly bodyguards also plowed into the floating rift, disappearing within its dark borders.

Finally, the hovering orb vibrated, and its intense white light returned to its original blue glow, bathing the corridor with its soft azure radiance. Spiraling downward in great wide loops from the ceiling, it too vanished into the shrinking void, and with a loud sucking sound, the void puckered out of heaven's existence.

"We have to return immediately," Da-Ved said to Aram. "His Majesty will have new duties for us."

Aram grabbed him by the arm. "Wait a minute, old friend. There's something I've been wondering about ever since the battle in the Golan Heights twenty years ago. Tell me something."

Da-Ved stopped and gave him a stern look.

Ariy'el quietly nudged Oreb. Putting a finger to his lips, he whispered, "Shhhh."

Oreb returned the gesture and gave Ariy'el a sly wink.

Meeting Aram's inquiring eyes, Da-Ved said slowly, "Okay. Go ahead. Ask away."

"Gathen went down like a ton of bricks that day you saved me and my command. Just what *did* you hit him with?"

Da-Ved was smiling now. "Oh, just my secret weapon, that's all." He feigned polishing his fingertips on his chest, then blew on them and smiled a conceited grin. "Why do you ask?"

"Whatever it was, it put his lights out...like right now! I've never seen anything like it. What was it?"

Ariy'el and Oreb drew closer. Da-Ved's exploit with the sling was well known, and his victory had not gone unnoticed by angels *or* demons. The story was legendary, and even now, Lucifer's minions gave Da-Ved a wide berth whenever his duties brought him into their orbit.

Oreb repeated the question. "Yeah, Da-Ved. Just what did you use?"

"Well, since you're my friends and since you asked, I'll tell you."

With a mischievous smile, Da-Ved pulled his shepherd's bag from his belt and opened it. "Open your hand," he ordered Aram.

Dumping the contents of the bag into Aram's considerable hand, he said, "There you go, *gen-u-ine* giant slayers. I've got four of them left."

In Aram's open hand were the remains of a large rusty spike. It had been cut into five equal pieces. but it was obvious that the pointed end was missing. Blotches of something dark and red stained the remaining fragments.

"I used the first piece to take out Gathen. It went through him like a hot blade through lard."

Oreb gave a low whistle.

"What are they? Where'd you get them?" Ariy'el asked.

"Yeah, come on. Da-Ved. Tell us."

"All right, but you can't tell anyone. It'll ruin my reputation as a warrior."

Pretending to look around as if not to be overheard. Da-Ved lowered his voice. "I picked up this spike at Calvary a couple of thousand years ago. It was a simple matter to divide it into five segments. Gathen didn't stand a demon's chance in heaven."

With that, he snatched the fragments from Aram's hands and deposited them back into his bag. Spinning on his heels. he set out for the Gate.

Ariy'el ran his hands through his long hair. "Whoa! I wasn't aware that Da-Ved was there that day at Calvary. Were you?"

Aram watched Da-Ved as he made his way to the Gate. "Yeah. I knew," he said in a lowered voice. "He doesn't like to talk about it much, though. It really bothers him. Or at least it used to. He was part of the Jerusalem Legion at Calvary."

Oreb's eyes opened wide. "*The* Jerusalem Legion?"

"Yeah. The one and—*only*—Jerusalem Legion," Aram said. "The Legion was ordered into the city by Miyka'el to act as a last-minute rescue contingency. The way Da-Ved tells it, it was nip and tuck there right up to the end.

"Da-Ved was there at Gethsemane, too, you know. He was part of a band of angels sent to minister to Yeshua in the garden the night before. But you know the rest of the story. His Majesty didn't call for the Legion's help and went all the way to hang on that curs-ed tree."

"How did the Legion let that happen?" Ariy'el asked.

"The Legion was formed out of the ranks of Guardians who have exhibited exceptional loyalty and obedience. Their fidelity is unquestioned, and they'll do whatever is asked of them no matter how repugnant.

"But Da-Ved took it hard—really hard. They all thought that at the last second, they were going to be allowed to dash in and rescue Him. I guess that's why Da-Ved is still assigned as one of God's scribes...to keep him close to the Throne.

"He tells me he's had some intimate conversations with His Majesty since then, and he's learned a lot about pain and tragedy. You know. Why He allowed Himself to be sacrificed. Why He didn't put up a defense. Stuff like that. How it was all part of His plan."

The large Guardian hesitated, a far-away look in his eyes. "I-I better get going. Something tells me this day's business isn't finished yet."

"May the Lord watch over you Aram," Oreb said in a hushed tone.

Ariy'el echoed his sentiments. "Yes. His peace be with you also."

Aram offered a large hand. "If—"

Oreb grabbed Aram's forearm. "We know. We know. It's the same with us. Now you better get going. We'll watch this gate until a replacement can be appointed."

Aram turned and took the long walk down the corridor entering into the sanctuary through the heavy door. As he entered, he saw that Da-Ved had already ascended to the altar and had presented himself to his Creator. Down on one knee, he was already receiving instructions for some new task.

Observing Aram's entrance, Yeshua called out to him, "Aram, come. I have a new mission for you and Da-Ved that concerns what happened here today."

Aram quickly descended to the courtyard and then ascended the second stairway to the top of the altar, and he too knelt to one knee, paying homage to his king.

"Aram, I summoned you and Da-Ved to the Throne during Lucifer's accusations because I wanted you to witness the truth of My Father. Da-Ved's been one of My scribes for many years and has access to knowledge of what's transpired throughout human history. Through his service, he's had an opportunity to learn and understand a great deal about human frailty and strength.

"But what of you, Aram? I need a messenger who can deal with humanity in a manner they aren't used to. What shall I expect from you?"

"Lord? Of all beings, You should know. Why ask me?"

"*I* know what you are capable of Aram, but I want *you* to be aware of your own abilities. Are you ready to find out what they are?"

"Yes, Lord. What is it You desire?"

"Excellent. Excellent. That's My Spirit. Now tell me. What have the scriptures recorded concerning My friend, Job? I want you to understand what happened with him so you'll understand what you're to do."

Aram scratched his head. "Uh, the way I understand it—the covenant between You and Job was tested by Lucifer to see if it would endure through any evil that transpired in his life. The covenant's power and Job's complete reliance on it dashed any hope Lucifer's generals might have had that an outright rebellion on Earth could be won by a direct force of arms on their part."

Aram paused as if finished, but his King pressed him to continue. "But?"

"But Lucifer's generals are clever too. They're not stupid. They know You love the people too much to abandon them completely to their sin nature. And obviously, You can't prosecute outright warfare against the rebels without going to war against the humans too. They're using that as a shield."

Yeshua motioned for Aram to continue. "So?"

"Sooo…because of their failure with Job, they quickly realized that if they were going to win their little rebellion, they were going to have to do it through deception, temptation, and through the traitorous acts of men. Since then, they have tripled their activities in these types of spiritual warfare. And most humans aren't even aware of the existence of these fallen spirits or ours for that matter. Why?"

"Lucifer doesn't know it yet, but My Father has just given him a great big headache. When he came in here today, bearing his false tales and weak accusations, We could see right where he was headed. My Father allowed him his day in court so all could witness once again Lucifer's spirit of rebellion and the iniquity that is in him.

"But My Father also felt He owed Job something in return for all that he suffered at Lucifer's hand. He's decided to send a messenger to Earth in a similar fashion that Lucifer once afflicted Job with. Terms of this brief visitation were allowed so Lucifer would think he had some control in the matter. You know how he's a control freak."

"And how," Aram agreed. "But I don't understand. Are you going to send a destroying messen—"

"No! No! Nothing like that! Ha! Ha! Just the opposite! I'm going to send a messenger of blessing."

"I'll go!" Aram and Da-Ved said simultaneously.

"Excellent! I knew you both would want to go. You know, the only term Lucifer wanted was that both of you would be on this mission. He insisted that you two leave the sanctuary of heaven and once again enter into Earth's atmosphere. He has some real hatred for you both."

"The feeling is mutual," Aram said quietly.

"It was explained to him in no uncertain terms that he wouldn't be able to interfere with your mission and that Miyka'el was going to send a detachment of Guardians to enforce a no-fly zone over the area.

"But I must tell you he'll try to work his revenge on you two if he gets the chance. One of you will have to take command of the Legion to provide the security needed to complete this operation. The other will be inserted incognito onto the planet. The messenger can't reveal to anyone his true identity, but other than that, I will entertain any means that you can conceive to consecrate this blessing to the community. I will give you free rein to operate as I want you to learn from this assignment as well. The blessing will be sanctified reciprocally to the messenger as well as to the mortals who will receive it. You don't have the capacity to understand that now, but you will later."

"How long will we have to convey the blessing?" Da-Ved asked. "Will this be a long campaign?"

"No. I want the blessing to be bestowed in a single Earth days' time—twenty-four hours. You'll be allowed to pick the day you wish to go, but the location of your arrival has already been selected. The churches have been preparing for revival there, and it'll be easier for you to operate in this small community than if I place you in a larger city. The local saints will be able to intensify your strength with their prayers and supplications. It may become dangerous.

"Now, which one of you do I send as My messenger? You decide."

Da-Ved said, "You go, Aram. You'll make an awesome messenger."

Aram rose to his feet, towering over Da-Ved. "I would love to be the messenger, Da-Ved, but no. You're the one. I know you want to go, and I'm in your debt. Besides, you're smaller. We're supposed to be incognito, remember? I'd be hampered by my size, limited to what I could do. The people would pay more attention to the messenger and not the message. No. You go. I'll fly cover for you."

"I guess when you put it that way, I'd have to agree," Da-Ved said.

Da-Ved then looked to Yeshua. "Your Majesty, you mentioned a visit to an old friend. Who?"

"Why, Job, of course," replied Yeshua with laughter in His eyes.

Da-Ved looked quizzically at Aram who answered him with wide eyes and a shrug.

*****

Several months passed on Earth, and North America transitioned from spring through summer and on into the late autumn months. Returning from an errand outside of the shelter of heaven, Da-Ved was finally summoned by the Son to attend Him at the Throne.

It was puzzling to Da-Ved. Aram's new responsibilities took him to Earth, and the date Da-Ved set for the implementation of the blessing was fast approaching. Plans needed to be made, and the two angels hadn't talked with each other for some time.

Over the last few weeks, Da-Ved's excitement turned to disappointment, and he tried to hide it as best he could. Now, at last, he'd been summoned to attend the Throne again, but he feared he was going to be replaced by another angel or, worse, that the mission had been canceled altogether.

Walking the long corridor to the gate, Da-Ved thought, *Guess I'll find out if His Majesty has changed His mind. I hope not.*

At last, he approached Se-Lah, the huge warrior who had replaced Aram as sentry.

"Greetings, Da-Ved! How is it with you today? Have you heard anything about your new assignment?"

Da-Ved looked up. "Huh? Uh, no, I haven't. I've been summoned to the Throne again, but other than that, I haven't heard a thing. I can't understand it. I thought this mission was supposed to rate top priority. I guess He's changed His mind."

A self-conscious grin spread across Se-Lah's wide face. "I'm sure He has His reasons. You'll just have to trust His judgment. Here. Let me get the door for ya."

Se-Lah grabbed the large handle and, with effort, slowly opened the door to the inner chamber. As Da-Ved entered, seven angelic trumpeters at the pinnacle of the altar announced his arrival with a staccato blast of their great shofars.

Thousands of cheering angels immediately stood to their feet and roared out a deafening tribute. He took three faltering steps into the chamber and looked for his friends for an answer. Se-Lah came up behind him and tapped him on the shoulder. Da-Ved looked up to the larger angel.

"Wh-Why?" Da-Ved asked.

Se-Lah bent low and shouted into Da-Ved's ear, "They are cheering for you, Da-Ved! Today you will be anointed by His Majesty! Be well, my friend!"

Se-Lah then gave the little angel a gentle push toward the altar and returned to his post, closing the great door behind him.

Da-Ved descended the steps to the courtyard, and the gallery continued their deafening ovation. As he crossed the courtyard and started his ascent to the altar, the cheering impossibly grew louder with every step he took.

Through misty eyes, he peered up the steps to the top of the altar and saw that the Son was standing there, waiting for him. It wasn't possible! The Son was standing there, cheering along with His angels. He was being recognized by His Majesty Himself.

Standing with Yeshua was Aram and an honor guard of fifty Guardians. They'd drawn their shimmering blades and held them at port arms across brass breastplates. Twenty-five pairs of angels arched their fiery wings high overhead, forming the traditional Arch of Triumph for him to walk through.

His eyes filled with tears. *This is impossible. The Arch is reserved only for humans.*

Speaking to himself, Aram whispered, "Well, well, well, if it isn't the mighty giant killer himself." He greeted Da-Ved with a grin and raised the smaller angel's arm in victory.

The packed galleries began to beat their war shields with their forearms, drumming out an intimidating cadence.

Yeshua walked over to Da-Ved, cupped his hands, and spoke into his ear. He then raised His hands as a signal for quiet. The huge amphitheater was immediately thrown into an eerie silence, and the atmosphere became charged with a feeling of great expectancy.

The Lord escorted Da-Ved to the Father now seated on His Throne. Aram followed at their heels.

"Father, Your messenger and his second have arrived. May I proceed with their anointing?"

"Yes, Son. Miyka'el is waiting to insert the messenger and to dispatch the security troops whenever you're ready. But I'm sure you'll have preparations to make first."

"Thank you, Father."

"Aram, Da-Ved, please approach Me."

The two angels knelt to one knee in front of their king. Even kneeling, Aram towered over Da-Ved.

Yeshua placed a hand on each of their heads. "I extend My blessing unto you. My anointing shall give you wisdom and understanding, and both of you shall be greatly empowered.

"The people will be able to engage with you, so Da-Ved, you will be in disguise. May you extend My blessing to all of Creation, to mankind, as well as to the heavenly Host. You shall have authority in all matters concerning your mission for the time of your visitation."

In Yeshua's hand were two small replicas of the silver keys hanging from His own belt. He gave one to Da-Ved.

"Da-Ved, you will be an extension of My authority while on this mission. With this key, you will have authority and dominion over death, sickness, disease, and all their forms and minions for the length of your stay. Thanatos will soon quake at the very sounds of your footsteps. Healings and miracles are yours to call upon.

"Aram, may you watch over Da-Ved, relaying to him from on high the power of the saints below. May their prayers and supplications supply you with all knowledge and wisdom concerning the principalities and powers of hell."

Yeshua then gave the other silver key to Aram.

"Aram, while Da-Ved is My messenger on this mission, I extend to you My authority over She'Ol and all his followers. May the mighty Leviathan tremble at your very shadow. Through My dominion, you will have access to the power of Elohyim, His Shekinah Glory, and His Throne. No weapon formed can come against you, and no spiritual force outside of heaven will be more powerful.

"For the duration of one Earth day, you will be one of the most powerful angels in the entire universe. Only Miyka'el will be your angelic equal. If you prove yourself worthy on this mission, I have a more onerous assignment planned for you in the future.

"Now, may My Father's countenance shine upon you and give you peace."

The Shekinah Glory at the base of the Father's Throne ascended from between His feet and flew overhead to Aram and Da-Ved. The ball of shimmering light then descended upon the two friends, anointing them with its fiery glow. Tongues of fire danced upon their heads, filling them with a soft white radiance, and they fell upon their faces.

With this physical weakness, Aram also felt a sudden surge of spiritual strength and power. His mind began to race with a new dimension of understanding of strategies and tactics of corporeal and spiritual warfare.

It was a feeling unlike he'd ever had before. Although physically incapacitated, he also felt energized as if he had been injected with some sort of heavenly growth stimulant.

When finished, the Glory lifted from the two angels and returned to the base of the Throne. Yeshua raised both hands into the air and spoke to the two angels again.

"Arise, shine, for the light is come, and the Glory of the Lord is risen upon you. For, behold, the darkness shall cover the earth, and gross darkness the people; but the Lord shall arise upon you, and upon you, His Glory shall be seen."

After several moments, Aram and Da-Ved finally regained their strength and rose to their feet. The amphitheater once again broke out into a thunderous exaltation of worship, singing songs of praise for the Father, the Son, and the Holy Spirit. The celebration of the anointing lasted for many hours, and the twelve massive doors creaked noisily as her stones sang out.

Earth! Earth was to receive a messenger.

A messenger of blessing.

And when the servant of the man of God was risen
early, and gone forth, behold, an host compassed the
city both with horses and chariots. And his servant
said unto him, Alas, my master! how shall we do?
And he answered, Fear not: for they that be with
us are more than they that be with them.
And Elisha prayed, and said, LORD, I pray thee, open his
eyes, that he may see. And the LORD opened the eyes of the
young man; and he saw: and, behold, the mountain was
full of horses and chariots of fire round about Elisha.

—2 Kings 6:15–17 (KJV)

CHAPTER SIX

The Arrival

SEASONAL CHANGE
EARTH, NORTH AMERICAN CONTINENT

During the summer months, Aram spent his time working closely with Miyka'el, developing a plan for Da-Ved's insertion into a selected community within the United States. After due consideration, the two agreed to send an advanced guard of warriors to Earth to determine the enemy's strength surrounding the city.

Sundown, December 24th, was the time and date Da-Ved selected to begin his day of visitation, and Aram used the autumn months to extend a defensive shield around the target's general location. Da-Ved still had no idea where he was going, but this information was on a need-to-know basis, and for now, he didn't need to know.

By October, the Legion was ready to move in with an occupying force. The demons native to the area were not aware of the infiltration of Aram's forces until their trap was set. No battle had taken place as the demons were far outclassed by these angelic warriors, and they'd been roughly rousted, pushed out, and denied entry back into the city and surrounding countryside.

Pharmakos, the viceroy in demonic authority over the territory, was outraged by the harsh handling of his troops and complained bitterly to Miyka'el about his loss of face as well as his access to his dominion. His complaints fell upon deaf ears, and Aram easily pulled the Prince of Addiction from the region.

With thirty of heaven's most elite warriors flying a mile-high security cap, the target was sealed and secured.

After witnessing Aram's easy subjugation of their governor, the principality's more tenacious demons begrudgingly became less insolent and more respectful to their powerful adversaries. It quickly became obvious to them that something unusual was afoot, and they decided to wait and see what was about to transpire. Besides, they were powerless to do anything else, and a restrained pacification finally settled upon the outskirts of the sector.

From the vacuum of the now almost demon-less environment, a new measure of spiritual insight and discernment matured within many of the human inhabitants. After decades of fruitless supplications, prayers began to be answered, and the local churches were strengthened in the faith and grew in numbers daily.

*****

As the winter months approached, Aram returned to report that the target city had been secured. As the time of departure approached, Miyka'el ordered Da-Ved and Aram to attend him in the Sanctuary.

The diminutive angel's appearance had been altered to allow him the anonymity needed to accomplish his covert mission. Gone were his angelic wings, leaving behind only two small nodules on his back over his shoulders.

Da-Ved was transformed in other ways also. Now that he'd experienced God's anointing power, he appreciated the precious freedom humanity had been endowed with and how powerful the humans could be if they would just walk in covenant with God. Very few men or women ever lived at this level of spiritual awareness and insight.

An invisible aura radiated from him, testifying to those whose eyes were spiritually astute that he possessed something very unusual, even for an angel. A single word easily described Da-Ved's transformation—*empathy*. The world was to be visited by a messenger of God's empathy, and he was carrying a blessing of tremendous power.

With his hair trimmed to a shorter length, Da-Ved also sported the shady stubble of a two-day-old beard. He no longer wore his leather kepi, and gone were his warrior's clothing and weapons, save for a small pouch hanging from a cord about his neck.

Clad in simple blue jeans and a gray sweatshirt, he also wore a navy-blue Peacoat and wool watch cap to ward off the chilly night air. On his feet were white athletic socks and a pair of work boots. Attired in this manner, he was now ready for the descent to the planet below.

Aram arrived and observed the Son addressing Miyka'el and a young man. As he approached them, he sensed something familiar about the mortal.

"Da-Ved! I hardly recognized you! I thought you were a human."

He ran up to Da-Ved who backed away cautiously.

"Easy there, big fella! I'm glad to see you too, but let's not kill the messenger before he delivers the message."

"It's been a while, Da-Ved. It's good to see you."

Miyka'el took a hard look at Aram. "Our final security sweep has been successful, I trust?"

"Yes, General. All is ready. We only await the messenger. I... uh...I've come to provide a personal escort for him."

Yeshua grinned at the sight of the unlikely pair. "Aram has risen in stature here since you last saw him, Da-Ved. Not many angels can equal his power and tireless energy. He's done an awesome job preparing the planet for you. My Father and I are truly impressed by what's transpired in the last few months. The Legion should be proud."

Aram bowed his head. "Thank you, Sire. I'll relay that to them. They take great satisfaction in any compliment coming from the Throne."

"Well, Da-Ved, are you ready for this?" Miyka'el asked.

The small angel smiled. "I've been looking forward to that question for some time now. Yes, I'm ready and anxious to go. By the way, where are we going anyhow? No one has told me, you know."

Miyka'el winked at his King, sharing some small secret between them.

"Are you sure you haven't been told, Da-Ved?" Miyka'el faked mock surprise. "I seem to remember a conversation not too long ago where you were advised of the whole plan. You don't remember?"

A puzzled look came over Da-Ved, and he looked to Aram for an answer. Aram looked away trying to conceal his laughter. Da-Ved stared at his friend in wide-eyed amazement.

"What? What's so funny?"

Yeshua said, "Da-Ved, you'll find out soon enough. Be assured that the place has been properly prepared and is awaiting your arrival."

Aram shook his finger. "Okay, partner, you have us full of questions, too, you know. Our brothers have been asking me why you picked December 24th for your day of departure. We realize the date's implications, but other than that, we're at a loss. What's the plan? Clue us in."

"That, my large friend, is *my* secret. You'll just have to watch it unfold."

Da-Ved turned to Miyka'el and asked, "If it's time, may we go?"

Miyka'el ordered, "Proceed, Guardians. Deliver the blessing, and be bold in your witness."

"Yeshua added in a hushed tone, "And My peace be unto you, Da-Ved."

Aram looked uncomfortable, a pained look upon his face. "Uh, Da-Ved. If you're ready, I'll have to carry—"

"I know. I know. You'll have to carry me because my wings are gone. So? Paul was once carried to heaven by an angel. Why shouldn't a blessing be carried to Earth in a similar manner? Let's go!"

Aram scooped up Da-Ved in his huge arms and, with a single downward thrust of his wings, was airborne. Soaring through one of the four large portals directly above the altar, Aram rapidly exited the cavernous chamber.

"The Lord has granted us priority clearance for this mission, Da-Ved. Let's use the shortcut to the planet. We'll be entering Earth's atmosphere in short order."

Stretched out across the Cosmos was Earth's rapidly approaching solar system. Minutes later, Aram sped past its outermost planets, and a small blue ball appeared to hang in front of them. It raced to them, growing in size with each passing second. Aram gradually slowed, then stopped to admire the small water-covered planet from just beyond its moon.

"Every time I see it from this angle, I'm awed by its creation," Da-Ved said.

"Me too," agreed Aram. "As well as its Creator. And this time, the humans will be awed with what you have in store for them, Da-Ved."

Two familiar figures darted from the far side of the moon to join them. "Hey, you two! Where've you been keeping yourselves?" Oreb asked as they drew near.

Da-Ved flinched in Aram's arms. "Oreb!"

At the rapid approach of Oreb's golden-haired companion, Aram said, "Ariy'el, what does our intelligence say? Is it safe for our final approach?"

"Yes, but Lucifer's troops have been on a planet-wide alert after their little soirée in the sanctuary a few months ago, and they've been watching for any unusual activity on our part. Lucifer couldn't help but know you're coming after we rousted his troops from the countryside. But he won't give us any trouble now. He knows your reputation and newfound strength, and he also knows Miyka'el is watching over us. He'll wait until the mission is completed or just about completed before he tries to move in. Boy, will he be surprised when he finds out what's happening."

"Don't underestimate him, Ariy'el. He's not stupid, and he's got a score to settle. I'm sure he has his scouting parties out also, and he's probably gathering intelligence on us as we speak. The situation is dangerous, so for now, let's concentrate on providing Da-Ved the security he needs, and then we'll decide what we're going to do about Lucifer later."

"Sure. It's just that I'm anxious to see how the blessing plays out. You may proceed to the planet now. Our troops have been alerted, and they're monitoring your approach."

Oreb shaded his eyes and looked towards the planet. "Local time is late afternoon, Da-Ved. Just as you requested. Big holiday tomorrow, you know. It's the evening before the day the saints traditionally celebrate the first tabernacle of the Lord. The day He came to dwell among them as a child."

"Your insertion point has been checked three times today and is secure," Ariy'el added. "We've picked out a spot in a small section of woods in the foothills near a road leading into town. I'm afraid you'll have to walk some."

"That's fine. It'll be good to stretch my legs a little."

Aram motioned to Ariy'el and Oreb. "You two go in first for a quick fly-by. Once we've landed, fly top cover for Da-Ved until I return and relieve you. Then you two can rejoin your troops."

"Yes, sir. Let's go, Oreb," Ariy'el said as he headed for the planet.

*****

DECEMBER 24 – 4:30 PM
EARTH, NORTH AMERICAN CONTINENT

A hundred miles southwest of Da-Ved's destination lay the city of Fresno, California. Located on California's central valley floor, the city's climate was a bit more temperate, and there were still days at this time of the year when people could walk about, wearing little more than a light jacket during the daylight hours. The sun was starting to set, and a cooling breeze chilled the air.

Several television sets in a modest appliance store window on Ventura Avenue were tuned to the same channel. The store owner had piped the audio portion of the broadcast to the outside storefront. A small crowd waiting at a nearby bus stop gathered around the display window to watch. The late afternoon newscast was on, and two attractive reporters were bantering back and forth with small talk.

"Well, Lisa, it appears either Santa has come a bit early this year or we have some goblins leftover from Halloween. It seems we're getting calls from the eastern ridge country in the mountains about lights in the sky again."

Lisa Silverton was in good humor. "I know, Dick. This has been going on for some time now. Maybe the elves have arrived a little early this year. If any of our viewers have seen anything unusual up there and would care to be interviewed, they might try calling our

Channel Six News Line, and our Sky Cam helicopter crew could follow up on this for a Christmas Day story. What do you think?"

The floor director cued for the break.

"I think it's time for our commercial break, Lisa. Stay tuned, folks, we'll be right back with the weather and sports up next."

Co-anchor Dick Cole turned to the floor director who signaled that they were off the air. In a lowered voice, Dick whispered, "Say, Lisa, you're not still on that UFO thing, are ya? Cause if you are, cool it."

Lisa whispered harshly, "I know what I saw, Dick. Or I think I know what I saw."

"That was three weeks ago, Lisa, and you said you had been drinking that even—"

"I had one lousy drink at a dinner party which was hours before I drove home through the hills."

"Let's not start that up again, okay?" Dick said, giving her a good-natured wink.

Her cheeks reddened, and she said, "Oooh...*men!*" She looked away to sort the papers on the desk in front of her.

The director counted down the end of the commercial break into her headset, and Tim Fossey, the local meteorologist, rushed to join Dick and Lisa at the news desk.

"Three, two, one—" She pointed to Dick.

"Say, Tim, what's it look like for Old Saint Nick and his sleigh this year? Any snow in the forecast tonight? Ha! Ha!"

Camera 2 was focused on the nearby weather set, but Tim always began his forecast in front of Camera 1 at the main news console with Dick and Lisa.

"Funny you should ask that, Dick, because I don't think Santa will have too much of a problem this year. Believe it or not, snow is in the local forecast for Christmas Eve."

Lisa and Dick both responded at the same time. "Really?" they asked together in amazement.

"Yep. A small weather system has stalled in the mountains, and because of a temperature inversion, it's going to stay low in the foot-hills tonight." He got up from his seat and walked the twenty feet to the weather set, trailing his control cord behind him. The camera-man at Camera 2 adjusted for a tighter shot.

"We'll probably get no more than a dusting here in the valley, but snow is definitely the word for tonight. And by the way," Tim said with a grin, "you can tell all the kids that our Accu-Trac Radar man is going to stay up all night, watching for any unusual radar blips above the Arctic Circle. We'll be sure to give them plenty of warning if we see Santa's sleigh heading our way so they can get to bed before he gets here."

*****

DECEMBER 24 – SUNDOWN
SEVEN MILES EAST OF THE TARGET CITY

Carl and Randy had a remote cabin up in the elevations east of the city. There, they cooked methamphetamine for the Devil's Own motorcycle gang in a clandestine drug lab. The crude lab was more of a shack than a cabin, and they had been attracted to it more for its seclusion than anything else.

The shack was perched seven miles from the nearest city at the edge of a small cliff. Here, they were far enough into the hills to provide the secrecy needed for their illicit trade but close enough to town to easily obtain most of the chemicals needed for their kitchen.

Their main means of transportation from town was an old jeep they parked out of sight near the base of the hill on a dirt road just off the main highway. In this secluded clearing, they also stored under camouflaged tarps two all-terrain vehicles which they used to move their supplies up the steep hillside on an old firebreak.

Always fearful of the police, they'd surrounded all but one approach to the shack with booby traps of pits laced with punji sticks and walls of hanging fishhooks.

The two had been fairly successful in that they were not greedy and so had never been caught. They only stayed in an area for a few months at a time and then moved on, never giving the local author-ities a reason for an investigation.

Even so, this location was unique. It was secluded, high in the countryside, and had a clear field of vision of the only paved road leading to town. Any approach by police would be easily ascertained, and the cooks could escape quickly on the two dirt bikes they kept at the shack, just for such an occasion. As a final precaution, a web of army surplus camouflage netting was suspended over the small building, making accidental discovery by air next to impossible.

They also pirated a small amount of power needed to cook the crank from a stepped-down power line strung up the hill years ago by the power company. The power line was needed to provide electricity to a remote repeater tower at the top of the mountain used by the local fire department's rescue squads. The ambulances used the tower to relay their weak radio signals over the ridge in order to talk to one of the larger trauma hospitals in the central valley.

Their setup was super-sweet, and they hoped they wouldn't have to move for some time. Carl had just returned from town and was unloading supplies from his four-wheel ATV. He was complaining again to Randy about their recent rash of bad luck.

"I can't understand it, Rand. It's unbelievable when you think about it. Man! First, our major buyer gets busted with the samples in his car, and for a stupid traffic ticket no less. Then the nearest hardware store where I get some of our chems goes out of business."

He grabbed a box filled with drain cleaner and headed toward the shack. "I can go elsewhere, but I need to spread out our purchases as much as possible. I don't want to make anyone suspicious, ya know? Now we're getting these electrical brownouts, and we'll probably have someone from the power company or fire department up here next week, sniffing around. It's been like that all over this part of the state. Every cook and grower I know has had some sort of bad luck since what? Late August? Early September? Nobody is making any money anymore!"

"Yeah, tell me about it," Randy said. "It's been real spooky, I'll grant you that. It's like we're under a curse or sumpin. Maybe we ought to move our kitchen—"

Randy turned and saw Carl looking up at the sky. In reflex fashion, Randy ducked down behind a tree.

"What is it? A chopper?"

"Nah. I don't know what it is. Here. Look, right over there."

"Where? I don't see anything."

Carl grabbed Randy and pulled him to the edge of the cliff, pointing down.

"Look down the hill toward the sun. See that patch of aspen trees between us and the road?"

"Yeah? So?"

Sweeping his hand skyward, Carl continued, "Now look straight up from there…about two thousand feet or so. See it?"

Randy strained his eyes. Squinting, he said, "What? What am I supposed to be looking at? Oh yeah! What is that? Man, what is that thing?"

Carl shaded his eyes with one hand. "I—wow! Did you see that thing move?"

"Yeah, it literally burned into the ground. What do you think it was?"

"Don't know. I didn't hear any crash. Some sort of freaky light. Ball lightning, maybe?"

The two men climbed up on a large boulder and peered over the cliff at the trees below. Randy put an arm on Carl's back, steadying himself, and leaned further out, looking into the gorge.

"No way, man. That thing hit in those aspens and all that grass. There's no fire. Hey! If anyone else saw that thing, it's liable to get crowded up here! We'd better leave. Maybe for good."

A frown spread across Carl's bearded face. "Man! Just like I was telling ya. We can't get a break. It's a curse, I tell ya. The gods are against us. It's enough to make ya go straight."

"We better scoot," Randy said as he jumped down from the boulder.

"Hey, how 'bout a little vacation? We've got a good stash saved, and we're getting ready to shut down with winter coming anyhow. It's a little early, but how's Mexico sound?"

"Dude! Sounds sweet to me. But we better move fast. Those chopper-heads won't be happy if they find out we're leaving. Ya know, they think they've got an exclusive on our goods, especially since things in the valley have been drying up lately."

Randy looked to the setting sun. "Let's go. It gets a little weird up here after the sun goes down. Grab any product we got left and turn off what you can. Maybe tomorrow, we can sneak back up here and get the rest of our stuff."

"Man! What was that thing?"

*****

APPROACHING EARTH

The Earth loomed in front of them, suspended in space, back-dropped by ten thousand specks of light.

"So, Da-Ved, are you ready to put on your cloak of humanity and fill your lungs with air?" Aram asked.

"Yes, as soon as we enter the atmosphere. I don't want to do that too soon."

"Okay, we'd better go. It'll take a few minutes."

Aram descended quickly and placed Da-Ved within a small copse of aspen in a secluded part of a wooded hill. The hill over-looked a two-lane road below their position, but traffic was sporadic this time of day.

Aram seemed preoccupied, more serious than Da-Ved had ever seen before. He was taking his responsibilities very seriously and per-formed a low-level fly-over first to check out the hillside. This was followed by a quick flip and a rocketing climb directly above the hill. Finally, Aram rolled over and corkscrewed in, descending the two thousand feet in seconds. Thirty feet above the ground, he spread and flared his huge wings, braking hard like an enormous eagle land-ing on some solitary perch. He gently deposited Da-Ved onto the ground.

Da-Ved stumbled but quickly caught himself. "Whoa there, Aram! Before you go, could you fly back up there and get my stom-ach for me? I think it's where you did that little flick and flip maneu-ver, near that little dark cloud!"

Aram ignored the taunt. "The road is just down the hill from here, Da-Ved. The town is to the west about seven miles. Sorry, I can't get you any closer than this, but my orders are to insert you here."

Da-Ved started to laugh. Silently, at first, then a chuckle broke out. Aram scowled. Da-Ved turned away from his friend and let out an audible chortle. Trying to stifle his laughter, he then let out a couple of snorts. Soon, he was bent over and convulsing with loud cramping horselaughs. Now tears were streaming from his eyes. It was infectious.

Aram broke into a grin, then chuckled. He laughed. Soon, he was bent over in laughter, pounding Da-Ved on his back.

When he finally caught his breath, he asked Da-Ved, "Wha-Wha-What are we laughing about?"

That sent Da-Ved into hysterics again, and Aram found himself so weak from laughter he unbuckled his armor and sword and fell to the ground. Soon, both angels were flat on their backs, knees doubled up, feet in the air, laughing hysterically.

Through sobs and gasps for breath, Da-Ved finally blurted out, "*You!* You big ape! You're so seriously stiff and formal. You're a *scream!*"

And once again, he broke down, pounding the ground, tears streaming from his eyes, letting out great war-whoops of laughter.

With that, Aram lost it again, loosing great guffaws and crying tears till he hurt and could laugh no more. Spent, they lay on their backs in a clearing amidst the trees, gathering strength for a few minutes.

At last, Aram sat up. With his knees flexed in front of him, his large wings trailed behind him up the hill. He stared westward towards the shrinking sun and became still. Da-Ved rolled over and, noticing his friend's quietness, sensed Aram was revealing a side to him he'd never seen before.

"What is it, Aram? What's wrong?"

"Nothing's wrong. I'm just concerned about the mission...and you. Lucifer is out there. Somewhere, waiting for you."

"I know. So? So is Miyka'el. So's the Legion. And you, Aram. I'm not worried. I'm...I'm *excited!*"

He leaped to his feet. "Let's get going, Aram. I know you've got things to do, so go do them. I'll be all right."

Aram got to his feet, wiping the dirt from his hands. He quickly donned his discarded armor and adjusted the scabbard upon his back, cinching it tightly.

"I know you will, Da-Ved. You'll do fine. Give 'em heaven!"

With that, Aram rose from the ground, hovering at treetop level. His seriousness had returned. Looking down at Da-Ved, he said, "I'll take one lap around the hill. Then, if everything checks out, I'll leave by flying towards the sun. When you see me go wait a couple of minutes, then head for the road. Remember, this one is for His Majesty. See you later."

He took one lazy lap around the perimeter of the hill, then streaked towards the setting sun.

Da-Ved brushed himself off, waited a couple of minutes, then trotted off toward the road. As he pushed his way downhill through the trees and undergrowth, he whistled an old church hymn he'd heard somewhere.

As the evening shadows lengthened, he started to feel very alone. The waning sunlight was turning everything into cool shades of gray, and the cold night air started to seep into his light clothing. He pulled the peacoat's collar up high around his neck and thrust his hands into its deep pockets.

The sky was flecked with vaporous clouds, and a drizzle began to fall, punctuating his footsteps with a forlorn melancholy. Sighing, he recalled the words to the tune he had been whistling and whence he had heard them—a funeral. The hymn mirrored his somber mood. Then he started to quietly sing his way to the road.

> Abide with me. Fast falls the eventide,
> The darkness deepens, Lord, with me abide.
> When other helpers fail and comforts flee,
> Help of the helpless, oh, abide with me.[2]

He looked up. Through the thickening clouds and among the first emerging stars shot two streaks of light. One object traversed from the east to the west, shimmering across the sky to the distant horizon. The second object streaked perpendicular to the first, traveling north to south. Its luminescent path was shorter. For an instant, a gigantic cross seared the sky.

"Oreb and Ariy'el!" he said, realizing he'd never been truly alone. He skipped to the last verse and continued the hymn.

> Hold Thou Thy cross before my closing eyes,
> Shine through the gloom and point me to the skies.
> Heaven's morning breaks, and earth's vain shadows flee;
> In life, in death, O Lord, abide with me![3]

The LORD said to Moses, "Speak to the people of
Israel, and tell them to make tassels on the corners of
their garments throughout their generations, and to
put a cord of blue on the tassel of each corner.
And it shall be a tassel for you to look at and remember all the
commandments of the LORD, to do them, not to follow after your
own heart and your own eyes, which you are inclined to whore after.
So you shall remember and do all my
commandments, and be holy to your God.
I am the LORD your God, who brought you out of the land
of Egypt to be your God: I am the LORD your God."

Numbers 15:37–41 (ESV)

CHAPTER SEVEN

Close Encounters

DECEMBER 24 – SUNDOWN
SEVEN MILES EAST OF THE TARGET CITY

With a little effort, Da-Ved descended through the undergrowth until he found pavement and headed west. The sky continued to cloud over, and the light drizzle turned into rain. Hunkering down, Da-Ved sought shelter under a tall pine tree near the roadway. He looked skyward.

Uh…this isn't exactly how I intended to enter the city, he thought.

A car sped by, not seeing the solitary figure obscured in the misty haze. Pressed for time, Da-Ved decided to try to hitch a ride with the next vehicle that came along, and within minutes, a small flatbed truck carrying a load of lumber emerged from around the bend. Da-Ved stuck his thumb out. The truck's brakes squealed noisily as the driver fought it to a hasty stop.

A sign on the door of the truck declared Cohen and Son Construction Company. The truck driver was a young man of about thirty, dressed in white coveralls, and wearing a baseball cap. He threw the passenger door open and yelled to the hitchhiker, "Hey, buddy! Are ya coming, or do ya *like* to walk in the rain?"

Da-Ved ran to the truck and hopped in. "Thanks for the lift. I was starting to get a bit wet."

The driver threw the truck in gear and gunned the engine. "No big deal…but in a little while, you would have been more cold than wet. The weatherman is calling for the white stuff tonight. It'll probably start soon this high up."

"Good thing you stopped then. I'd hate to spend the night up here."

"Yeah, and I almost missed you. You seemed to appear out of nowhere."

"Yeah, I guess I must have just walked out of the trees as you came around the bend. Talk about timing."

Reaching under his seat, the driver pulled out a silver thermos bottle. Without taking his eyes off the road, he handed it to Da-Ved and shifted into second gear.

"You must be freezing. Here, have some coffee. It's still hot."

Da-Ved took it and poured a cup of the steaming liquid into the thermos' metal cap.

The young man was talkative. "My name's Danny. I'm heading towards town, but I turn off before I get to the city limits. I suppose you're going farther than that."

The cup was hot, and Da-Ved cradled it carefully. "Yes, and you can drop me anywhere. I'm just thankful for the ride." He sipped the coffee. "Mmmm. This hits the spot."

Danny looked him over. "You're traveling kind of light, aren't you? I don't mean to pry, but I didn't see any knapsack or bedroll."

"No, it's not what you think. I'm not that far from home. I just need a ride."

Danny shifted into third gear, and the transmission whined as the truck picked up speed. "I didn't catch your name."

"I'm sorry. The name's Da-Ved. Are you Cohen?"

"That's Cohen *and Son*. I'm the son part. So what'cha doing up here in the foothills, tonight of all nights? Heading home for Christmas?"

Da-Ved chuckled and said, "I'm surprised by your name you'd even know that tomorrow is the holiday."

Assuming a hurt look, Danny replied, "Why, I'm shocked, Mr. Dave. Everyone knows tomorrow is Christmas. Not that I care, mind you. But this *is A-mer-i-ca*!"

In a more serious tone, he added, "The missus does care, though. Our family is that all-American household everyone talks about but no one ever truly sees. And we've got all kinds of religion at the Cohen home.

"Take my father, for instance. He was always quoting scripture from the Tanakh. And my wife, Kim? Her family is from Korea. Met her over there while I did a hitch in the army. And check this out. Her family are all Buddhists, and she's a Southern Fried Baptist! What a hoot!"

Da-Ved tried hard to not spit out a mouthful of coffee while he stifled a laugh. "I'll bet it gets confusing around the holidays. Do you have any kids?"

"And how! I've got three. Two girls and a boy. And you bet it does. Get confusing, I mean. But we all get along. We're Americanized. Somehow, we manage to blend Christmas, Chanukah, and all the other holidays together.

"I don't take the religious part too seriously though. My family's all right, but I can't stand the smug hypocrites in organized religions. You know what I mean?"

"Hmmm," Da-Ved mused.

Danny glanced at his passenger. "Hmmm? What does hmmm mean?"

"I was just thinking. You remind me of someone I know. At least your outlook on religion does."

"Anyone I know?"

"No. Just someone like yourself. Another carpenter. Come to think of it…He's Jewish too. And like you, He doesn't care much for pious hypocrites. I don't think He's too fond of religion either."

"Sounds like my kind of guy. I'd like to meet him someday. Maybe we could get together and start an anti-religious movement or something. Hah! Bet we could get rich doing it too!"

"Sorry," Da-Ved said, "you're too late. He's already started one. But He's always looking for new members."

"That's just great!" Danny said with faux disappointment in his voice. "I think of a way to start a new religious movement and maybe make some easy money, and someone has already gone and done it. Bet his initiation fee is steep too."

Da-Ved gave his companion a mischievous grin. "No, there's no membership fee, but eventually, you do tend to make a large investment. But it's all right because the benefits are fantastic. Ha! Ha!"

The rain became heavier, and Danny turned on the wipers. They drove on for a few minutes in silence, save for the rhythmic movement of the wiper blades. Da-Ved then noticed a white tassel, a foot-long tzit-tzit fringe from a prayer shawl hanging from the truck's rearview mirror.

"I thought you didn't take all this religious stuff very seriously," Da-Ved said, nodding toward the tassel.

"Oh, that. How do you know about that stuff? That was my grandfather's. He died two years ago come January. His passing was peculiar, too, you know?"

"Oh yeah? How so?" Da-Ved asked.

Danny's voice had a slight tremor to it now. "My grandfather was dying of cancer and wasn't doing very well with the doctors, the chemo, and all that stuff. He hated hospitals and he wasn't shy in letting anyone know it.

"Gramps didn't take any bull from anyone. Not after what the Nazis did to him in Germany. He was the youngest in his family and the only one that survived the war in Europe. But he was tough as nails, that old man. After the war, he moved to America, married, and built this company out of nothing. My dad went into business with him when he was old enough. They did pretty well too."

"What happened? Did your grandfather become religious at the end?"

"Yeah. But I never understood why."

"Something must have happened," Da-Ved said. "What was it?"

"Mmmm...are you sure you want to talk about this? It's not a good story."

"Yeah, if it doesn't bother you too much. I want to hear about the tassel."

"All right. My folks were both killed in a car accident about ten years ago. Grandma died long before that, and I was the only family

Gramps had left. I can tell you... We didn't see eye to eye on most things. And he'd spent all his time building the family business, so he didn't have many close friends. He had no one to lean on besides me and my wife, and he wasn't too sure of my Korean Christian wife.

"But then Kim got him to read some scriptures from Yesha'yah. Oh, sorry. That's Isaiah to you. And some other stuff from her Christian Bible. You know...that...that New Testament stuff."

Da-Ved nodded. "Yes, I'm familiar with it."

"At first, I thought it was kind of pitiful. It was like he was a drowning man reaching out to grab a life preserver, a log, anything that would float. He devoured that book in the little time he had left and he kept going back and forth from our Jewish Bible to that Gentile Bible.

He kept talking about the name of God written on a thigh and something about a king and some other such nonsense."

"Interesting," Da-Ved said. "What do you think he meant by that?"

Danny rubbed the back of his head, dislodging his cap, and mussing his thick red hair in the process. It fell across his eyes.

"Who knows? The only thing I know is he was a hard man that led a hard life. He hated the religious holidays...said it was for the weak. In my entire life, I don't recall ever seeing him go to any services at the synagogue.

"I guess the Nazis finally beat the religion out of him. But he respected the old ways, even though he no longer had any use for them."

A puzzled look came over Da-Ved's face. "That sounds somewhat strange, don't you think?"

Brushing the fallen hair from his eyes, Danny said, "Yeah, he was funny that way. Gramps was proud of Jewish culture and supported our local synagogue financially. He jealously guarded his family's memory and their traditions and wouldn't allow the Nazis to destroy everything from his early life. Even though he had no use for it himself, he raised his family in the religion and made the boys attend yeshiva classes.

"The Rabbi used to come by the house a couple of times a month, and they would play chess while debating the existence of God. When I was little, I used to sit on the floor by the hearth and listen to them argue."

With a hushed voice, Danny whispered, "It made me uncomfortable to see Grandfather get religion at the end."

Holding the fringe in his hand, Da-Ved asked, "But what about this tassel?"

Danny coughed and wiped his nose. He shifted in his seat to sit more erect.

"Oh, that. That came off Grandfather's tallit—his prayer shawl. In actuality, there are four tassels in all. One for each corner of the shawl. We learned that the name of God is tied with special knots in the tassels. Gramps knew about the Scriptures from his boyhood education and from arguing with Rabbi Goldberg, but I never kept up with it much after my early teens.

"Come to think of it, the fringe does hang low when you're wearing the tallit. It brushes up against you on your thigh, but how that fits into what he was talking about I'll never know. Whatever Kim told him seemed to help because a peace seemed to come over him, and he died easy a month later."

The small angel held his tongue, and an uneasy silence momentarily filled the cab.

Danny looked away but then returned to his story. "My wife's a good woman, and she became very close to my grandfather in the few weeks before he died. They used to have long conversations during the day when I was away at work."

"What did she tell him?" Da-Ved asked.

"I don't know, but it sure seemed to make a difference to him. I guess religion has its place after all."

"I don't think so, Danny. You were right the first time. All religions are deceptive in that they allow people to think they can earn their way to heaven. You can't work your way there. Sounds to me, though, that your grandfather got to talk to the right person before he passed away."

"You think so? Go figure. We buried him wrapped in his tallit like he wished, but he wanted me to have this one tassel and that old Gentile Bible."

"So. There it is, just hanging there like a missing piece from some crazy jigsaw puzzle."

Danny flicked it with his finger and watched it swing back and forth from the mirror.

"Kim says someday, she'll get around to telling me about it when I'm ready. Ha! Ha! Can you imagine that? A Southern Baptist Korean girl telling *me* about a tallit. Me...who was bar-mitzvahed when I was thirteen. She's going to tell me about a tallit? That'll be the day."

"Did you ever read that Gentile Bible?" Da-Ved asked.

"Nah. I got it, though. It's right there in the glove box. Here."

Without taking his eyes off the road, Danny reached over, popped open the compartment, and took out a small leather-bound book.

"Hey, sorry, but I'm coming to my turn off. The city limits are just down the—"

Glancing at his passenger, Danny found he was alone in his truck, and he hit the brakes hard.

The vehicle skidded to a stop and stalled, and he let it coast to a stop onto the berm of the highway. Throwing open his door, he charged out of the truck and ran to the back of his load.

"Dave! Dave!"

Searching the highway, Danny looked for signs of his injured passenger lying somewhere nearby on the ground. The road stretched out behind him for a quarter mile, but his passenger was nowhere to be seen. He hadn't fallen out. He'd simply disappeared.

Danny pushed his cap to the back of his head. "What's going on?"

Returning to his seat, he shifted the transmission into neutral. He sat for a minute, pondering his bizarre encounter when he noticed a small medallion hanging next to the tassel on his rearview mirror.

Now where'd that come from?

Danny sat in the truck in shock, the wipers beating a monotonous tattoo on the windshield. A car rushed by, spraying his truck with a large rooster-tail. The spray from the passing vehicle entered through his side wing window, drenching his arm and already damp coveralls.

"Ahhh!" He flinched as the cold water shocked him to his senses.

Looking at the medallion, he saw there was something inscribed upon it. It read simply "Numbers 15:37–41." He flipped the medallion over and saw another engraving. He recognized this second inscription as verses from the Gentile Bible referring to the book of Revelation. The inscription read "Revelation 19:11–16."

With fumbling hands, Danny grabbed the leather book on the seat and opened it to the scripture in Numbers. It referred to God's first instructions concerning the tallit and for the way His people should live. He removed the medallion from the mirror and examined it more closely.

"What the heck?"

He searched the table of contents and found the other scripture at the back of the book. He flipped through the pages, found the verses, and began to read.

Danny blinked and read it again. He looked out the window with a faraway look on his face. Then his eyes misted over, and he couldn't see the road anymore.

He tore the tassel from the mirror, clasping it to his chest. He cleared his throat and whispered, "I-I don't believe it."

The young carpenter wiped his eyes and sat there for a full ten minutes, reading and rereading the verses. At last, he started the truck, threw it into gear, and turned off onto the side road.

Danny Cohen was headed home.

For the wrath of God is revealed from heaven against all
ungodliness and unrighteousness of men, who by their
unrighteousness suppress the truth. For what can be known about
God is plain to them, because God has shown it to them. For his
invisible attributes, namely, his eternal power and divine nature,
have been clearly perceived, ever since the creation of the world,
in the things that have been made. So they are without excuse. For
although they knew God, they did not honor him as God or give
thanks to him, but they became futile in their thinking, and their
foolish hearts were darkened. Claiming to be wise, they became
fools, and exchanged the glory of the immortal God for images
resembling mortal man and birds and animals and creeping things.

—Romans 1:18–23 (ESV)

CHAPTER EIGHT

Three

DECEMBER 24 – 5:00 PM

Da-Ved instinctively grabbed at the arms, encircling his waist, and hooted with amusement. "Ha! Ha! Oreb, I thought you were going to rejoin your unit. Your timing's excellent."

The dark-skinned Guardian slowed, then hovered in mid-flight to watch the small truck maneuver onto the side road. It quickly sped away into the distance.

"I was headed that way. I was just returning when I saw you hitchhiking. I thought it might be a good idea to hang around a little while, so I caught a ride with you on top of the truck's cab. That was an interesting conversation you just had with that human. I heard the whole thing."

Oreb landed to deposit Da-Ved onto the main highway.

"It *was* interesting, wasn't it? I only hope his curiosity is aroused now, and he heads home for that long talk with his wife."

"*Cur-i-osity* aroused? Ha! Da-Ved, I pulled you out of there so fast he never saw you leave. I'm sure the conversation at that house is going to be very unusual tonight, to say the least."

"I hope so, Oreb. And thanks. I can manage from here. You better head back to your troops. They'll be wondering what happened to you."

"Yeah, I'm sure Aram has things for me to do. Be careful."

"Thanks, I will. I'm almost to town now, so I should be fine. I'll catch you later."

Oreb leapt into the sky and streaked away, leaving a slight contrail. The rain dissipated, and a stiff wind blew in from the high country, drying the tarmac. Several miles closer to town now, the road grew to a four-lane highway divided by a grassy median strip.

Lights were starting to turn on in a few scattered homes below in the valley. Da-Ved spotted a signpost and made his way to it. As he drew nearer, he could see the sign indicated he was approaching the city limits to a small town.

Great! I finally get to see where I'm going, he mused.

When he got within twenty feet of the sign, he grinned. "So that's the big mystery."

Revealing his destination, the sign read

> JOB, CALIFORNIA
> CITY LIMIT
> POP 17,252   ELEV 4,682

The temperature fell, and with the wind at his back, he made for the heart of the city. The majority of the city's population was nestled within a mountain valley in the Sierra Nevada Mountain Range running near the California-Nevada border. To the west of this elevated valley stretched the greater Central Valley between the Sierra Nevada's and the other California coastal ranges.

*****

Before the turn of the twentieth century, Job had been a boom-town called Silver Hills. The town had flourished because of a rich silver strike, and it had been one of the more successful mining districts in California.

After the fertile silver vein pinched out in the summer of 1888, the town had all but crumbled along with the mines. When bleak times came to Silver Hills, a handful of die-hard prospectors had hung on as well as a few sheep ranchers and farmers. The tenants who lived closest to the land had long before recognized another type of treasure hidden within the surrounding beauty of the forests, meadows, and streams. With their roots sunk deeply into the land, the more steadfast residents managed to keep Silver Hills from completely becoming a ghost town.

Nevertheless, the economic loss of the mine hit the townspeople hard, and many of them left to seek their fortunes elsewhere. That was when the name of the town changed. Reeling under the loss of the silver from the played-out mine, the shopkeepers nicknamed the town after the seemingly cursed biblical figure—Job.

The name stuck, and Job remained a sleepy little valley throughout the first half of the twentieth century. But California was destined to grow, and her expanding population would eventually spill out across the state. Suburbia eventually knocked on Job's door, and the small town slowly began to awaken from its long slumber.

As the population of the state swelled, a multitude of professional people, frazzled from their long daily commutes in the big cities, began to move into the mountain valley. The nouveau riche caused Job's housing prices to rise, and the city endured a growth spurt into the '70s and '80s. Wealth brought taxes to Job and, with taxes, came normal community amenities such as safety services and schools.

Job slowly evolved into somewhat of an eclectic society. The farmers and sheep ranchers continued with their agrarian way of life living close to the land, and a few solitary homes of the well-to-do sprung up on the rural hillsides. But for the most part, the community was stretched out along the valley floor within the city.

*****

DECEMBER 24 – 5:00 PM
JOB, CALIFORNIA

Sheriff Deputy Thomas Branford left the house a little early to avoid another confrontation with his wife. She just couldn't understand his aversion to the holiday season, and he didn't feel like explaining it to her again.

At one time, Tom had been a dedicated churchgoer and model family man, but that was a long time ago. His faith in church and family began to erode the summer his older brother failed to come home from the war in Vietnam. Robert's Dustoff chopper had been shot down near the DMZ in 1972, and his body had never been found. Tom had prayed that his brother would eventually be found alive in a North Vietnamese prison camp, but when the American servicemen were finally released after the war, he'd not been among them.

Being listed as an MIA was worse than a KIA as far as Tom was concerned. There had been no closure, no finality for his family... or for him.

Tom's father died of a stroke the following year after his brother had been reported missing, and the two tragedies ripped the heart out of him. That's when he discovered that his religious faith was all a sham. His faith had been misplaced in his family's religious traditions, and his shallow religious roots could no longer sustain him in his dungeon of despair.

He tried to keep up appearances at first by continuing to attend church services on Sundays, but he saw this to be too hypocritical, and six months later, simply stopped going. Over the ensuing decades, his belief in a loving and merciful God wilted like fruit withering on a sun-scorched vine.

Now his children were grown, and he was nearing retirement. Spiritually, his antiseptic life seemed to have no meaning or purpose, and the Christmas holiday season became too much for him to bear.

It'd been a cold ride to the sheriff station, and he was glad he decided to bring his heavy crew sweater for his evening shift. He changed into his uniform in the department locker room, then headed to the small kitchenette where the smell of hot coffee was strong and holiday cookies were sure to be found.

Pouring himself a cup of coffee, he dumped in a spoonful of artificial sweetener and stirred it with a plastic stick. He pitched a few coins into the kitty and walked from the break room to the dispatch office where he joined the other members of his shift. Two other deputies were being briefed by the offgoing shift commander on what had transpired over the last eight hours. They greeted Tom with good-natured ribbing.

"Tommy boy! What are you doing working Christmas Eve? We thought with all your seniority, you'd be off tonight."

"Yeah, Tom. I thought John was working tonight."

"There you go, thinking again. It's just another work night to me. My kids are pretty much grown, and John's kids are still little. Besides! He's giving me two for one. I work this shift tonight, and he works two shifts for me when I go deer hunting next fall. Works for both of us."

Deputy Jeff Workman gave the other deputy a nudge with his elbow.

"But, Tom… Christmas Eve? Isn't your family going to church together tonight? We thought that was a big thing with your family."

Tom winced as he sipped the hot coffee, almost spilling it. "I'll say it is. And this gives me an excuse to duck out of another long boring sermon about some lame wise men and screwy shepherds chasing a stupid light in the sky. I mean, how dumb can you get? Shoot! You know, if that Christmas story is true, it probably didn't happen the way it's usually told. Those poor dorks most likely saw the moon or Venus through a patch of moving clouds or something. It makes the stars and moon look like they're moving when the clouds are only blowing across them in the wind. And the day you catch me chasing after a star along with some nerdy shepherds is the day I throw in the towel and start attending church again. No, sir. You won't find me talking to any angels tonight."

Jeff surrendered, backing away with both hands palms up. "Okay, okay, Tom. We've got the picture."

He pulled a quarter out of his pocket. "I'll flip you for the jeep. The weatherman is talking snow tonight."

Tom waved him off. "No, thanks. My squad car has brand-new snow tires, and I'll take it over that rundown piece of junk any day. It's *all* yours!"

They all laughed and headed out the door to check their patrol vehicles.

*****

DECEMBER 24 – 6:00 PM
OUTSKIRTS OF JOB, CALIFORNIA

As Da-Ved trekked into the outer boundaries of the city, he noticed that a vehicle had pulled off the highway and parked on the un-mown grass of the median strip. Making his way towards the car, he could see by its headlights that a young woman was out of her small convertible and was looking at something lying in the grass. As he approached, he saw that the something was a small animal.

Holding a compact cellular phone, the woman turned at the sound of Da-Ved's footsteps. "Hey! Wow, you scared me there, coming out of nowhere like that," she said, holding one hand to her heart.

"I'm sorry, I didn't mean to sneak up on you. What's so interesting?"

"Oh, someone hit a coyote. She's lying over there in the grass, hurt."

"She?"

"Yeah. She's got babies too. They're hiding in the tree line just over there. See? By that big rock."

A second vehicle pulled off the road onto the median; a blue gumball light revolving on its roof cast the roadway with its garish illumination. A white-hot spotlight started to pierce the darkness around them.

Trying to escape the light's penetrating glare, the coyote winced in pain. Her ears flattened back, and she bristled, baring her fangs. She growled at the approaching police officer.

"Oh no," the woman said in a hushed voice. "I called for the forest ranger, not the sheriff's department. What idiot sent the cops out here?"

"You call this in?" the deputy said to Da-Ved.

Before Da-Ved could answer, the young woman spoke, "*I...* called it in, and I didn't call for the police. Where's the ranger?"

"I guess out on another call, Miss. What have you got there? Hurt coyote? You hit 'em?"

By her tone, it was evident that the young woman didn't like police officers. "Nooo, I didn't hit her! I found her crawling off the road after someone else hit her. I stopped to help."

"And who might you be, Miss?" the deputy asked.

"I'm Erin Matheson. I live down the road in Job."

"So...what did you have in mind, Erin? For the coyote, I mean."

"I was hoping the ranger would stop and take her to a vet or something."

"A vet? Don't let the sheep ranchers hear you say that. I suppose you know they don't like coyotes much around these parts. Why don't you two head on home now? I'll take care of this."

Da-Ved looked at Erin. Her eyes pleaded with him to do something. He turned to the officer. "Deputy—"

"Branford." finished the policeman. "Tom Branford."

"Well, Officer Branford. What are our options here?"

"Options? What options? You have an animal in pain here. It's only humane to put her down. Besides, the animal's a varmint, probably preying on livestock and such. Then there's the rabies to think about."

He walked back to his car, reached inside, and unlocked his shotgun from its gun rack.

"She's got babies!" Erin cried, pointing to two young coyotes hiding a few yards away in the scrubby trees lining the side of the road.

Deputy Branford checked the weapon, making sure the safety was on. "Even more reason to put her down, I guess. Fewer varmints preying on the sheep that way."

Walking back to the coyote, he pumped the gun once, chambering a shell.

"The ranchers wouldn't like it knowing we let a coyote and her whelps go. Sorry, but I have to get back on patrol."

Erin moved towards the animal but stopped when it started to growl. She cried and clutched at her phone, not knowing what to do. She bent to kneel on the ground.

Da-Ved edged to the side of the road, placing himself between the coyote and Deputy Branford.

"Deputy, any other night you could do this. But tonight, you can't. Tonight, you don't have to."

"Huh? Why don't I have to?"

Erin jumped to her feet. "Yeah! Tonight is the night for miracles, you know," she said, wiping her eyes.

"Hey, if I don't put her out of her misery, what do you suggest I do? Do you think some fairy godmother is going to come along and wave a magic wand or something?"

His demeanor softened. "Look, miss, I don't want to euthanize the animal. I just don't have any choice in the matter, that's all."

"Yes, you do, Tom," Da-Ved said.

"How do you figure that? What are my other choices?"

Da-Ved turned to look at the coyote lying in the grass. "If the coyote isn't hurt, then you won't have to put her down, will you?"

"No…no, I guess not. But I can see she has a compound fracture of the right front leg and her side is all staved in. Look. She's going to die anyway. For crying out loud, she's dying now. Probably got a punctured lung by the look of her rib cage and the blood she's coughing up. You're just prolonging her misery, and the pups are going to starve then too."

Turning back to face the deputy, Da-Ved said, "But you agree if she's not hurt there's no need for the shotgun, right?"

Erin was shaking her head. "No. Don't play games with—"

Da-Ved cast her a look that cut her off. He turned back to face the deputy again. "Well, Deputy?"

"Okay, yeah. If she weren't hurt, I wouldn't shoot her. But—"

Da-Ved turned and walked to the tall grass, keeping his body between the police officer and the coyote. The coyote reared back on its hind legs and bared her fangs at his approach.

As Da-Ved drew near, the animal became quiet as if recognizing a long-lost friend. With her tail wagging between her legs, she rolled onto her uninjured side and peered up at Da-Ved. He reached down and gently placed his hand upon the animal's injured ribcage. His other hand grasped her broken foreleg. The coyote snuggled her muzzle up to him and whimpered.

From their vantage point, Erin and the Deputy could only see Da-Ved's back as he knelt to examine the injured animal. A soft blue light appeared to emanate from somewhere close in front of him, but they could only see its afterglow as it quickly faded away.

Erin gasped. "Oh! What...what was that?"

Da-Ved stood, cradling the coyote in his arms.

"Huh? What the heck?" Deputy Branford said as he lowered his gun.

"I guess she's not as injured as we thought she was," Da-Ved said with a grin.

"Must have just had the wind knocked out of her," Erin added.

The coyote yelped once, looked up at Da-Ved, and licked his face. Da-Ved scratched her behind her ears and placed her on the ground. She just sat there, looking up at him, making no move to leave.

Looking directly at the coyote and without speaking, Da-Ved nodded towards her pups hiding in the trees.

Seemingly, the coyote understood Da-Ved's gesture, yelped again, and ran off to gather her pups. Once she'd made sure they were all right, she headed up into the rocks and the tree line beyond with her two pups in tow.

In a mild state of shock, Deputy Branford said, "Say, Mister. Just who are you? What did you—"

Erin grabbed Da-Ved's arm. "My boyfriend has a way with animals, Deputy. No law against that, is there?" She looked up into Da-Ved's eyes and whispered, "Follow my lead."

The deputy watched as the coyote led her pups into the tree line. "I could have sworn that the coyote was hurt bad. Look at the bloodstains where she was lying. The grass is still wet with it.

Da-Ved walked with him back to his patrol car. "I guess her wounds are just superficial now, Deputy. Besides, it's like the lady said. Tonight is the night for miracles, isn't it?"

"Some would say it is, but my sergeant isn't going to believe it," Tom said as he unloaded a round.

Erin giggled. "So tell him something he will believe. We have to be going now. Merry Christmas, Deputy Branford!"

He laughed and said, "And a happy Halloween to you, Miss Matheson."

The patrol car's radio crackled, then a female voice called out from it, "Station to car thirty-four."

Deputy Branford leaned through the driver's window and reached for the mic.

"Car three-four, go."

"Car thirty-four, go to channel two."

Tom reached in and switched his police radio to channel two.

"Car three-four on two," Tom answered the dispatcher.

"Are you in service yet, Tom?"

"That's affirm, what do ya have?"

"We have a report from up on the eastern ridge. Those bright lights in the sky again."

Tom shook his head in disbelief, an embarrassed look on his face. "What kind of lights?" he asked his dispatcher.

"Not like the other night, Tom. This one's not moving. Supposedly, it's just sitting there."

"Sitting where, Marge?" he asked with growing annoyance.

The radio sputtered a few seconds of incomprehensible static.

"Sitting where?" he inquired again.

"They say it's just hovering, like some kind of UFO thingy... directly over the town, Tom."

The deputy hung his head low and whispered into the mic, "Who is *they*, Marge?"

"Some sheep ranchers over on Three-Toed Ranch."

"Three-Toed Ranch? That's Hector Gonzales' ranch, isn't it?"

"That's correct, Tom. Just southeast of town."

"Ten-four, I'll be heading that way in a minute. Car three-four, going back to channel one."

He hung up his mic and said, "What a night, and my shift is just beginning."

Turning to Da-Ved, he said, "You won't believe this one. Some sheep ranchers have seen a light or some such nonsense hovering over the town. Now they'll probably have me chasing the moon or a star. What a way to spend Christmas Eve."

"Oh, I don't know," Da-Ved said. "Seems to me to be the appropriate way to spend Christmas Eve. You know...chasing a star reported by shepherds and all."

Tom Branford suddenly appeared uncomfortable and looked off towards Three-Toed Ranch up on the ridge. Lost in thought, he didn't say a word. A sudden breeze kicked up, and he shivered.

"Deputy?" Da-Ved called.

He turned and said, "Yeah. I guess when you put it that way. Okie-dokie, folks, I have to get going. I want to check it out. You two have a safe holiday."

He climbed into the cruiser and locked the shotgun in its rack.

From high in the tree line, a coyote punctuated the night air with a long mournful howl while Deputy Branford drove off to find his star.

"Mister...um...oh for goodness' sake! I don't even know your name. Can I give you a lift somewhere?" Erin asked.

"Yes, if you're headed into town, I would appreciate a ride. And my name's Da-Ved."

"Da-Ved? Are you European? I know, French! Right? You're not from here, right?"

"Something like that," Da-Ved said.

"I knew it! I just knew it. My horoscope said I would meet someone interesting over the holidays. And here you are. The miracle man. You know, I could tell you were special right off when you first walked up. I could tell by your beautiful aura. I can see them, you

89

know. Everyone has them. Auras, I mean. You can tell by a person's aura if he's a good person or not. At least I can."

"Seriously? And what does mine look like?" Da-Ved asked.

"Yours is an exquisite shade of red. It's quite beautiful."

"Erin!" Da-Ved pronounced her name like a father catching a small child in a lie.

"But I *can!*" Her eyes averted his, and she stared at the ground. With a lowered voice, she whispered, "At least I used to be able to see them."

Da-Ved bent down until their eyes met. "I can tell you're interested in spiritual things, Erin. Why don't you tell me about them?"

She looked into his eyes and said, "You can? Because that's true. You know, I meditate every day."

She pulled at a small piece of crystal suspended from a silver necklace she was wearing, twisting it slowly between her fingers.

"My roommate at school…Kelly? She gave me this. It's supposed to enhance my connection to the universal cosmic mind. It's a lens of some kind."

"A lens?"

"You know. To help focus your spiritual energy."

Da-Ved gave her a skeptical look. "Does it work?"

"Not too well lately, I'm afraid. Nothing seems to work since I came home for the holidays. It's as if I'm caught in some sort of spiritual vacuum or something."

"You're home for the holidays? From where?" Da-Ved asked.

"Yeah. I'm a junior at UCLA. I just came home about ten days ago for Christmas break. But it's been kind of a drag."

"So have you always been interested in your own spirituality?"

"No, not at first. I only became interested in it after I took a paranormal psych course my freshman year as an elective. It was very interesting. Some of my profs are super cool and are into that stuff. Then, last year, I took a course in meditation and started meditating almost every day. After that, things just seemed to click. But since I came home on winter break, I can't seem to connect. My mantra doesn't seem to work anymore." She giggled nervously, then added, "It's like I'm under some sort of an attack."

"Erin," Da-Ved asked, "did you ever stop to think that since you came home, maybe you're just free of those things at school that were blinding you? Spiritually, I mean? Maybe you've been given a second chance to find what you've been searching for."

She put her hands on her hips, pretending to inspect Da-Ved from head to toe and said, "You know, you're a pretty heavy dude, Da-Ved. It's easy to talk to you about spiritual matters, and I saw how you talked with the deputy. Would you like to go grab a cup of coffee? There's a diner just up the road a little way. We can continue our talk on the way, and you can explain what you did with that coyote."

"Sure, Erin. But I can't talk too long. I have to be moving on in a little while."

The pair got into her small sports car, and she pulled out onto the road, expertly shifting through the gears. Large fluffy snowflakes started to fall.

"Snow! I just love the snow, don't you, Da-Ved? We get snow up here every year. I always miss it when I'm away at school. I heard on the news tonight that the big valley may get a little tonight too. Bet that will be a Christmas they won't soon forget down there."

"Yeah, I like the snow too," Da-Ved agreed. "It's pure, clean, and falls from heaven."

As she drove, she teased her new friend. "Don't tell me you're into that heaven nonsense? Ha! Ha! And I just came to the conclusion that you weren't such a geek after all! Maybe I'd better wait on that opinion."

Da-Ved threw up his hands in mock protest. "I didn't mean that the snow was actually falling from heaven. It's just an expression. But I do believe in heaven. Don't you?"

"Not since high school. My parents used to make me go to Sunday school and all that junk. Man, was I ever brainwashed!"

"And you've seen the light since?"

"Sure enough, friend! My roommate's aunt is totally immersed in the New Age movement. She's supposedly been reincarnated several times, you know. Dale, her boyfriend?—is one of the grad assistants at school, and he channels a spirit guide named Jade. I went to one of his channeling sessions at the student union last quarter.

It was freaky and kind of scary, but once I got to know him, it was pretty cool."

"Erin, what about the Bible?"

"Oh yeah! That's cool! Yeah, all my friends believe in it too. But you know, that's just one book. There are all sorts of other religious books and philosophies, too, you know. They all have something positive to say about God."

"But the Scriptures say that it is appointed unto men once to die, and after that comes judgment. The Bible doesn't teach that people live and die over and over again, trying to work out their karma as reincarnation does."

"It does? Once, huh? Hmmm? You're starting to sound like my older brother. He and his wife have been going to one of those repressive mainline churches over in Fresno. He's always saying stuff like that. So the Bible mentions judgment, huh? I wonder if Kelly's aunt knows that. Is there anything else the Bible disagrees with? I mean with New Age beliefs."

"Well, since you brought it up, Jesus taught that when you pray not to use vain repetitions but that you should pray for what you need specifically. The Lord's Prayer is a good example of *how* to pray, not *what* to pray."

"I suppose you mean chanting my mantra over and over again is out, right?"

"Yes, Erin. You know, there is a God out there waiting to meet you. But you won't find Him in New Age teachings or any other religion."

She frowned. "Oh...is that so? I suppose you think that the only way to heaven is through Jesus. Well, I believe that Jesus was a great teacher and one of many great avatars that walked our planet in the past, but there were many other avatars besides Jesus. The more enlightened teachers were all Christs in their fashion and taught that we could all ascend to Christ Consciousness. They all preached a way to bliss, but not necessarily the same way. What about them?"

"There's one huge difference between them and Jesus, Erin."

"And what's that?"

"Those great avatars, as you call them, all died and are still in their graves. No one denies that. But those who follow Jesus believe that He rose from the grave and is alive to this day. I think that gives Jesus the edge, don't you?"

"Hey! I never thought of that. But wait…doesn't the Bible teach that there are many paths to God?"

"Not at all. The apostle Luke wrote that there is no other name under heaven by which you can be saved. Luke was referring to the Jewish Messiah, Jesus."

The diner was just ahead, and Erin pulled into the driveway, parked the car in the back lot, and turned off the lights and ignition. She set the parking brake but didn't get out. Erin then shifted in her seat to look more squarely at her passenger.

Snapping her fingers, she said, "Now I have you! You said Jesus was a Jewish Messiah. Christians believe that Judaism was replaced by Christianity. So why have a Jewish Messiah?"

"It's because most Christians haven't taken the time to investigate and understand the ancient Hebrew scriptures, what they call the old covenant. Jesus didn't replace the old covenant. He simply fulfilled it. Every jot and tittle of it.

"Isaiah described the coming Messiah and his sacrificial atonement for mankind. And Jeremiah spoke of a new covenant made with the house of Israel and with the house of Judah. All these scriptures quote the books written by the ancient Jewish prophets. You owe a great debt to the Jewish people, the elder aunts and uncles of all Christians. They are God's chosen people. The Messiah couldn't help *but* be Jewish. And by the way, Jesus isn't His actual name. In Hebrew, it's pronounced Yeshua."

"But aren't the Jews sort of…like…ah…enemies…or something? Didn't they kill Jesus? Or Yeshua? Ooh…whatever!"

"I'm ashamed to say that too many Christians share that same belief with you, Erin. Too many people and for far too many centuries. It's been the cause of much pain and bloodshed. No, they are not adversaries, Erin. Zechariah claimed that the Jewish people are the apple of God's eye. And, technically, they didn't kill Jesus."

"But I thought—"

"Yes, the religious leaders petitioned Pilate for His execution, but it was the Romans who executed Him by crucifixion. The Jewish method of execution at that time was by stoning. But in a larger sense, the Romans didn't execute him either."

"You don't talk like anyone I ever met before, Da-Ved. Now you've got me all mixed up. I'm not sure what to believe anymore."

A tight whirlwind of blowing leaves gyrated across the parking lot, enveloping the car. Opening her door, Erin said, "Oh my. It's getting cold out. How about we go get that coffee?"

The diner was on the outskirts of town, and the usual supper crowd was already thinning out. They walked in to find a couple of rough-looking truck drivers occupying the short stools at the front counter, but a few tables were unoccupied. They took off their coats and slid into a vacant booth.

A young man occupied the booth across from them. His hands were folded and his eyes were closed. His lips moved silently. A couple of truck drivers at the counter were watching him and cracking jokes about what he might be praying for.

"Hey! Sylvester! Praying for a new car? You sure need a new one! Ha! Ha!"

The other trucker joined in. "Yeah, Sly. Then you could drive from one side of town to the other without breaking down. Wouldn't that be something? And then maybe you could pray for a replacement for that old rundown church bus you drive on the weekends."

The waitress scolded them into silence. "C'mon, you two. You should be ashamed of yourselves. It wouldn't hurt for you to put your hands together once in a while, too, you know!"

"Aw, come on, Leeny. We're just having a little fun."

"Yeah, we don't mean anything by it."

"If you two don't stop bothering my customers, you're going to have to leave, hear me?"

The two answered as one, sounding like two small boys in school being scolded by their teacher. "Yes, m-a-a-m."

She approached the young man and asked, "Can I get you anything, Sylvester?"

He opened his eyes and looked up. "Uh...no thanks, Leeny. What I need you can't give me. Guess I best be going anyhow. I've got a busy night in front of me. I'll get my bill at the cash register."

He plunked down a small tip on the table and walked to the men's room.

The waitress cleared his table and then brought over two menus to her new customers.

Erin peeked over the top of her menu, catching Da-Ved's eyes. "Want anything to eat, Da-Ved? My treat."

"Coffee is fine."

Erin handed her menu back to the waitress with a five-dollar bill. "Just two coffees, please."

"Okay, hun, I'll be back in a minute. I just have to run a few customers through the register first, then I'll be right back."

Erin nodded her approval, and the waitress went back to the counter.

Playing with a sugar packet, Erin wrestled with her uncertainty, attempting to put her next question into words.

Da-Ved smiled with anticipation. "What?" he asked.

Finally, Erin asked in a subdued tone, "The thing is, if the Jews and the Romans didn't kill Jesus...who did?"

"Why, you did, Erin. You along with every other person on this planet. It was you who nailed Him to the cross with your sins."

Erin's mouth dropped open. "Sins? *MY* sins?"

She giggled and said, "You *are* some kind of dinosaur, aren't you? For the love of Pete, Da-Ved, don't you know that the notion of sin is as outdated as the horse and buggy? Just about all of my psychology professors would laugh and say that sin is an old worn-out religious concept. It's been discarded. And my friends would say we can find our way to true spiritual harmony by reason, philosophy, and science. All the psychologists I ever studied rejected the notion of sin. Is the Bible that big on sin, Da-Ved?"

"That's one of the biggies, Erin. The apostle Paul said that everyone has sinned, and John tells us that if we say we haven't sinned, we deceive ourselves. The Bible also warns that the wages of sin is death."

"But I'm a good person," Erin said. "You said yourself that I was spiritual. I like all kinds of people, and I do nice things."

When Da-Ved didn't reply, she added with a tone of growing desperation, "Look, I stopped to help with the coyote, didn't I? Doesn't that count for something?"

He gently took her hand in his and said, "I guess it would depend on what you use for your standard for goodness, Erin. The Prophet Isaiah said your self-proclaimed righteousness is like a filthy rag. I suppose God has pretty high standards."

"But—"

"And if there is a day of God's judgment coming, Erin, do you think your psychology professors, even with all their knowledge, education, and great intellect will be able to reason or debate their way out of it?"

She shook her head. "I...I don't understand."

"Look, the best way I can explain this is the way I once heard a pastor explain it."

"Who would that be? Anyone I know?"

"Maybe. He was a pastor from Florida named Kennedy. He said, 'God is Holy, and mankind is sinful. If that was all there was to the problem, then God could solve it very easily. He would just send everyone to hell. However, God is also a God of infinite love. And because He loves mankind, He sent His own Son into the world and laid upon Jesus Christ all of man's guilt and sin. And then God poured out all of His wrath for sin upon His own Son. Jesus Christ suffered infinitely in body and soul on your behalf and paid the penalty for your sins.

"'The problem for you is simple. Your sins are going to be punished by God. The question is, are they going to be punished on you in hell for eternity or on Jesus Christ at the cross? If you prefer the latter, you need to abandon all trust in yourself and repent of your sins and receive Him into your heart as Savior and Lord. You have to trust in His atoning death and perfect life as your only hope for salvation. This is what's called the Good News.'"

Erin started to speak but couldn't quite find her voice, and she pulled her hand away. Her voice became a hoarse whisper and now had a slight tremor to it.

"But if the other religions are untrue, why did I have such success with them at first? And why did it all fall away when I came home for Christmas?"

"Come on, Erin. Think about it. Didn't you learn anything in that Sunday school when you were a little girl?"

Regaining her voice, she coughed, then said defensively, "I guess so…yeah. We were taught a lot of stuff. We learned that there was a fallen angel named Lucifer and that he caused some sort of commotion a long, long time ago. Supposedly, the angels that followed him became demons or something. I think they were supposed to tempt people to sin, but I thought that was all fairy-tale stuff. You don't mean that fallen angels or demons really exist, do you?"

Da-Ved's grin caught her off guard. "Why do you think your mantra worked for you if it's against God's will for men to pray that way? Don't you see? You just repeated your mantra over and over again until you made your mind go blank. Once you were zoned out, it was easy for something else to step in to fill the void, so to speak."

"O-kay. I…think I see. But then why isn't my mantra working now? What's blocking it?"

"Nothing is blocking it, Erin. Nothing at all."

She sat quietly, thinking for a moment.

"If…then…then if you're right, that can only mean one thing," she said.

"And what's that?"

"For some reason, I'm free of any outside spiritual influences. If what you say is correct and my mind was being manipulated by some sort of spiritual force, then it, or they, must be gone, and I'm on neutral ground right now."

Da-Ved leaned forward and asked, "And what will you do with your neutrality, Erin?"

Tears welled up in her eyes. Pulling out a crumpled tissue from her purse, she dabbed at her eyes. Her mascara started to run, turning the tissue black.

"I guess…I guess I've been misled. I guess I should ask God for forgiveness. I didn't understand. I'm so sorry—"

She stopped in mid-sentence. With her newfound remorse, the scales that had spiritually blinded her fell from her eyes, and she saw Da-Ved for more than what she'd seen previously.

"Why you do have an aura, Da-Ved! It's so blue! And so beautiful! Just…who…are you?"

She reached out to touch the soft azure glow enveloping him, and when she did, she fell forward, falling into a deep slumber.

Da-Ved caught her and leaned her against the cushioned backrest of the booth, positioning her so she was wedged upright into the corner of the wall and the booth's enclosure. *Her true spiritual quest is just beginning,* he thought.

He grinned as he thought about Erin, Danny Cohen, and Tom Branford. Turning his eyes upward, he whispered, "It's starting already. Three, Lord."

"Three!"

Be not forgetful to entertain strangers: for thereby
some have entertained angels unawares.

—Hebrews 13:2 (KJV)

CHAPTER NINE

Angels Unawares

As the waitress approached with their coffees, Da-Ved quietly reached for his coat and got up to leave. Seeing Erin sleeping peacefully in the booth, she said, "Oh my, she's asleep. You two must have been on the road for quite a spell."

Da-Ved nodded. "Yes, I believe she's come a long way today."

Leaning over the table, Da-Ved read the server's nametag on her blouse. "Look, Eileen, is it? I was walking into town when Erin here was kind enough to stop and offer me a ride. I have an appointment I need to keep tonight, so I have to be going.

"Could you watch over her for about a half hour or so? Give her some time, and she'll wake up on her own. Tell her I know she's on the right path now. She'll know what you mean. If it's all right with you, that is."

Eileen placed the coffees on the table and bit her lower lip. "Well…okay…but my shift is over in an hour. If she doesn't wake by then, I'll have to wake her."

"Great. I appreciate it."

Da-Ved pushed through the door and stepped outside, letting a blast of chilly night air into the diner. The two truck drivers sitting at the counter pivoted on their stools to glare at the culprit, but Da-Ved had already vanished through the doors and into the darkness beyond.

Pulling his coat tightly around him to ward off the biting wind, he buried his chin in its oversized collar. The crunching of gravel behind him caught his attention, and he turned to see a dirty yellow taxicab approaching the street from the empty side lot. A sign on the taxi's door advertised that the cab company also provided parcel shipping services to the community.

The driver rolled his window down and hollered, "Hey, buddy, I'm dead-heading back to town if you want a ride."

Da-Ved recognized the cab driver as the young man who had been praying in the booth in the diner. He raised his voice and said, "Sorry, friend. I don't have any money for a fare."

The young man waved him closer. "I figured that. I'm going that way one way or another. Makes no difference to me if I have a fare or not. The ride's yours if you want it."

Da-Ved raised an arm in grateful acquiescence. "You talked me into it," he said as he opened the passenger door and slid into the front seat. The door closed with a loud pop and a grinding sound.

The cabbie laughed. "That door's been written up so many times I've stopped complaining about it. Folks usually sit in the back, so it doesn't get used much. Are you just passing through town? Or do you want me to drop you somewhere?"

Da-Ved rubbed his hands briskly in front of the open heater vent. "I came to visit a friend for the holiday, but I'm not sure where he lives. I hope I'll recognize the place if we get into the right neighborhood."

"Fine with me. I'm heading back to the depot at town center, and then you're on your own. Okay?"

"That would be great, thanks."

"Don't mention it. It's too cold to walk very far tonight. By the way, my name is—"

"Sylvester. I know. Sorry, but I couldn't help overhearing those two taunting you in the diner. Does that happen often?"

"No, not too often. Anyhow, I don't pay any attention to it. And call me Sly. I hate Sylvester."

Da-Ved noticed a small sign fastened to the car's dashboard. It read "*Jesús es el Señor.*"

"I like your sign," Da-Ved said. "*Habla español?*"

"*Solamente un poco,*" Sly said with a grin. "I guess I under-stand it better than I speak it. My girlfriend, Sofia, is fluent in it, though. So you like my sign, eh? The pastor of our church had these signs printed up, so I stuck one in the cab. It usually starts up a conversation."

He gunned the engine, and the car lurched out of the parking lot.

A few minutes later, Da-Ved noticed the countryside was becoming less rural. City streetlights flooded the darkness with their harsh illumination, and the business district quickly dominated the landscape. Giant candy canes hung from every other streetlamp, and almost every store window contained either a Christmas tree or a Santa Claus. The streets were awash with garish-colored lights.

Da-Ved shielded his eyes with a hand and asked, "They just don't get it, do they?"

"I'm afraid not," Sylvester said. "If they could just see—"

"See what?" Da-Ved asked.

"Oh, how material their lives have become, I guess. How people have removed Christ from Christmas. They would be so embarrassed."

"But aren't people the same just about everywhere?"

Checking his rearview mirror, Sylvester said, "Not necessarily. The people from our church don't have much in the way of material wealth, but they *are* rich in a spiritual sort of way. Pastor Reyes can really preach the Word too. And you should see the kids.

"Our youth group raised fifteen hundred dollars this summer holding car washes and collecting aluminum cans. Would you believe they sent the money to a sister church in the Dominican Republic last month as a Christmas gift?"

"Wow! That's great," Da-Ved said. "Sounds like your church is doing a good job with the kids."

"And most of these kids aren't from well-to-do families either. For the most part, their own Christmas trees will be pretty sparse tomorrow morning, but it won't matter to them. They have the real Christmas spirit right here," the young cabbie said, tapping his chest.

"Can I ask you something personal?" Da-Ved asked.

"Yeah. I guess so. Depends what it is."

"What were you praying for back there at the diner? You looked like you made a connection."

"Did I? Gee, I guess I did. I don't exactly understand what's been happening here in Job, but it's been pretty neat…at least lately. This may sound a little hokey, but we've had the beginnings of a real revival here in Job. And I'm not talking about having some silver-tongued huckster working the locals into an emotional frenzy for a week either."

Da-Ved thought for a moment. Recalling all the summer preparations made for his arrival, he asked, "How did it begin?"

"It started a couple of months ago, unexpectedly, and quiet like. And not at any church, mind you, but at a small Bible study held at someone's house."

"A Bible study?"

"Yeah. This group started praying for a certain person's release from alcohol, and within two weeks, she quit drinking and turned her life completely around. I hear it kind of freaked them out a little since they hadn't expected results so soon. It grew from there. They began to pray for people and situations and started seeing their prayers answered almost weekly."

Sylvester flipped on his left turn signal and turned the wheel.

"Hearts are being changed here, and God has become very real to us. It's weird. I've never seen anything like it before. It's like…like all the churches have been blessed or something."

"So you're saying your prayers are being answered. What were you asking for back there in the diner?"

"Oh, just a couple of things. I was praying that the revival would continue to grow."

"And?"

"And that somehow, somewhere, I could deliver some Christmas presents to some of the poorer kids of our congregation."

"Do you think that God would grant such a request?" Da-Ved asked.

"Yes, quite honestly, I think He would," Sylvester said with a nod. "But it makes no difference if He does or doesn't. He's already given us the best present possible. You know. His own Son. And,

103

anyhow, the Bible tells us to give thanks whatever our circumstances. Gifts or no gifts."

Da-Ved sat quietly, enjoying the ride and the company. They soon arrived at the town square where a forty-foot Christmas tree was erected in the center of a small park. Resembling a scene from a Charles Dickens novel, Christmas carolers wearing clothes from another century sang carols near the tree. Snow started to collect on the ground, and the grass would soon be covered. The men held lanterns and wore long coats, tall top hats, and scarves. The women wore long skirts and bonnets and carried choir books.

Other religious displays were also on the commons, including a large nine-candle menorah. A tall clock tower at the north end of the commons rang out seven times.

Sylvester pulled into a parking spot in front of the large well-lighted Millard Department Store. A few harried customers were rushing in and out of its doors, shopping for last-minute bargains.

The cab sputtered and coughed. With a shudder, the engine raced for a few seconds, then shook to an uneasy idle.

"Sorry, I have to drop you here. The garage is just around the square and down Third Street. Does anything look familiar to you yet?"

"No, not yet. But I'm sure I'll find him." Da-Ved gave the car door a hard shove, and its rusted hinges opened with a creaking groan.

"Thanks for the ride, Sly. You have a Merry Christmas. I hope your prayers will be answered."

He banged the door closed, and swirling snow blew up from the street momentarily, enveloping him in a billowing white out. When it cleared, he was gone.

Sylvester leaned forward, looking up and down the street, but Da-Ved was nowhere to be seen.

He scratched his head. *Where'd he go?*

Checking his mirrors, he backed the cab out of its parking spot and pulled into traffic, heading towards the garage on Third Street. A chorus of "Joy to the World" seeped through the cold air across the park, into his car, and he started humming along with the carolers.

The traffic signal turned red, and Sylvester fought to keep the car from skidding into the intersection. The light from a streetlamp reflected brightly from something metallic at the rear of his car. Unknown to Sylvester, the generous-sized rear seat of the ancient checkered Marathon was silently filling with small gifts and toys. Children's hats, coats, shoes, and other new apparel also manifested out of thin air into the trunk of the old cab.

Peering up at the traffic light, Sylvester said to himself, "What a week. If it gets any better, I'll probably end up talking to an angel or two."

The light turned green, and he glanced at his watch. "Holy cow! It's after seven! I'll be late for church if I don't get moving."

He gunned the engine and headed to the garage. This time, the car didn't protest.

*****

DECEMBER 24 – 7:05 PM
DOWNTOWN JOB, CALIFORNIA

In front of Millard's Department Store stood a tall black man dressed in a cheap Santa Claus suit. Next to him was a sizeable cast-iron kettle suspended on a chain from a metal tripod. A sign attached to the tripod declared that the money in the kettle was to be given to the homeless through one of the city's local charitable organizations. A few coins and small bills barely covered the bottom of the pot.

Da-Ved watched the man at work for a few minutes, ringing a small handheld bell as he attempted to solicit donations from the local shoppers. It was no use. Either they had no money or didn't care to contribute to the charity. They seemed to look through the bell ringer as though he were invisible.

At last, his patience wore thin, and the Santa became more aggressive in his approach.

"Hey, pal. How 'bout something for the kettle?" he asked one man as he came out of a nearby store.

"Beat it, ya bum! Ya smell like a brewery!" snarled the startled shopper.

"Hey, man, I haven't touched a drop for five years now. What da ya say? How about helping someone a little less fortunate than yourself?"

The shopper had his hands full of newly purchased gifts. They were gift-wrapped and piled high in his beefy arms. The man's abundant chins held the pile tightly so as not to drop them.

"I'd like to, fella. But things have been kind of tight this year. Maybe next year." Red-faced, the shopper turned and quickly walked away.

The crimson-clothed Santa kicked snow after the man. "Yeah, go ahead. Run home to your castle and pull up the drawbridge, ya lousy crud."

He peered up towards the night sky and said, "Yeah, I know. I know. I'm sorry. But you better do something pretty quick, Lord, or we're gonna go under."

Da-Ved approached the large elfin figure from the street. "How are you doing, Santa? Having any luck?"

"What's it to ya, buddy?" the Santa asked.

"Nothing. Just making conversation. I'm looking for someone who lives near here."

The black Santa glared back at Da-Ved. "So? I don't have time for no chitchat. I gotta fill this thing before the nights over or the bank is gonna close us down next month."

Da-Ved drew nearer. "Why don't you move the kettle over here by this tree next to the building? There's more people walking by that way, and you'll be out of the wind. Come on. I'll help you."

Deftly removing the kettle from the tripod, Da-Ved moved the arrangement to the sidewalk near a small Christmas tree. He rehung the kettle next to a large display window and stepped back. A string of shoppers filed out of the department store, and each one dropped in a small donation.

"Hey, thanks, pal. I owe ya one. It's not too bad here either. At least the wind doesn't bite so much over here."

Da-Ved stomped his feet and rubbed his hands together. "Yeah, it is a cold night. That's for sure. I just arrived in town and need help finding someone's house. I'm not sure where he lives. Can you give me a hand?"

"Sure. If I can. I don't know everybody in town, you know. Whose house are you looking for?"

"Job's," answered Da-Ved.

"Job's House? You're kidding, right?"

"No. I'm not kidding. Do you know where—"

"Sure, I know. Who do you think I'm working for?" Santa asked. He spun the kettle around to show Da-Ved a small sign attached to it. It read:

All proceeds will go to JOB'S HOUSE—a nonprofit shelter run by the Interfaith Council of Churches of Job serving God and the homeless.

"Yeah, that would be him all right," Da-Ved said with a laugh. "Where is his house located? Is it far?"

"Not too far. See that alley behind me? Take the alley for two blocks and turn left. It's just down the street from there. It's a big old Victorian house with a wrought iron fence. You can't miss it."

"Thanks. I hope your night's work will be fruitful."

"Me, too, man. The churches help out as best they can, but it's been a bad year for some folks. A few of them always seem to pass through here. Sometimes they're at the end of their rope, and that's when we step in."

A young woman carrying a bulging shopping bag walked by and dropped in a small donation. She greeted them with, "Merry Christmas, gentlemen," and continued on her way.

The Santa returned her greeting, "Thank you, Miss. Merry Christmas to you too!" He turned back to Da-Ved. "I know what it's like. I've been there. If it hadn't been for Job's House, I probably wouldn't be here talking to you right now."

"Oh? Why is that?" Da-Ved asked.

"The people there are great, and I was a real mess when I first came to Job. They cleaned me up, dried me out, and helped me regain my self-respect. And they introduced me to someone who changed my whole life. Hey, if you're going to Job's House, maybe I'll see you there later tonight. We can talk some more. What do you say?"

"If I'm still there when you get back, that would be fine," Da-Ved answered. "But I don't plan on staying in town too long."

A clinking noise behind them caught Santa's attention. He whirled around to see a stream of gold and silver coins erupting out of the kettle into the street.

"What the?" Santa gasped. "Do you see what I s—"

Turning to catch his companion's reaction to the queer phenomena, he discovered he was alone.

"Hey!" Santa shouted. "Hey! Where'd ya go?"

Spinning completely around, he saw that, indeed, he *was* alone. He ran to the alley and looked down its cavernous walls to the well-lighted street two blocks away. If Da-Ved had been in the alley, his silhouette would have been obvious, cast against the streetlights at the end of the alley. But he just wasn't there.

A loud clang rang out, and the Santa turned from the alley to see that the weight of the filling pot had broken the chains it had been suspended from. The kettle was now upturned, and a small amount of wet sand and seaweed had also splashed out onto the pavement. The pot continued to breathe coins as the silver and gold flood spread down the sidewalk for several feet.

The hair on the back of Santa's neck stood on end. "Hallelujah!" he cried. "No one is *ever* gonna believe this! No one!"

He dropped to one knee and looked skyward again. He whispered in a failing voice, "Thank you, Lord. I shoulda known you wouldn't let us down. I'll never doubt you again."

*****

Da-Ved turned left at the end of the alley and briskly walked east on Liberty Street. With each step, he progressively shed the veneer of invisibility he had cloaked himself with. In a few seconds, he was visible once again.

He noticed he was traveling through a less affluent part of the city. A few buildings here and there were abandoned and boarded up, and a few rundown taverns and restaurants lined the street. They were doing a brisk holiday business, and peals of riotous laughter came from some of the more boisterous establishments.

Da-Ved continued his easterly journey, passing open doorways and dimly lighted backstreets as he walked. Crossing an alley, he heard what sounded like a prayer mumbled from behind a heavily dented trash container. He heard it again, low and thick as though through numbed lips.

"Help me, Jesus."

Stepping into the alley, he looked behind the dumpster and saw a man half sitting, half lying in the wet alley. His head and upper back were propped up against a brick building with his feet splayed out in front of him. Eyes half shut, the man's hands fell to either side of his body. His left hand grasped a half-empty bottle of clear liquid. With his chin resting on his chest, he kept mumbling, "Help me Jesus."

In the alley with him were two small scaly demons who were tormenting the man. One used a long red stiletto-like dagger, jabbing it into the man's head. With each thrust, the man winced as some unpleasant memory penetrated the alcohol-induced haze he'd tried to shroud his mind with. As each pain-soaked memory oozed back into his numbed consciousness, his eyes fluttered, and he grimaced. In self-defense, he lifted the bottle to his lips and swallowed a little more of his liquid medication.

The other demon held a short spike fastened to the end of a serpent-shaped shaft with which he speared the man in the heart every time he took a swig from the bottle. This, too, caused the man pain, but it was a physical pain that made him clutch at his chest from time to time.

"Help me, Jesus," he muttered again as he endured the invisible onslaught.

Instinctively, Da-Ved ducked down beside the dumpster. Examining the alley, he sensed another presence nearby. He whispered, "Who's there?"

"My name is Arioch," whispered back the unseen entity.

From within the dumpster emanated a flash of bright light, and a Guardian materialized from out of the container, revealing his presence to Da-Ved. At one time, his appearance may have been intimidating, but for now, the angel seemed to be lacking in something.

Arioch crouched low, next to the dumpster, so as not to be seen by the attacking demons. His once white robe was discolored and threadbare through long years of service and oppression. One wing seemed to hang at an odd angle, and he walked with an obvious limp.

He carried a somewhat tarnished and badly dented shield in his left hand. It bore a foot-long diagonal gash across its face where it had once deflected a slashing battle cleaver. His only other weapon was a longsword sheathed in a tattered scabbard slung across his back.

The disheveled Guardian seemed to be exhausted and somewhat puzzled with the appearance of possibly another angel.

"What goes on here?" Da-Ved demanded. "This place is supposed to be secure. Where did those two come from? And why are you here?"

Arioch seemed surprised by these questions. "Ah, if you don't mind…I'll ask the questions. Who are *you?* If you are mortal, how is it you can see me, one of God's Holy warriors?"

Da-Ved replied, "I'm not mortal. Like you, I'm a messenger of God sent to complete a special task here in Job. Haven't you been briefed?"

The Guardian bristled. "Briefed? Who has time for briefings? It's all I can do to keep my charge alive. I've been with him for over forty years, but I'm afraid I'll be seeking a new position soon."

Da-Ved sat quietly for a moment, studying the man and his tormentors. Finally, he said, "It looks like he's been a heavy responsibility."

"You can say that again," the lanky angel said. "He's been through the wringer. I'll say that much for him."

Commenting on Arioch's rumpled appearance, Da-Ved said, "He hasn't exactly been through it alone, has he?"

"No. No, I've been there through it all with him, and I'm not ashamed to say I'm at my wit's end. I'm glad you're here to witness my final failure."

Da-Ved stared back at the weary angel. "What do you mean failure? And how is it these two haven't been driven out of here?"

Arioch scowled and said loudly, "Why would they be driven from here?"

Snapping a finger to his lips, Da-Ved whispered, "Shhhhh! Keep it down until I can figure out what's going on here."

And there were in the same country shepherds abiding
in the field, keeping watch over their flock by night.

—Luke 2:8 (KJV)

CHAPTER TEN

Shepherds

DECEMBER 24 – 7:30 PM
OUTSKIRTS OF JOB, CALIFORNIA

The weather turned worse as Tom Branford drove his squad car into the higher elevations. It started to sleet, making the road slippery, and he kept the powerful cruiser's speed in check. At last, he came to the open entrance gate of Three-Toed Ranch and pulled off the paved road onto the ranch's main drag.

He continued to push the squirming squad car up the meandering drive for the quarter-mile journey to the main residence. There, he found two men waiting for him in a small jeep parked in front of the house while a third was just coming out the front door.

The third man wore a red beret and sported a closely cropped white beard. In one hand, he grasped a small flask and a gnarled old cane in the other. His gait was hampered, and he seemed to favor a leg.

A solitary light illuminated the lot at the front of the house, casting deep shadows beyond the nearby trees. Falling sleet glistened in the white light's stark illumination. The lot had been freshly plowed, and snow was pushed up around its perimeter.

The man with the flask seemed excited and rushed up to Tom as he exited the cruiser. "Ah, bueno, it's my good friend, Deputy Branford. How are you, mi amigo?"

Tom loved to tease the old man, so he pretended not to hear the greeting and used his anglicized name. "George? You old goat, what are you doing up here? I thought you'd be long gone this time of year. Don't you usually take the herd down the east side of the mountain into Nevada for the winter? How come you're still up here?"

Jorge Martinez looked over his shoulder and motioned to the two men getting out of the jeep.

"This is what I get for taking this gringo under my wing when he was a young toro and needed a summer job. Now he has no time for me and wants to know why I am still on the land of our ancestors. His older brother would never talk this way to me."

Tom took his friend into his arms, and the two embraced with laughter and hearty backslaps.

"It's good to see you, amigo! How's the family? Is that Jesse I see back there? Jesse, is that you? Come here so I can get a look at ya, boy!"

An athletic-looking youth came close to the two old bears and was quickly grabbed by the bigger man and placed into a powerful headlock. The trio tussled for a short time in good-natured fun.

The sleet changed to snow again, and the heads of the three men were speckled white. Their breath came heavy in great puffs of condensed vapor. Too tired to continue the struggle, Tom called a truce. "Here! Here! Is this any way to treat the Law? Stop now or I'll have to run you two in."

Tom now noticed that the other man standing by the jeep was thinner and a bit smaller than Jorge and Jesse. Holding the struggling wrestlers in two headlocks, he peered at the diminutive figure. "George, who is that over there, laughing at us? Another grandson? "

Talking from under Tom's left armpit, Jorge bellowed, "Yes, you slippery gringo. But not mine. That's Hector's thirteen-year-old grandson, Felipe. Let me go, and I'll introduce you."

Tom let his two opponents loose, only to be pelted by a shower of blows to his right arm by Jesse. "Jesse, hold up! Hold up, old son! George, this grandson of yours has done some growing. What have you been feeding him? I see I'm going to have to take you two on one at a time from now on. Stop it, Jesse! Boy, if you don't stop it, my arm's gonna fall off!"

Jesse broke off his attack and gave Tom a jovial slap on the back. "Good…to see you…again…Mr. Branford." He paused to catch his breath. "I guess…it's been a few years, hasn't it?"

"I'll say. The last time I saw you, you weren't much bigger than Felipe here. George, you say Felipe is Hector's grandson?"

"Sí. Yes. Felipe, come here and meet Deputy Branford. When he was your age, he and his brother used to work for your grandfather. Deputy Branford used to be taller, but I wore his legs down some, making him walk these hills for four summers."

Felipe came near and offered his hand to Tom. "My grandfather has spoken of you before, Deputy Branford. Always with much laughter."

Tom Branford took the youngster's hand and shook it. "Nice to meet you, Felipe. Your grandfather used to make me laugh too. How is he? Is he up at the house? I'd like to see him again."

"Oh, he's fine, fine," Jorge said. "But no, he's not here. And it's a good thing for you too, old friend. He may be older than me, but if he'd set his hooks into you, you'd soon know it. You wouldn't manhandle Hector Gonzales the way you manhandled Jesse and me. He'd be a match for you, even at *his* age."

Tom laughed at the banter, then asked, "I take it he's with the main herd at winter pasture?"

"And where else would he be?" Jorge asked. "Besides, the weather there is much nicer than up here in the winter."

"Then what are you doing up here this time of year? Haven't you finished closing up the house for the season?"

"No. We are not closing the house this winter. You know Hector. He's always trying to improve the sheep. He asked us to stay the winter with a small herd he crossbred with a Cheviot ram. They're a hardy breed and do well in high altitudes. We're going to see how they take to the cold weather up here."

"Why bother, George? There's nothing for the sheep to eat up here in the winter. Everything is buried under the snow. You'll have to feed and water them every day."

"I know, but Hector still wants to breed a sturdier strain of sheep. And besides, Hector is a rich man. He has the money to throw away. And it will be good to spend a winter with my family and still be employed. We're not complaining."

"So where are the sheep?"

"They're in the lower pasture behind the house. The shelters are not far from there."

The handie-talkie hanging from Tom's web-belt hissed static, reminding the lawman to move on with his investigation.

"Hey, I just remembered, I'm up here on a call. Don't tell me you're the reason that I had to run all the way out here. You guys report seeing some weird lights up here?"

Felipe bounced on his toes with excitement. "Tell him, Señor Martinez! Wait till you see, Deputy Branford! Wait till you see!"

"Sí, we have seen lights up here," Jorge said reluctantly. "But we always see lights up—"

Jesse interrupted, "Just tell him, Abuelo."

Tom grimaced. "Tell me what? So help me, George, if you're running that still again—"

"Ha! Ha! And what if I am, gringo? It gets cold up here on the mountain, you know. A man has to have something to keep his bones from freezing. But, no, that is not the reason we called you."

"Confound it, you old coot, then what am I doing up here?"

Jorge looked away uncomfortably, staring at the trees surrounding the parking lot. "The boy. He has...that is...*we*...have seen something that is—*como se dice—inusitado?*" He looked to Jesse, and Jesse spoke.

"Unusual."

"Sí, that is the word. Unusual."

"I hope you three haven't dragged me up here just to admire the moon."

Felipe grabbed Tom's arm. "No! No, Deputy Branford! Señor Martinez is right. We have seen many illuminations up here since early autumn. They are...very beautiful. But this is different. It's not the same."

Tom looked skyward. "Just where is this...this...this...whatever it is?"

"You can see it near the overlook," Jesse said. "We'll have to climb up to the old sheep trail."

"Way up there?" Tom said, turning toward the mountain. It'll take half the night to go there and back. I have better things to do. Besides, the weather's getting worse."

Looping his cane around Tom's arm, Jorge pulled him close. "Look here, Thomas. You're one stubborn son of a ram, you are! I am, as you say, a taxpaying citizen, and I want to report something. It is your duty to investigate it."

Jorge's eyes softened, and he lowered his voice. "See, Thomas? It has stopped snowing. We can take the jeep up to the high pasture and then cut through the woods on foot to the sheep trail. It will only take a half hour that way. Since you're up here, you might as well have a look. Si?"

"Okay, you old goat. But I had better not stumble upon that still. Hear me?"

They all laughed and headed toward the jeep. Tom abruptly turned and headed for his car.

"Wait a minute. I'd better tell them I'll be off the air for a while before they come looking for me." He opened the driver's door, reached in, and picked up the mic. "Car three-four to dispatch."

His radio emitted only hissing static. He called again. "Car three-four to dispatch."

The dispatcher's voice came back, somewhat muffled. "Go ahead, car thirty-four."

"Marge, this is Tom. How do you read this unit?"

"Four by five, Tom. You okay?"

"Yeah, I'm good. Listen, Marge. I'll be out of the car for a bit, so I'll be off the air. My portable won't transmit back to the base from way out here, so you won't hear from me for a little while. Don't get excited and send out a posse looking for me, all right?"

"All right, Tom. Be careful."

"Ten-four, Marge. I'll be fine. I'll be with George Martinez."

"Okay, that's different. Tell Mr. Martinez I said Feliz Navidad. Base clear."

He shed his portable radio and lightweight uniform jacket, tossing them into the back seat. Walking around to the rear of the cruiser, he unlocked the trunk and reached in to grab the heavier hooded parka he always kept there for nights when the weather turned bad. He also found the two-piece leather and wool mittens he kept in an interior pocket of the heavy coat and put them on. Swapping his uniform cap for a wool watch cap, he prepared to climb the mountain from the old road to the overlook.

The jeep pulled up to the police car, and Jesse rolled the driver's window down. "Come on, Tom. Let's go."

"Just a second, I forgot something."

Rummaging through the trunk's contents, he found the army-surplus ammo-can he used to store survival gear in. Popping its latch, he reached inside and grabbed a pair of small binoculars and placed them in his parka's inner pocket. Looking up at the sky, he said to himself, "What a night."

Jorge moved to the jeep's back seat to sit with Felipe, and Tom climbed in to sit up front next to Jesse. The jeep skidded out of the parking lot onto the main drive. Jesse then picked up the dirt road to the upper pastures and headed for the old sheep trail. The sheep trail was actually an ancient game trail, but the ranchers used it to move the sheep from one pasture to the next during the spring and summer months.

The jeep rattled around in the frozen ruts of the rugged dirt road, and the accumulated snow made the driving treacherous. Tom cautioned the young driver, "Slow down, Jesse! This old bucket needs to cart us up *and* back down again, you know. I'm not one for wanting to walk back in the dark in this weather."

In fifteen minutes, the meandering road ended, and a wall of fir trees sprung up in front of them.

"End of the line," Jesse said. "We walk from here up through those trees to the lower ridge. It will be an easy walk to the overlook from there."

Tom grabbed the large flashlight he'd removed from his squad car and got out. Jesse reached under his seat, retrieved a smaller flashlight, and gave it to Felipe. Jorge stuffed the metal flask into a small canvas rucksack, reached for his walking stick, and worked his way out through the front door after Tom.

Felipe had already hopped out through the rear window and was waiting for them at the tree line. "C'mon, you slowpokes! I want to go see if it's still there!"

Jesse looked at Tom with laughing eyes. "Felipe! You come back here. Your parents won't like it if we don't bring you back home in one piece."

The older boy walked around to the rear of the jeep and reached in for the .30-30 lever-action Winchester that was always kept there in a leather case.

Looking at Tom, Jesse explained, "You never know what you'll run into up here. We were tracking a cat up there late this afternoon when we saw the light. C'mon, let's go."

The trees weren't thick, but in the partial moonlight and on a steep grade, it was tough climbing. When they broke through thigh-deep snowdrifts, they climbed in single file.

Felipe quickly found the vertical trail they'd made earlier in the day. Jorge instructed him to follow it so the climbing would be easier in the heavy snow. Felipe and Jorge took turns breaking trail and soon outdistanced the two other climbers.

"Your grandfather never seems to get tired," Tom said.

"Why should he be tired?" Jesse said with a grin. "This is his backyard. It's been his backyard for the last seventy years, and he's used to these higher elevations and the steepness of the mountain."

"Yeah, I guess. I only get up here for a few days every year for deer season. I never seem to be in shape for it no matter how much preseason conditioning I do."

They continued their upward ascent until Tom motioned for Jesse to stop.

"Time for...a break...Jesse. You're gonna kill me...if I...don't catch...my breath."

Jesse looked at Jorge up ahead, breaking the trail with Felipe. "What's the matter, Deputy Branford? Can't you keep up with that old man up there?"

Tom stopped and, leaning against a sapling, gasped, "No. And neither...can you...you young...he-goat. Now I'm...taking a break. How much farther...is that old trail...anyway?"

"Not much farther. Just up to the next ridge. I'll bet Jorge and Felipe have already found it and are waiting for us."

"Give me a minute. I'm not...as young as...I used to be."

Tom unzipped his parka a few inches. "Phew!"

"Sure," Jesse said, "but you're missing quite a view."

"I'll bet, Jesse. I haven't been up to the overlook...since I was a boy...but I remember that it was quite...a sight."

"And the town has grown quite a bit since you were a boy, Deputy Branford. Wait till you see it."

Tom grabbed for a young sapling in front of him and continued the ascent to the game trail. In ten minutes, he and Jesse climbed out of a large clump of aspens and found Jorge and Felipe waiting for them on a large rock a few yards from the path. Tom climbed up onto the rock, sat down, and asked, "Where...did you two...go? Is there an elevator...up to here?"

"Yeah. Don't tell me you and Jesse actually *climbed* up here?" taunted Felipe. "That Jesse. He *can be* cruel."

Jorge looked down the trail towards what appeared to be a clearing fifty yards away. "We are almost there, mi amigo. Rest a minute, and then we go."

The trail was buried in a foot of snow, but it was evident that large animals regularly used it to traverse the mountain. A narrow path tramped down its middle made it an easy walk.

The wind whipping through the trees caused snow to cascade from the branches onto the hikers. Tom reached down and pulled the parka's zipper back up to his chin. Pulling his watch cap tightly over his ears, he signaled to continue with their journey.

"Let's get this over with Jorge. I'm beginning to think this was a bad idea."

Jesse shouldered the rifle and took the lead, proceeding down the well-worn path. Felipe scrambled off the rock and ran to catch up with him.

Jorge slowly made his way back to the trail. Stopping to brush the snow from his coat, he said, "You will not think it was a bad idea when we get to the overlook, mi amigo. Vamos."

As Jorge and Tom neared the overlook Felipe cried out to them. "It's still here, Señor Martinez! It's here! Come see!"

Tom scanned his powerful police flashlight onto the surrounding trees, lining the trail, trying to see what Felipe was so excited about. The tightly focused beam stabbed several yards into the underbrush but revealed nothing. He spun the ring at the tip of the flashlight, and the penetrating spotlight became a softer floodlight.

The wider beam did not penetrate as far into the trees, but the light was projected onto a larger section of woods. As he approached the overlook, Tom could see that Felipe and Jesse were on their knees and not looking *at* the trees but out—towards the city.

Jorge said quietly, "Turn off your light, Thomas."

Tom snapped off his flashlight, knelt to the ground, and crawled to the edge of the precipice in the dark. Below, the city of Job sprawled throughout the valley. It had grown some since Tom last viewed it from here, and the valley was beautiful as seen from the overlook. The gentle illumination from the city and small farms kindled the countryside into a patchwork of soft light and warm shadows.

"It's beautiful, but I don't see anything to get so exci—"

From the corner of his eye, Tom became aware that the others were not looking down *into* the valley but *out* over it. His eyes climbed slowly from the valley floor skyward.

At last, he saw it, and his breath caught in his throat. Directly over the city glimmered a light. It seemed close, hovering, like a silent helicopter.

Tom whispered, "What is that thing? I don't hear any engine noise."

"*That*, Señor Branford, is what we wanted to show you," Felipe said.

Jorge came up behind Tom and prodded him with his cane. "Did I not tell you, Thomas? Do you still think that this was a bad idea?"

121

Stunned, Tom simply asked, "How long has it been here?"

"Only since a little after sunset," said Jesse. "But we have seen other lights since late fall. We've seen many lights all throughout the valley."

"Where?" Tom asked.

Jesse scrambled to his feet. "Everywhere. In the valley. In the meadows. The woods around the farms. Sometimes in the high country. Everywhere. Not every night but almost every night."

"But you said this one was different. How is it different than the other lights you've seen?"

"The other lights move about—low, through the tree line," Jesse said. "Most of the time, they follow the natural lay of the land. It almost seems as if they are trying to stay hidden. They come and go through the creeks and hollows as they move through the valley. But you can only see them if you're up here in the high country. *This* light—is out in the open and high—over the valley."

"And not moving," added Felipe.

"And not moving," Jesse repeated.

Tom stood. "Aw, it's just a planet. Probably Saturn. Don't you boys know the night sky by now?" he said, brushing the snow from his knees.

Jesse pointed to a star-like object behind them shining through the partial cloud cover in the western sky. "Saturn is over there."

Tom turned to look at the planet. "Oh, yeah, I guess it is." He looked back to the light hanging over the valley. "Then what the heck *is* that thing?"

"I do not know, Thomas," Jorge said. "But I do not think it's from our world."

Just then, the shimmering object emitted a burst of intense light, and two iridescent beams plummeted earthward from it. For a brief second, twin pillars of light stood, connecting the object to the city. Their red and blue hues burned shadow images onto the retinas of the four witnesses.

Felipe jumped to his feet. "Wow! Did you see that?"

Wiping his eyes, Jesse cried, "Yeah, man! What happened? Did it leave?"

"No, it's still there," Tom said. "But it looked like something dropped to the ground from it."

Looking to where the rays descended, Felipe asked, "What's down there?"

The seamiest part of the city, Tom thought.

Jorge let out a hoot and, with cane and rucksack held overhead, began to sing and prance about.

Puzzled, Tom and Felipe looked to Jesse.

Beats me, Jessie motioned silently.

Tom asked, "Hey George, what gives? Why the song and dance?"

Jorge lowered his hands to his hips but continued prancing about, kicking at the snow. "None of you understand, do you? Ha! Ha!"

"Understand what, Gramps?" Jesse asked.

Jorge chuckled, laughing at some unseen joke. "Como no! Job is going to be paid a little visit…I think."

For whosoever shall call upon the name of the Lord shall be saved.

—Romans 10:13 (KJV)

CHAPTER ELEVEN

Redemption

DECEMBER 24 – 8:00 PM
THE ALLEYWAY, JOB, CALIFORNIA

Da-Ved peered over the top of the dumpster, keeping a wary eye on the sadistic demons. Motioning towards the other side of the container, Da-Ved whispered to Arioch, "Now, quickly, tell me about them. I need to know what I'm dealing with here."

Arioch's eyes softened. "Quickly? You want to know about them quickly? How do I account for a lifetime of suffering in just a few sentences?"

"Just hit the highlights, Arioch. It's important."

The wounded angel's demeanor grew cold, and he shivered as he recalled the struggles of the man's life.

"That poor wretch lying there is James Townsend, and he's had a hard and miserable life. When he was a young man, he saw his wife and child die when their apartment building burned to the ground. He tried to rescue them but was overcome by the heat and smoke of the fire, and his face and hands were horribly burned. He barely survived."

"How did he get involved with those two?" Da-Ved asked, motioning towards the demons. "Who are they?"

Propping his shield against the large trash container, Arioch sat down, leaning his back against it. "Those two? They're Shekar and Asthenes. They were assigned to torment James right after the fire."

"What brought about their authority to manipulate him?" Da-Ved took a quick look over the top of the dumpster. "I mean, how did they gain control of the man?"

"After the fire, James spent months in a hospital, recuperating and then enduring many operations and skin grafts. And he's never recovered from the loss of his family. The spiritual scars he carries within him are far worse than those he carries upon his flesh. The enemy knows James's weaknesses, and they use them to their advantage."

"Weaknesses? What weaknesses?" asked Da-Ved.

"Every day, James struggles to escape his agonizing past by numbing himself with alcohol and drugs, but he's never been able to rid himself of the guilt he feels for not dying with his family. He's become addicted, and it's slowly killing him.

"Those brutes torturing him have been with us since the second month after he was released from the hospital. Once they realized that his will had been weakened, they took up permanent residence with him. At first, they came to him, disguised as a soothing chemical balm, but eventually, they gained the upper hand and became his masters and tormentors."

Arioch grimaced and proceeded to massage his thigh for a few seconds. Carefully flexing his knee, he checked its range of motion. "As soon as the alcohol numbs his pain, Shekar there jabs his memory, making him recall the guilt and remorse he's trying to escape. And Asthenes has been trying to kill him by working on his weakened heart.

"He's suffering malnutrition from years of self-abuse, and his body is just worn out. It's deteriorated to where it can no longer heal itself. And the worst of it is he doesn't care." He looked off into the distance, not speaking.

Da-Ved waited a moment, then whispered, "Go ahead, Arioch. I'm listening."

"Oh, sorry. It's just that for all the misery in his life, there seemed to be a glimmer of hope for a short time when James's pain and mental anguish finally became too much for him. He began to realize that if he was ever going to find a modicum of peace in his life, he was going to have to undergo some sort of transformation."

"What did he do?"

"He started to pray for help on a daily basis. Within a week, a young minister befriended him, and they talked off and on for several days. James found new strength in their friendship, much to the chagrin of those two," Arioch said, nodding at James's assailants.

"And through the counseling of this new friend, James was persuaded to attend evening services at the mission house just down the street."

"I'll bet that was tough," Da-Ved said.

"You can say that again. At first, James was reluctant to go, and of course, Shekar and Asthenes wanted no part of it. But with some firm encouragement, I was able to loosen their hold on him enough that in a state of desperation, he sought out the counseling services at Job's House."

"With no complaints from Shekar or Asthenes?" Da-Ved asked with a sly grin.

"Oh, believe me, they howled and put up quite a fuss, but strangely, for the first time, I was empowered by the prayers from the local saints. They must have been fasting and in earnest prayer for James because I have never felt such raw unfettered power before for this man.

"And the scriptures are eagerly preached here. Hearing the Word of God for the first time, James received the faith to fight his physical addictions."

"Yes," Da-Ved agreed, "the saints here are serious and have been praying for revival for years. Because of their many petitions, His Majesty has sent a special envoy to Job. During the past few months, this city has been quietly secured and is awaiting his arrival. That's why you're experiencing new authority in James's life, Arioch. Didn't you know?"

"No. Not exactly. I knew something was going on in this valley because Lucifer's troops have been on the run ever since late summer. All the pestilence that has plagued this city has been rooted out and banished, including Shekar and Asthenes. Even the Warlord

Pharmakos has left the territory. I knew when Pharmakos was evicted, something big had to be in the works, but I didn't know what it was."

"But if Shekar and Asthenes were banished from Job, what are they doing here now?" Da-Ved asked.

"That's a good question. At the time, it was a big relief to me to be rid of them. In a few days, James's body started to respond to the absence of their attacks. With adequate food and care provided by Job's House, he started to gain some of the weight he'd lost due to his wretched lifestyle. His face no longer seemed quite so gaunt. and the spark of life returned to his eyes. James was finally at the point where he was free to pick up the pieces of his life, but he still needed spiritual healing."

Da-Ved said, "Don't tell me. I can guess what happened next. He wanted his independence again, didn't he?"

"Yes," Arioch said with a frown, "he foolishly tried to move on too soon. Without the continued support from the shelter, he had nothing to sustain him."

Da-Ved glanced over the top of the dumpster to check on the attacking demons. "Go on. Finish it," he said.

"It was bound to happen sooner or later, and James wasn't prepared for it. A few weeks ago, he came across a half-empty whiskey bottle he'd hidden somewhere and was tempted to take a drink at a difficult time in his new life. His old companions were invited back into his world when he succumbed to this impulse and have become worse than before. And despite the prayers of the saints, when James extended that new invitation to Shekar and Asthenes, I lost whatever authority I had gained over them concerning him.

"You may not believe this to look at me, but at one time, I wouldn't have had any problem with a hundred of those little imps. Now, in my weakened condition, it's all I can do to keep James alive, and I feel him slipping from even this safeguard."

"But what about our security patrols?" Da-Ved asked.

"Ha! I've seen the teams move very quietly through the city, but these two cowards hide whenever a security sweep comes through here. After they've gone, they're right back at him again.

"Just last week, I encountered a patrol and informed them again of the presence of James's tormentors. They told me their authority only covered uninvited guests, and they could do little to assist me. I was advised that a special messenger was to arrive soon and that I might take it up with him, but I don't think he'll come in time."

Da-Ved asked, "Just how did those two regain the upper hand?"

The pain etched on Arioch's face revealed the years of bitterness and failure he had endured. He replied with a faltering voice, "The problem...is...is...that James's deliverance was never followed through...to where he accepted His Majesty as his Savior. God has no final claim on him, and Asthenes and Shekar can come and go as they please, seeing as how God's Spirit hasn't taken up residence within him.

"He's almost comatose now, and it won't be long before I'll no longer be able to shield him from their more deadly assaults. Soon, they'll kill him. I-I fear I've failed him."

"Not necessarily, Arioch. *Almost* comatose is not the same *as* comatose, and while there is life, there's always hope."

"How? He's slipping away minute by minute, and they have the greater claim on him. By what authority do we intercede for him now?"

Da-Ved cupped an ear. "By listening, Arioch. Just listen."

"Listen to what?" the desperate Guardian pleaded.

"Listen to James. Don't you hear him?"

Arioch rose from his seated position and cocked an ear towards the supine figure in the alley. "What? He's just mumbling."

Da-Ved ordered, "*Listen!* There is the opening, Arioch. We can deal with them now." Da-Ved stood, revealing his presence to James's assailants.

Instantly, Asthenes' arm froze in midair as he drew back for another thrust upon the unconscious mortal. Instinctively, the two demons whirled from their victim to confront the small angel, their weapons held ready. Shekar arched his furry back like a spooked cat.

"Whooo are yoouu?" he hissed. "And vhat doo yoouu v-a-n-t?"

"Ha! Ha! What a sorry pair you two are," Da-Ved said. "I'm going to enjoy watching Arioch take your prey from you!"

Asthenes whipped his spear towards Da-Ved and cried, "Nooo! He is ours! You cannot have him!"

"Arioch, you say?" sneered Shekar. "Humph! He's a coward."

Revealing his presence, Arioch stood and walked straight through the dumpster to stand beside Da-Ved. His left wing drooped a little, and he walked with a prominent limp, but his countenance was still that of a warrior.

His long blade sang sweetly as he slowly unsheathed it. It momentarily flooded the drab alley with an eerie celestial light.

Unnerved by the presence of a second angel, the two powerful demons simultaneously took a step backwards, defensively guarding their prey.

Sizing up his adversaries, Asthenes' yellow eyes darted from one angel to the other. Then Shekar pressed their attack. "Stay back, Guardiansss. You have no dominion here. He iss ourss. Arioch…we have been witshh you a long time. You sshould be happy. It will all be over ssoon, and you will finally be done with ussss!"

Arioch grabbed his shield and boldly approached the pair. "You have not won the battle—yet," he said.

Da-Ved also drew closer to the two demons. "We have a claim on this one, and we will have him."

"*NOOOOOOOOOO!*" screamed Asthenes as he rushed wildly towards the two angels.

Perceiving that Da-Ved carried no weapons, the scaly spirit sprang at him first. Spotting the small pouch hanging about Da-Ved's neck, he came up short from the defenseless messenger. "You… You…You are…*Da-Ved?*" he asked in a low whisper.

Shekar's weapon clinked noisily as it fell from his grasp to the pavement. His eyes wide with alarm. He too asked, "Da-Ved? You are"—he gulped—"*Da-Ved?*"

Arioch took a faltering step backward as he eyed his diminutive companion. His grip on his weapon became a little firmer, and he seemed to stand a little straighter.

"And what if I am?" Da-Ved answered with a question.

"YOOU HAVE NO CLAIMM!" howled Asthenes. "It is too late for you. The fool has summoned us back into his life and he is ours. Be gone, Guardians!"

With that, he turned and raised his spear for one last thrust into the chest of the defenseless human.

Directly extending to the earth from the bright object overhead, two pillars of red and blue fire rapidly descended into the alley. Simultaneously, a blast of wind rushed from above, knocking over several trash cans to fill the street with blowing papers and trash. Alighting behind Da-Ved appeared Ariy'el and Oreb; their flaming swords bathed the alley in an unearthly glow.

Da-Ved acknowledged the two angels and turned his attention back to the demons.

"Our claim on the mortal is also by his invitation," Da-Ved said as he pressed the issue. "If you will only stop your quibbling and listen, you will know I am right."

The belligerent demons turned to stare at their victim. The bottle had fallen from James's hand and lay in the street next to him. Without exposing themselves to attack, the fiends backed towards the human so they could hear his mumbled slurred speech. Over and over, James drunkenly kept repeating himself. "Help me, Jeshus. Save me, Je-shus. Help me, Je-shus. Save me, Jee-sus."

"*NOOOOOOO!*" Whirling on his clawed feet, Asthenes rushed at Arioch. The bony spikes and ridges lining his back were now fully erect, and a poisonous black liquid oozed from the tip of each spike.

The resonance of honed steel filled the air as Arioch's blade flashed defensively. The charging demon's disembodied head rolled eerily through the dumpster, only to stop within a puddle of muddy water near the alley's entrance. There it melted, popping and sizzling out of existence.

As the headless body tumbled to the ground, it turned white-hot, spurting a black substance from its neck. The putrid odor of brimstone permeated the air, and the demon's carcass ignited, incinerating into a snow-like ash before it could hit the pavement.

Shekar immediately broke off his attack. Outnumbered four to one, the wily demon slowly backed away as the white ash fluttered to the ground.

"Lord Pharmakosss will hear offf thisss robbery," he said. "Youu two will ssufffer greatly for thiss ins-ssult!"

Ariy'el and Oreb lowered their weapons. "You may have some trouble locating Lord Pharmakos, Shekar," Ariy'el said. "I don't think he's even in this county anymore. If you do find him, please let him know that Ariy'el and Oreb were also present today. We would be most willing to accommodate him…at his leisure, of course."

Shekar stooped to pick up his dagger but found that Oreb had placed a heavy foot upon the serpentine blade. Shekar hissed his disapproval, and his clawed hand recoiled in horror. Scrambling to his feet, he retreated from the alley, passing through a parked car, and then veiled the direction of his escape by walking through the brick wall of a nearby building.

Oreb motioned to his companions and pointed to the retreating demon, "Please don't go away mad, Shekar. Just go away!"

Arioch approached Da-Ved and asked, "You are the angel called Da-Ved?"

"Yes," Da-Ved said.

"And you're the special envoy also?"

"I guess you could say that."

Arioch sullenly resheathed his sword. "What do we do now? I've not completed my assignment, and my charge can't possibly receive the truth in the condition he's in."

"That is not entirely correct, Arioch," Da-Ved replied. "His Majesty has given me great power and authority for the short time that I'm here. It will be under unusual circumstances, but we'll be able to talk with James, and if he is willing, he will receive the Good News. But as always, redemption will be a decision he'll have to make of his own free will. You understand, we cannot force him to accept it."

Da-Ved placed a hand gently upon the inebriated man's eyes and ordered, "James, awaken!"

He backed away to stand with his companions.

James Townsend's body shivered. His eyelids fluttered and then opened, and for a moment, he lay still as if awakening from a deep sleep. At last, he sat upright and found that he was confronted by four angelic beings. James gasped and covered his disfigured face with deformed hands.

"Where am I? Who are you?" he asked.

Da-Ved replied, "You are here with us in this deserted alleyway. James. We're friends. You don't have to hide your face anymore. We have something important to tell you."

James rubbed his sunken eyes with the heels of his hands. Rising to his feet, he muttered, "I must be dreaming...or drunk. Yeah, that's it. I'm still wasted."

Arioch shut his eyes in frustration. "No. James, your flesh is still poisoned with the alcohol and drugs you consumed tonight, but for now...you are not drunk."

An intense and palpable fear swept over James with the sudden realization that the entities confronting him were real. Teetering on unsteady legs, he cried out in a faltering voice, "Please...go...go away!"

Quickly advancing to his side, Arioch said, "Fear not, James, we bring you tidings of great joy from He who is the Alpha and Omega, the First and the Last."

Peering up at his Guardian, James asked, "I don't understand. What does that mean?"

As his legs regained their strength, he slowly got to his feet. "And how can I be poisoned with alcohol as you say...but not be drunk?"

"It means," said Arioch, "that you are not in your body. My friend has arranged that for the moment, your flesh cannot interfere with the message we have to give to you."

Pointing to something behind James, Arioch said in a sharp voice, "Behold!"

James turned to see the body of a man lying on the ground behind him. Cautiously, he approached the supine figure and then noticed a gin bottle lying near an opened disfigured hand. Gasping in sudden recognition of himself, his hands sprang to his eyes, shielding them from the impossible vision before him.

Looking up to his Guardian's face, he asked, "How can this be?"

Da-Ved motioned to Arioch to bend low and whispered into his ear, "Arioch, he is *your* charge. You fought many battles for him. It would only be proper for you to tell him."

"Thank you Da-Ved. You honor me."

Looking at his body, James asked, "Does this mean I'm dead? Have I died?"

"No, James," said Arioch, "your heart beats and your lungs continue to breathe. Your flesh still lives. But as the apostle Paul once experienced, your spirit is temporarily unfettered by the confines of your body. You are a very lucky man on a very special night for this to have happened to you."

With his eyes riveted on his physical body lying before him, James asked coldly, "What do you want?"

At last, Arioch thought. "James, you may not know this, but I have been with you for a long time. A very long time. I have witnessed all the sorrow and pain you've endured and the many degradations you've inflicted upon yourself. Several battles have been fought to protect you from the Evil One, and you've finally arrived at the supreme moment foretold of every human life. As one who invisibly ministered to you over the years, I only wish for you to receive the Good News of He whom I serve."

"You're talking about God, aren't you?" James asked. "Are you… are you…angels?"

"Yes, we're angels sent by God to help you. I am your Guardian."

James looked away. "A few weeks ago, a preacher tried to tell me about God and the Bible and other stuff, too, I guess. I didn't understand it all but when he talked about God, it was almost as if I could reach out and touch Him. I guess I should have listened to him better, but I thought I could find my own way after I cleaned up a little."

"James, don't you know you'll never understand it all and you'll never find your way to God alone? How can a mortal man possibly understand He who is infinite? Just know this: that He loves you and wants you to be at peace with yourself and with Him."

For the first time in years, James started to weep and hid his face in his hands. "How can I be at peace with myself?" he cried. "Don't you understand? I lost my family! I let them die!"

He looked up, and spittle ejected from his mouth as he screamed, "I couldn't save them when they needed me most! How could God love me when I abandoned them?"

Arioch reached out to place a compassionate hand upon his shoulder. "He knows of your pain, my friend."

"How? How could God possibly understand *my* pain?"

Bitterness rose in his voice. "You say you are my Guardian. Well, just where were my family's Guardians the night they died? Why would a loving God let my wife and little boy die that way?"

Arioch knelt to one knee to look James squarely in the face. "Their Guardians were there with us, James. I know because I saw them leave with your family as they escorted them into His presence. I can't say why your wife and child died. Or, for that matter, why you lived. I only know that as created beings, we have a limited view of eternity…as though looking through a darkly tinted glass.

"I'm here because while your wife was alive, she prayed for you daily. And, like myself, there are many other angels serving God in this city. We've watched over you.

"For centuries, angels have faithfully served as ministering spirits to the human race. Understand me, James. There is a great struggle for men's souls between God and the father of lies. Sometimes we are assigned as Guardians and can take an active role in the lives of mortals. Other times, we are only allowed to be witnesses to their struggles with evil. We don't understand why it is this way, but we defer to God's profound wisdom and judgment in these matters."

"But—"

"You ask heart-rendering questions, James, but I'm sorry…I don't possess the wisdom you seek. I've heard the sweet songs of the Pleiades and the harmonic strains of Orion when He spoke the stars into existence. But I can't tell you how He laid the foundations of the Earth or where He set the boundaries of the oceans. Job also asked such questions of God, but no one can understand His ways.

"And James, He understands your agony because He's felt that same pain. There was that one time when the Father abandoned His Son and allowed Him to perish, too, remember? I was present when your preacher friend told you about His sacrifice at Calvary."

"You mean that fairytale about the resurrection wasn't a hoax? It really happened?"

Pointing to Da-Ved, Arioch said, "Ask him. He was there. He saw Him die…and rise again."

"Did you?"

Da-Ved nodded. "Yes, James. I was in Jerusalem that week with a large company of Guardians.

And we were ready to do whatever was necessary to save Him from the agony of that Roman cross. We were fully prepared to destroy this planet if it would have kept Him out of the Destroyer's hands, but we weren't allowed to play a part in His plan. We were sixty thousand strong, but not a single angelic finger was lifted in His defense."

Da-Ved's voice became huskier. "Our hearts were sorely rent by what transpired that black day. He refused our help, and we saw Him bleed and die on that accursed tree. The Father turned His back on His Son, and all creation rebelled against the Creator. The earth shook, and the celestial servant candle you call the sun even refused its light for a time as the world was plunged into spiritual darkness. And He did this…*for you.*"

With a faltering voice, James asked, "Why?"

"Because He loves you," Arioch said. "He's been waiting for you to come to Him so He could heal you spiritually. He knows you've suffered a tremendous loss, but you need to go to Him for redemption. Just ask Him. Turn to Him and ask for forgiveness, and your name will be added to His book."

James screwed up his face. "Book? What? What are you talking about?"

"His book James. It's called the Lamb's Book of Life."

James slipped to his knees and bent forward, resting his head upon the pavement. He began to cry, releasing the grief and anger he'd carried within him for decades.

Rocking to and fro, he cried out, "Oh God. Oh God. I'm sorry. I've been such a fool. All those years…wasted. Please forgive me, Jesus. Please take away this pain. I can't handle it any longer."

While his emaciated body was racked with the ravages of his miserable existence of living on the streets, his spirit-body convulsed violently with guilt and despair. "Oh, Jesus, save me," he said. Falling to his side, he curled up into a tight ball of sin and hopelessness.

Oreb and Ariy'el joined Arioch and Da-Ved, taking up defensive positions surrounding James. Hearing their Lord's name upon the lips of a sinner petitioning pardon from their King, the four angels bowed their heads reverently. With the power of God's redemption pouring into the valley from on high, the quartet grinned at each other with knowing smiles.

A flood of God's mercy and redemption washed over the frail mortal, enveloping him in infinite love. Multiple waves of a warm crimson tide gently stripped layer after layer of sin and shame away. James's spiritual body started to resonate with soft white light, and ever so slowly, he uncurled from the fetal position he'd locked into.

Undergoing a miraculous spiritual metamorphosis, his disfigured hands sloughed off dead skin and mangled bones, revealing hands made whole. Overcome by his transfiguration, he wept quietly, thanking God for his spiritual healing and regeneration.

Finally, James sat up to reveal a healed and restored face. His spirit had been made whole by the redeeming blood of the Lamb—Yeshua, the Messiah.

James spoke to Arioch. "What is your name?"

"Arioch."

"Thank you, Arioch. Thank you."

"How do you feel?" Arioch asked.

"As if I've been reborn."

"You have," Oreb answered. "That you have."

Looking at his unconscious and deformed physical body lying on the other side of the alley, James asked, "Do I have to go back?"

"Do you want to go back?" Arioch asked. "I am willing to spend as many years with you as the Lord will allow, James."

"There's not much to go back to, Arioch. I have no friends or family. My physical body is weak and crippled, and it's been a long time since I've felt whole. I'm all alone there. No. No, I want to be with Him. Please don't make me go back."

"I'm sorry, James, but it's not up to me. I don't know what will happen, but I know you have to go back for at least a short time. Your spirit must reunite with your soul and body once more. But I do know this: He will do what is best for you. You don't have to be afraid, no matter what the future holds."

"Will I remember you?" James asked. "Will I remember our meeting?"

"I'm not sure what His Majesty has planned...for you *or* me. But I suspect that since your salvation is rooted in our unusual circumstances tonight, I believe that, yes, you will remember us. Are you ready, my mortal friend?"

"I-I guess so."

Perceiving his hesitancy, Arioch asked, "What's the matter, James? What are you afraid of?"

"This is happening way too fast. I don't know what to make of it all. Are you sure God will continue to forgive me? How does He know I'm not faking my repentance?"

"Because His Word says so, James."

"You keep talking in riddles. What Word are you talking about?"

"Oh, that's right!" Arioch said. "You haven't had much time to learn any of it, have you? It's written in the Scriptures, James, that the Word of God is quick and powerful and sharper than any two-edged sword. It pierces even to the dividing of your soul and spirit and discerns your thoughts and the intentions of your heart. All things are naked and open to the eyes of God.

"He knows that your repentance is for real, James. We all know it. Is that good enough for you?"

A wide smile on his newly restored face revealed James's answer before he could speak. "Yes, yes, it is. And thank you again, Arioch, for all your years of service and for...you know. Telling me the truth about Him. I'll try not to forget you."

With a shrug, he added, "I guess I'm ready now."

Arioch placed a large hand over James's face, and he fell into unconsciousness once again. Catching him up, the Guardian carried James's spirit body to be reunited with his physical body. Da-Ved was there, waiting.

With authority from the Throne, Da-Ved converged James's spirit, body, and soul into one whole living being again. Although his physical body never regained consciousness, a smile formed upon his disfigured lips. The human took a long deep breath, then exhaled slowly. He took another. And then another. Gradually, James's respiratory system became more inhibited by the depressants working within his system.

Arioch looked to Da-Ved. "What is to be done? Will he live?"

"No," Da-Ved said. "The Lord just revealed to me that it was decided before I arrived. He was to die this day no matter what the outcome here. You served your King well this night, my friend. Another precious name has been added to His book."

While they stood watch over James's physical body, the three listened sympathetically as Arioch related the many battles he had endured as James's Guardian. As he talked, the alcohol and barbiturates in James's bloodstream reduced his rate and volume of air exchange by depressing the respiratory center in his brain stem. His pupils became fixed and dilated, and the carbon dioxide in his blood increased to a dangerous level. James's buffer systems were long since overwhelmed, and his respiratory system struggled in the last stages of life. His lungs expanded shallowly, and his rate, rapid at first, became more infrequent.

Other systems now started to be affected by the failing respiratory system. His blood pressure fell precipitously as James's pulse became weak and thready.

His skin became cold to the touch and took on the pallor of death. Eventually, the lack of oxygen caused James's heart to arrest, and his circulatory system quickly collapsed. With his brain deprived of oxygen, death came in minutes.

A final slow exhalation came forth, and James gave up his spirit. With his disfigured face fraught with excruciating pain, he clutched at his chest and sat bolt upright. Just as quickly, the pain was gone, and an expression of relief and surprise flickered across his eyes. His face was perfect once again.

"Hey! What gives? I thought you said I was going back."

Arioch answered, "You did, James. But you're back with us again."

James got up from the ground, no longer feeling the biting cold in his bones. Looking about, he said, "It...it doesn't look like I've been gone too long."

Spying his lifeless body nearby, he gasped. "Oh! I...guess...I guess I didn't make it, did I?"

Ariy'el came over and put his arm around him. "You made it where it counts, James. You can go home now."

"Can I?" he asked. "When?"

Da-Ved answered him. "Right now, James. You can go right now. Arioch will escort you right to His Throne."

"His Throne? God's Throne?"

Smiling, Da-Ved said, "Sure! Oh, you've nothing to fear. Now there can be no judgment for your sins, remember? If you're foolish enough to bring them up, He won't even know what you're talking about."

Turning to Arioch, Da-Ved said, "I have to go. I have other responsibilities tonight. Oreb and Ariy'el will escort you to the present Commander who is flying the security cap for this mission. If that is agreeable with you, from there, you can go on with James to New Jerusalem."

Arioch offered a large hand to the small angel. When Da-Ved took it, Arioch pulled him close and whispered. "I'll miss you, friend. I hope we'll serve together again."

Taking James in his powerful arms, Arioch addressed his escort, "Guardians, we're ready. Let's go home."

The trio's flaring contrails scorched a dazzling pathway through the lower atmosphere. For the briefest of moments, streaks of blue, red, and yellow burned vertically in a spiral fashion from the alley towards the shimmering object suspended over the valley.

Now when Jesus was born in Bethlehem of Judaea in the days of Herod the king, behold, there came wise men from the east to Jerusalem, Saying, Where is he that is born King of the Jews? for we have seen his star in the east, and are come to worship him.

—Matthew 2:1–2 (KJV)

CHAPTER TWELVE

The Wise Man

DECEMBER 24 – 8:30 PM
THE OVERLOOK

Four sets of human eyes witnessed the pinwheeling lights rising from out of the city.

"Look!" cried Felipe. "Here they come again. Hey, there's three of them this time."

Standing on a small knoll behind them, Jorge watched, leaning on his cane for support. His beret and shoulders were speckled with newly fallen snow.

Jesse's voice betrayed the apprehension he felt. "What is it? Are we being invaded or something? Shouldn't we tell someone? The authorities?"

Tom shook his head. "What am I, chopped liver?" he muttered to himself.

Pulling a mitten off with his teeth he unzipped his parka and reached into its inner pocket to retrieve the small binoculars. Raising the instrument to his eyes, he said, "Now, let's see what we can see."

He fine-tuned the knurled knob between the eyepieces and focused the instrument upon the rising objects.

"Quick! What do you see? What do you see?" Felipe asked.

Jesse stared at the rising objects. "Yeah, what are they?"

Tom lowered the binoculars and pulled out a handkerchief. Wiping the lenses, he said, "I don't know. The glasses must be too warm. They're fogging over. I can't see too well. They'll have to acclimate to the cold a bit."

Once again, he raised the optics to his eyes to solve the mystery. He scanned the horizon for a moment.

"There they are. Yep! There's three of 'em all right. There's a yellow one going straight up...and the other two are red...and...blue. They're not going straight up with the yellow one, though. They're kind of twisting about it as if they're trying to keep it between them as they rise, like they're guarding it or something. All of them are leaving colorful trails—"

His voice caught in his throat. "Ahhh!"

Jesse grabbed for the binoculars. "Let's see! Let me see!"

Awed into silence, Tom passed him the binoculars without taking his eyes off the lights climbing into the sky. Jesse grabbed and fumbled with them, almost dropping them in the snow.

Losing sight of the lights momentarily, he asked, "Now where are they? Oh! There they are."

Raising the binoculars to his eyes, he said, "Now...let's see... hmmm."

A sudden updraft blew a wall of white powder up and over the cliff, interrupting his view.

"What the?" Jesse backed away from the gusting wind and blowing snow.

Tom turned to look at Jorge who hadn't spoken a word since the objects initiated their skyward ascent. The old man was smiling, oblivious to the dusting of snow covering him.

Felipe sprang forward and grabbed the binoculars out of Jesse's hands. "What did you see, Jesse?"

Jesse surrendered the binoculars without protest. "You wouldn't believe me, Felipe. You'll have to see for yourself."

Tom asked, "Jesse, just what did you see, boy? Tell me."

"I-I don't know for sure. It's...snowing a little out there...and the lights make it hard to see clearly. They're moving and twisting around so much."

Tom came up behind him and whispered in his ear, "It's all right Jess. I don't trust these old eyes of mine either. But just between you and me, what *did* you see?"

"Feathers!" screamed Felipe. Looking through the glasses, he exclaimed, "I-I can see feathers!"

Jesse swallowed hard and looked to Tom nervously.

"And why not?" Jorge asked. "What did you expect?"

Tom glanced over his shoulder. "Say, George, you seem to know more than you're letting on to. What gives? Do you or do you not know what those things are?"

"Yeah, Gramps," Jesse said, "what are they?

Jorge shrugged. "What does an old toro know?"

"Ahhh…he doesn't know any more than we do," Tom said with disgust.

Waving his cane at the policeman, Jorge said, "You do not *want* to know what they are. Or you already know and are afraid to admit it."

"Then what are they, Grandfather?" Jesse asked.

"Are we not observing the end of the season of Advent tomorrow? Are we not shepherds watching over our flock by night?"

Raising his cane and pointing to the curious light hovering over the valley, Jorge asked, "Are we not witnessing a new star in the heavens?"

He climbed down the snow-covered knoll and grabbed both of Tom's upper arms in the iron clasp of hands made strong from decades of shearing sheep.

Looking Tom in the eye, he said, "And you, my gringo friend. Are you not searching for something? Something you lost some time ago? If you are a wise man, you will find it again. Here. Tonight. On this mountain."

Letting go of his friend, he watched the mysterious illuminations as they danced in their upward spiral, winding a path towards the flicker of a tiny golden sun.

Tom turned to stare as the three lights rose from the city. He answered his friend in a low whisper, "If only I could, Jorge. If only I could."

*****

DECEMBER 24 – 8:30 PM
THE MIBTSAR

In addition to Oreb and Ariy'el, Aram's security force consisted of twenty-eight winged warriors. These Guardians monitored Arioch's ascent from the city and were waiting to congratulate the victorious trio and to greet the precious human soul they now carried. Ever vigilant, they circled Aram's command post in two tight concentric circuits forming a winged fortress called a Mibtsar. Handpicked by Miyka'el, each of these twenty-eight Guardians carried the golden shield of the Jerusalem Legion.

The outer screen of sixteen angels slowly circled the inner screen. The inner screen warriors leisurely cycled in the opposite direction like a wheel revolving within a wheel. Although small in size, this compact circular citadel could easily withstand most demonic onslaughts.

Four main sentry posts were located just to the outside edge of the revolving outer wheel. Each of the angels manning these positions carried special shields as badges of their rank within the Legion.

Using this formation of warriors as a command and control platform, Aram monitored the valley below. Normally, a fortress such as this was employed solely in the spiritual realm for the pulling down of enemy strongholds, and when used in conjunction with the prayers of a region's saints, this configuration of angels was truly a fearsome spiritual weapon.

Indeed, the Prophet Daniel recorded the overthrow of a demonic overlord called the Prince of Persia by Miyka'el using a similar battlement. The fighting had been fierce during that intense encounter, but after three weeks of combat, the territorial spirit finally fell to Miyka'el and his winged juggernaut.

Besides having the ability to operate within the spiritual realm, the Mibtsar could also engage with the material universe. The vortexes that could be produced by this fortress could easily tear a planet apart by simply playing with its magnetic fields and gravitational tides.

But if a more localized decimation of the planet's surface was preferred, then frozen rocks from the asteroid belt located just beyond the sun's fourth planet could be snared and hurled to the Earth's surface with devastating accuracy. The Mibtsar was locked, cocked, and ready to rock.

As Commander of this Angelic Host, Aram coordinated Da-Ved's ground-based security detail from this airborne platform. He no longer carried his huge fur-covered shield, longsword, or staff but had exchanged them for the commander's smaller shield and gladius of the Legion. His shield now bore the image of the Ark of the Covenant, a symbol of the seat of God's grace and mercy.

Ambient starlight refracting from the shields of these circling warriors caused a flickering motion to any eye who should witness their movement. When viewed from Earth, the Mibtsar resembled just one of the many celestial phenomena normally seen in the night sky.

*****

DECEMBER 24 – 8:30 PM
APPROACHING THE MIBTSAR

"Arioch, just where are we going again?" James asked with more than a little apprehension in his voice.

The Guardian looked down at the human in his arms. "Ah, James, that is an interesting question. Under ordinary circumstances, a redeemed mortal isn't aware of their Guardian's presence as they are escorted to one of heaven's twelve gates. Usually, the trip is instantaneous, and the redeemed simply awake to find themselves in the Great Hall awaiting an audience to the Throne. But as I said before, you have been blessed on a very special night.

"Do you see that bright object just ahead? It's called a Mibtsar, and it's the fortress of the heavenly Host for this province. Nothing will move in this sector tonight without his knowledge or permission. We'll have to check in with him before you can go home."

"Home," James let the word rattle off his lips. "That word had no real meaning for me before, but now it genuinely feels like I'm going to go home. I can't believe it."

As the small troupe neared the star-like object, it became obvious that it was a formation of immense warriors. James asked, "Arioch, just how big do angels get? Each one of them look like they could take on a whole army by themselves."

The eastern sentry carried a shield that had the image of a lion inscribed upon its face. He called out and descended to greet them. "Hail Arioch!"

Arioch stopped his ascent momentarily and looked to the Lion Sentry. "Ke'phiyr! It *is* you. I thought I recognized your voice." He continued to rise to join his friend.

Two more Guardians approached, allowing a small gap to form in the outer wheel. The other sentries stayed at their posts. Guardians from the inner wheel systematically peeled off to fill in this outer breach. Simultaneously, the inner circle's six remaining warriors shifted positions, falling back to make a smaller and tighter inner wheel.

Ke'phiyr detained Arioch at the Mibtsar's outer angelic ring, but Oreb and Ariy'el obediently continued to the wheel's center to report to Aram.

As they advanced, Aram asked, "What is your report, Oreb?"

"Another of the redeemed comes home, Aram. Our king has won another one."

"That's good. His Majesty paid dearly for them. I should think heaven will be a noisy place tonight.

"But what of Da-Ved? Did you see him? Is it safe for him to continue his mission with the enemy regathering outside the city?"

"Ha! Don't worry about him," said Ariy'el. "The enemy is terrified of him. We saw him stand unarmed before Asthenes and Shekar, and they *still* refused to attack him."

Aram scowled. "Those two always *were* cowards."

"Well, you don't have to bother about Asthenes anymore," Oreb said. "The Guardian on station there dispatched him to the Abyss when the fiend foolishly attacked him."

"Who was the Guardian?"

Oreb looked beyond the nearest sentry to the outer containment ring where a small but noisy reunion was in progress. "Arioch was the Guardian. He still handles his sword well."

Aram's eyes followed Oreb's gaze to the distant wheel of angels. "I thought that there might have been a human casualty since Arioch returned with you. How is it that the human has won the victory if Arioch also returns at this time? Shouldn't Arioch remain on Earth as his human's protector?"

Oreb turned to his commander. "Today is the day of salvation for the mortal James Townsend. It just happens to be the day he also goes home to the Father."

"Was it that close?" Aram asked.

"Yes," Ariy'el added, "and if Da-Ved hadn't been there, it wouldn't have happened at all."

Folding his arms across his chest, Aram asked, "I don't suppose *you* two had anything to do with it?"

"Oh, let's just say we backstopped them," Ariy'el said.

"And we were polite too," Oreb added. "We sent along our regards to Lord Pharmakos."

"Ooh yeah, I'll just bet you did. I take it Da-Ved is continuing with his mission? Are there any signs of the enemy within the city?"

"No, you can relax, Aram. If Lucifer were around, I'm sure we would have seen something of him by now."

"Never underestimate that snake," Aram warned. "He's very cagey and more than a little dangerous. It would be just like him to lay low for a while until we drop our guard. That's when he'll strike. When we feel safe and secure. And once you are in his coils, he will crush and constrict you until he is able to absorb you. Never forget that. Now get back to your posts...and stay alert."

Oreb looked at Ariy'el and asked, "I'll take top and you take bottom?"

Ariy'el feigned a pained expression and said, "You always get top. I want the top. Come on. It's my turn."

"Oh, all right," Oreb said as he flew to the Serpent Sentry position directly below the spinning aviary fortress. With that, Ariy'el took the high position as Raptor Sentry.

As they departed, Aram called out, "Ke'phiyr! Shareth!"

The Lion and Servant Sentries quickly reported to their commander. Ke'phiyr asked, "Sir?"

Aram's demeanor hardened as he gave his sentries new orders. "I've redeployed our Serpent and Raptor lookouts. While they are at their posts, I would like an intelligence sweep east and west. You two explore our outer sectors and report any new enemy activity you come across. Be careful."

*****

As Ke'phiyr and Shareth redeployed, Aram signaled for Arioch to approach him.

"Greetings, Arioch. It's good to see that you escort your charge as one of the redeemed."

"Thank you, sir. His name is James."

James squirmed in Arioch's arms. "He-Hello, sir."

"I'm happy to meet you, James. You're on a grand adventure, aren't you?"

James swallowed hard and nodded.

"What do you have to report, Arioch?" Aram asked. "I expect you're on your way home."

"Yes, sir, but I have to confess, Da-Ved helped win the victory. My charge was almost lost."

Eyeing the sword hanging on Arioch's back, Aram said, "I've heard of the skill of your blade, Guardian. Sometimes, when faced with the evil of the day, the only thing one can do is to stand. And judging from the looks of your wing and that fair-sized slash across your shield, I'd say when you make a stand, you don't back up much, do you?"

"It was a minor wound, Aram, and it will be worth it if my hardships have benefited the expansion of His kingdom. I only hope that on my return to the celestial city, there will be a place to serve Him near His Throne."

"I don't think that's going to be a problem," Aram said with a knowing smile. "I have a pretty good idea what your next assignment will be like. He has a special post for those Guardians who've been wounded in His service and need time to heal. I think you'll enjoy it."

"Thank you, sir. I hope so. I know that whatever it is, it will definitely be interesting."

"We've been monitoring this valley for days, and I can assure you, it's secure," Aram said. "You're free to continue with your journey. Just be aware we are on high alert while Da-Ved is below. Be careful."

Arioch turned and looked at the assembly of angels encircling them. His eyes jumped from Guardian to Guardian.

"I don't think Lucifer would dare try a direct assault with the team you've assembled here. He might have more assets than you could successfully defend against, but he'd have no planet left to rule if he challenged this Mibtsar outright. And I've heard of the grudge he holds for you and Da-Ved. He wants you two more than he wants this human. No. If his attack comes, it will probably be on the planet below...where Da-Ved is. We'll be fine. By your leave, sir?"

"Take him home, Arioch. I only wish I could be there with you to witness his entry. That will be a sight to behold."

*****

DECEMBER 24 – 8:30 PM
THE OVERLOOK

"Hey!" Felipe shouted. "Those lights just merged with that... that...UFO thingamajig...whatever it is."

"If I didn't know better, I'd call it the mother ship," Jesse added. "Soooo...now what?"

The four stood quietly watching for a few silent minutes. Tom used the respite to pray silently, *Oh Lord. If only I could believe again. But I can't. I'd like to, but I just can't. If you're really out there tonight, please show me the way. Please...give me a sign or—*

A silent explosion of light discharged from the stellar object, and the four spectators flinched as an immense violet halo radiated from its center.

Simultaneously, an iridescent red blur rocketed straight up from out of the center of the apparent detonation. At the same time, a burning ethereal blue ball plummeted to take up a position directly below it. There was no sound or shockwave, but a few seconds later, the object flared again. This time, two golden orbs raced horizontally to the east and west.

"Did you see that?" Jesse yelled. "Gramps! Tom! Did you see that?"

A coyote howled from somewhere below them.

Tom stiffened as he remembered the bizarre encounter with the injured animal earlier in the evening. An immediate draining feeling overcame him, and he felt all his spiritual resistance leave as the haunting echoes of the coyote faded away.

That...I did see, Tom thought. *That I surely did.*

"What do you think it means?" Felipe asked.

"It means...it's time to go," Tom answered a little more loudly than he had wanted to.

He lowered his voice and added, "I can't stay up here all night. I gotta get back to work. Come on. Let's get going."

"Oh, shoot! It's just getting interesting!" Jesse said. "Where do you have to run off to, Tom?"

"Well, for one thing, I have to get back to my patrol. And for another, I just might swing by my wife's church for a few minutes after work."

Tom glanced up to the top of the mountain behind him. "I know when I'm licked, George."

The old man raised his cane in victory and smiled.

A wise man and three shepherds left the overlook and made their way back to the old game trail. The blowing wind and snow had almost obliterated their tracks, but it was of no consequence. Jorge had long since memorized every inch of the mountain, and they were soon moving through the trees, making their way down to where they had abandoned the jeep.

A few seconds after they left the overlook, a single yellow light streaked silently from the flickering object towards the Earth's moon. Its only witness was a solitary coyote as she sat guarding the entrance to her den in the valley below.

*****

DECEMBER 24 – 8:30 PM
THE ALLEY

Da-Ved watched the three Guardians soar out of the alley as they escorted James to the Mibtsar. He then strolled the length of the narrow street, making sure he hadn't overlooked anything that might hold a clue as to what his mission might encompass. Thinking of the spiritual struggle that had just been wrestled there, he sat on a trash can to study James's body. To the undiscerning eye, it would not appear that much of a victory had been won in this alley this night.

In a puddle of water amidst the filth and debris of the street lay James's cold dead body, uncouthly propped against the brick wall of a rundown building. An empty bottle lay just beyond the reach of his outstretched hand.

He frowned with the realization that much would be made of what appeared to be James's pointless demise by the local authorities and news media, especially because of the holiday season.

Working his way back through the alley, he returned to the street from which he'd come and then headed east for Job's House a few blocks away.

*****

DECEMBER 24 – 9:00 PM
DEPARTING THE MIBTSAR

"James, this may be a little unpleasant for you," Arioch said. "Your eyes won't be able to fathom the speed or the dimension we're about to travel. I'll go slowly at first, but I must accelerate to a velocity your mind won't be able to comprehend, and it will probably compensate for it."

"How?" James asked.

"You won't remember the journey. Are you ready?"

"Yes, let's go, Arioch."

Departing the spinning citadel, Arioch first headed for Earth's natural satellite as a reference point so James would have something finite to fix upon. At a pace with which human intellect could still function, James witnessed the moon's speedy approach and then just as quickly saw the lunar landscape shrink to a small white dot behind them. His Guardian then accelerated to a mind-numbing speed after which time, gravity, and the universe contorted into a new dimension. James's defensive mechanisms kicked in, and he swooned.

*****

EARTH TIME: DECEMBER 24 – 9:20 PM
THE CORRIDOR

Like so many countless times before, a deceased human soul awoke to find itself in a dark place on a cold and hard floor. The soul sensed that it was in a vast chamber of some kind, but the only available light source appeared to be far away. Finally, James remembered his identity and the strange odyssey he was on. Unable to recall just exactly how his Guardian had brought him to this place, he struggled to his feet and stumbled towards the light.

Anxiously, he called out to the darkness that engulfed him. "Arioch, where are you?"

A voice from the inky blackness answered, "Right behind you, James. I'm still here."

James stopped. "I can't see you. Why are you hiding?"

"I'm not hiding. I'm just making sure you don't walk this way. There's a hidden gate here you're not supposed to open."

James resumed his march in the other direction towards the distant white glow. "Why not, Arioch?"

"It would be bad. You don't want to come this way. Don't worry, I'm right behind you."

"Am I going in the right direction? Should I stop?"

"No, don't stop, James. You're doing fine. The redeemed always walk toward the light. They seem to sense the correct direction to go. I guess they're drawn to it."

"What about the lost?" James asked. "Wouldn't they set out for the light too?"

"No, James. They never get to see it. They never arrive on this side of the Dark Gate."

As they walked along, the room became more illuminated, and James picked up his pace. At first, he perceived they were in some sort of dark tunnel, but now he realized they were traversing a long stone corridor.

"Arioch, why is it so dark in here? I can barely see the ceiling."

"We're good. We're heading to the end. Just keep going."

They walked through several doorways, but the far end of the hallway was blocked by an enormous white door. James turned to see his Guardian limping along a few feet behind him and stopped. "You're injured!" he cried.

"You had a hard life, my friend. You were a difficult assignment."

James lowered his head, averting his eyes. "I'm sorry, Arioch. I had no idea."

"No mortal does, James. Don't even think about it. It comes with the territory. But cheer up. Your race will soon be over. We're almost home."

They continued in silence for a few minutes, then James asked, "What's on the other side?"

"The other side?"

"Yeah. You know…the other side of that door I'm not supposed to open."

"Oh. Sheol is on the other side of the door. It's a dark place at present occupied by a number of cruel devils. You wouldn't like it."

"Sheol? I never heard of it. What's Sheol?"

"Sheol is 'the grave' in the Hebrew tongue. It's an ever-expanding place of outer darkness where there is wailing and gnashing of teeth. It's a place where the lost are all alone. And it is there that they await the coming judgment."

James stared into the oppressive gloom of the hallway he had just traveled and shivered with a sudden chill. As they neared the end of the passageway, he found that their way was blocked by a massive pearly-white door. The whiteness of the door became almost blinding, but he could also see that a towering watchman stood guard in front of it. He slowed down and whispered, "Arioch, look. Will he open the door for us?"

Arioch prodded him forward. "It'll be all right, James. I'm here to make sure you finish this journey. Don't be afraid. The guard's name is Mal'ak. He will let us pass."

James turned to stare again into the dismal blackness they had just traversed.

"James, I know something is bothering you. What is it?"

"If I had arrived on the wrong side of that...that...Dark Gate by mistake, would I have been able to open it?"

"Do you think God makes mistakes?" Arioch asked.

"Hypothetically, I mean."

"Hypothetically? It wouldn't happen."

James was insistent. "But if it did?"

The lanky Guardian prodded James again. "If it did, then I guess that somehow, yes, it would be opened for you."

"How do you know?"

Mal'ak answered for Arioch in a great booming voice, "Because neither death nor life nor angels nor principalities nor powers, things present, or things to come nor height nor depth or any other creature shall be able to separate you from the love of God, which is in His Majesty, Yeshua, the Messiah! Greetings, James. I've been expecting you."[4]

James ducked behind Arioch like a scared child. Peeking around Arioch's legs, he asked the enormous sentry, "You…you know my name?"

"Yes, James. I've been appointed to receive you and Arioch into His inner chambers. I am Mal'ak, watchman of the Judah Gate."

Mal'ak was an imposing sentry. At fifteen feet in height, his slender physique easily towered over both his visitors. He wore a full-length white robe made of a seamless coarse cloth tied off at the waist by a scarlet rope. A pair of jade-green eyes set off his untamed fiery red mane, and a pair of oversized wings of royal blue arched over his head. They cascaded behind him, trailing to the floor. Crisscrossed upon his back hung a huge longbow and a large quiver of thick arrows. He grasped a bulging goatskin bag in his left hand.

"Arioch, I have words for you from His Majesty. He's very pleased with your service and desires to meet with you later."

A toothy grin spread across Mal'ak's broad face and he held out the bag for Arioch to take.

"For now, he wishes you to partake of this refreshment as a token of His appreciation. It's good, my friend. It's from the River."

Wide-eyed, Arioch took the sloshing bag from a gigantic hand that dwarfed his own.

"Arioch?" James whispered.

"Yes, James?"

"Is-is my family beyond those doors? Will I be able to see them again?"

Mal'ak said, "Oh, I think a small reunion has already been planned, James. Now if you will allow me, I'll herald your arrival to His Majesty."

Gesturing towards the doorway, he added, "All paradise awaits you just inside this gate."

James took a deep breath and said, "I guess…I'm ready."

The grinning giant reached down, grasped the huge handle of one door, and opened it just a crack. Deep angelic voices immersed in a praise melody belted through the cleft and reverberated down the hallway.

"I love this part," Mal'ak said in a loud voice. Pulling hard, he swung the door outward into the corridor.

Arioch pushed James to the entrance where they both peered into the sanctuary.

James's eyes opened wide, and he faltered at the door. Multitiered balconies teemed with thousands of angels of all sorts and sizes. As the door opened, the galleries fell silent, and all eyes in the sanctuary were now riveted upon James, heaven's newest citizen.

From the middle of this great chamber rose the altar, and upon this elevated platform sat the seven-branched Golden Lampstand and God's Throne. Stationed at various locations around the altar were winged musicians who continued to play their instruments softly in the background.

As James entered, the orchestra stopped playing, and the Son rose to His feet. He clapped his hands and proclaimed, "At last, well done, my victorious servant! Well done! It's good to have you home!"

A deafening cheer exploded from the galleries accompanied by thundering applause which lasted several minutes. The lengthy exaltation slowly evolved into a song of praise glorifying Yeshua which also told of James's personal victory. James became overwhelmed by the wondrous splendor displayed before him, and he cried unabashedly.

Arioch looked to Mal'ak who gave him a confident thumbs up. The songs glorifying the Son and honoring James also told the tale of Arioch's battles and spoke of his loyalty to God and to angelic victory in the face of overwhelming odds. James now caught a small glimpse of the hidden mystery of God's wisdom which had been ordained since before the world had been created.

The final emotional straw came for James when he spied two angels stationed on the landing between the two large scrolls. The Guardians stood side by side, feet spread apart with hands on their hips. With their wings expanded tip to tip, they effectively blocked his upward path to the altar.

Two familiar figures emerged from behind these titanic warriors and, hand in hand, quickly descended the stairs to the courtyard. James sank to his knees as he recognized his wife and son, and Arioch reached down to strengthen him. Together, they descended the stairway to the misty courtyard where a tearful but joyful homecoming took place.

An ancient poem put to music was beautifully sung by the myriad of angels witnessing the family's glorious reunion. As mortal hugs and kisses were exchanged, celestial harpists played, and the Host sang:

Praise the LORD!
For it is good to sing praises to our God; for it is
pleasant, and a song of praise is fitting.
The LORD builds up Jerusalem; he gathers the outcasts of Israel.
He heals the brokenhearted and binds up their wounds.
He determines the number of the stars; he
gives to all of them their names.
Great is our Lord, and abundant in power; his
understanding is beyond measure.
The LORD lifts up the humble; he casts the wicked to the ground.
Sing to the LORD with thanksgiving; make
melody to our God on the lyre![5]

Once again, the galleries broke into rumbling applause as son and wife took James by the hand to lead him up to the altar's summit. As the small family ascended from the courtyard, the two Guardians standing at the landing formed the traditional fiery winged Arch of Triumph for James to walk through. The ancient chamber resounded thunderously when Arioch added his own wings to the arch as James entered into God's presence.

For the word of God is quick, and powerful, and sharper
than any two edged sword, piercing even to the dividing
asunder of soul and spirit, and of the joints and marrow, and
is a discerner of the thoughts and intents of the heart.

—Hebrews 4:12 (KJV)

CHAPTER THIRTEEN

Spirit

DECEMBER 24 – 9:20 PM
JOB'S HOUSE

Pastor Timothy Witherspoon was alone in the front drawing-room of the old Anderson residence. The mansion had been a boarding house back when Job had been a bustling boomtown, but when the town's mines failed, it too fell upon hard times. The once magnificent house eventually became a speakeasy, and as it deteriorated, it eventually was abandoned by its owners. For several years, its only inhabitants were vagrants and winos, and the building was ultimately condemned and scheduled for demolition by the city.

The vision of two elderly sisters, Lucy and Nora Anderson, saved the old house from the wrecking ball in 1979. With financial assistance from local churches, they converted the huge home into a halfway house for men recovering from drug and alcohol abuse. Several congregations continued to pledge their financial support for this ministry, but funding continued to be a never-ending struggle.

Clara Rogers poked her head through the library's ornate oak doors and found the young pastor looking out the large front window.

"There you are, Timothy. I've been looking all over for you. Come on. We're going to have some hot chocolate and roast marshmallows in the fireplace."

Deep in thought, Pastor Witherspoon gazed out into the shadows. The wind had picked up, and snow was starting to blow through the fence and bushes that lined the front of the property. It fell against them, creating a small but burgeoning drift.

Hearing his name, Tim turned to see Clara standing in the wide doorway leading from the library.

"Huh? What's that, Clare?"

The older woman entered the drawing-room to share his view of the street corner. Seeing the blowing snow, she said, "My, that looks cold and foreboding tonight, doesn't it?"

When Tim didn't respond, she drew closer and spoke in a hushed voice, "What's the matter, Tim? Thinking about James? Come on, you did what you could. You have to stop beating yourself up about him. He'll come back when he's ready. You know that. You can't make them change. They have to do it themselves."

"I know, Clare, but look at that," he said, nodding at the falling snow. "He's out there in that mess, probably holed up somewhere in that alley of his. He'll be lucky if he doesn't come down with pneumonia tonight."

Clara sidled up to him and gently took his arm. "Look, you told him he's welcome here anytime if he needs help, didn't you? He's a grown man. It's his choice."

Irritation crept into the young pastor's voice. "I know. I know. Believe me, I know. But he was so close. So close. I honestly thought he was going to cross over the night of the rally. He only needed a little more persuasion. Why did he have to go and find that stupid whiskey bottle? It's my fault. I lost him."

The small woman dropped his arm and exclaimed, "Timothy Witherspoon! You should be ashamed of yourself!"

Eyes aflame with indignation, Clara continued her barrage, "You don't win them and you don't lose them. That's the Lord's work, and don't you go taking credit for His labor. All you do is plant the seed and maybe turn the soil over a bit. Don't you ever forget that."

"Yes, ma'am. You're right. I just feel like I have to do something is all. I can't just sit here wondering where—"

A solitary figure traipsed out of the dark alley into the Liberty Street intersection and walked briskly toward the house. Tim strained to see who it was through the blowing snow. The shadowy figure seemed to hesitate at the streetlight for a moment or two as if conversing with someone just out of view. Tim looked left and right but could see no one else in the street. Losing his timidity, the person crossed the street and walked directly to the main gate.

"You don't suppose—"

Clara stood on tiptoes, stretching to peer out the window. "Could be, Tim. He's the right size, but he walks like a younger man. No. I don't think so. But go and see. He's coming through the gate. Go see."

*****

Da-Ved walked the last few blocks rapidly, making good time. During his short trek to the house, he discerned only three other Guardians who acknowledged his presence with a friendly gesture or salute. These were the local Guardians of Job who were assigned to make sure no enemy forces were lingering about to challenge his advancement into the city.

Da-Ved emerged from the narrow alley into the main intersection of Liberty Street. The wind was gusting now, and blowing snow made it difficult to see the next street sign a block away. He pulled his wool cap down tight over his ears.

Beckoning to him across the street was a well-lit three-story Victorian house, and a tall figure partially emerged from within a nearby streetlamp as he approached.

"Peace be unto you, Da-Ved. We've been expecting you."

Da-Ved stopped dead in his tracks. "Whoa, where did you come from?"

He slowly turned around, scanning the street. Unable to discern anyone else in the immediate vicinity, Da-Ved asked the winged figure, "Who...is...we?"

"Aye!" exclaimed the Guardian as he extruded himself from the lamppost. Bending at the waist, he gestured with a sweeping motion to the entire street with one hand. *"We!"* he repeated to the neighborhood.

At this signal, a Guardian rose from inside the large house across the street to stand upon its roof. Another angel ascended from below street level, issuing through a covered manhole. One by one, Da-Ved counted fifteen Guardians on the block as they emerged from their concealments.

Da-Ved laughed. "I never thought about how many of us there might be in Job. You mask your presence well."

"Aye, Da-Ved. We have served here many years, waiting just for a night like tonight. Aram has informed us of your mission and instructed us to make this a secure place for you. We're pleased His Majesty has selected our city to extend a special blessing to its citizens and hope to be of assistance to you in any way we can. I am Shamar, the watchman of Job. Welcome."

"Thanks, Shamar. It's good to know I have friends close by. I'll call you if I need you, but I've got to go."

"Aye, Da-Ved. We'll stay close."

As Da-Ved crossed the street to the large house, walking along its aged wrought-iron fence, each Guardian silently raised a flaming sword in tribute. Approaching the front entrance, Da-Ved noticed a small weathered plaque fastened to the gate. It read:

> The Praise Gate to JOB'S HOUSE
> Violence shall no more be heard in the land, wasting nor destruction within the borders: but thou shalt call thy walls Salvation, and thy gates Praise.

Looks like this is the place, Da-Ved thought. *May we always enter His gates with praise.* He reached over and unlatched the gate. Pushing it open, he made his way up the walkway to the porch. As he thumped up the wooden steps, the front door opened, and he was greeted by a cautious young man.

"Good evening, sir. May I help you?"

"Sure," said Da-Ved, "I'm looking for someone."

"Yes? And who might that be?"

"That's my problem," Da-Ved said. "I'm not exactly sure."

Awkwardly, the two stared at each other in silence for a few seconds.

A matronly voice floated from somewhere behind the man at the door, "Boys! Boys! It's freezing out there. Please ask the gentleman in, Tim, and shut the door. I'll get you two something hot to drink while you talk."

"Oh yes. You're right, Clara. I'm sorry, won't you come in? It *is* pretty cold out there tonight."

Da-Ved stamped the snow from his feet. "Thanks. I'd appreciate it."

Once inside, Tim shut the door and asked, "Can I take your coat? Why don't you come into the library and warm yourself by the fire? I'm sure Clara will find us there sooner or later with some cocoa."

"Thank you, but I don't wish to intrude. As I said before, I'm trying to locate someone, and I thought that he might be here."

"Oh, you're not intruding. Not tonight. Come in. Come in."

As they entered the library, Da-Ved saw several men of various ages standing around an old upright piano. Their inept attempts at harmonizing kept them all laughing. A large pile of holiday cookies was rapidly growing smaller.

Tim ushered his guest to the fireplace where they sat upon the built-out stone hearth. The fire crackled and popped while they talked.

Da-Ved removed his cap and held his hands to the warm fire. "Ah, that feels good."

Tim placed his guest's coat on a nearby chair and asked, "Yes? You were saying you're not quite sure who you're looking for."

"First off," Da-Ved began, "allow me to introduce myself. My name is Da-Ved. I'm sorry if I seem brusque, but I'm rather pressed for time. I'm leaving town in a few hours."

"Okay, Da-Ved...is it? How can we help you? Can you describe this person? As you might imagine, we have many visitors throughout the year."

"Yes, I'm pretty sure I know whom I'm trying to track down. I know he's not too old, some kind of minister. I believe he works with homeless men. That's why I came here. Do you know him?"

Warily, Tim leaned backward, looking over his guest. "Maybe. That depends. What do you want with him?"

"I'm afraid it's a personal matter. If you could just help me contact him, I would truly appreciate it."

Timothy's tone became aloof. "Look, mister, it's Christmas Eve. We're in the middle of a celebration here. If you're down on your luck, you're welcome to spend a few days with us as long as you're not in trouble with the law. Otherwise, can't this wait until morning?"

"No, I'm afraid not," Da-Ved said. "I'll be long gone by morning. It's important that I find this man. You see, I recently met a friend of his. I'd like to talk to him about this friend. I'm afraid I have some troubling news."

"Who's the friend? Maybe I know him."

"Yes. I suppose you might. Do you know a James Townsend?"

The color from Tim's face drained. He leaned forward and, in a strained voice, answered, "Yes. Yes, I know James. What about him? Is he all right?"

Da-Ved perceived the sudden pain in Tim's eyes. Playing his trump card, Da-Ved asked, "Tim, can we go somewhere quiet to talk? I have something to tell you."

Tim stood. "You know my name. How do you know my name? And you know James. Say, what's this all about? Where *is* James?"

Backing into the room from the kitchen, Clara interrupted them with two steaming mugs of hot chocolate. "Here you go, boys. They're hot, so don't burn yourselves. So, Timothy, what does our young guest want?"

Tim folded his arms across his chest, and his eyes narrowed. "I was just going to find out. Why don't we go back into the kitchen? We can talk privately there."

Not taking his eyes off their mysterious guest, he added, "All right, Clara?"

Taken aback at Tim's sudden dark demeanor, she said, "Why, I guess so, Tim. Go ahead. I'll keep everyone out for a while. But you better be quick about it. I won't be able to keep the men out of there for long the way those cookies are disappearing."

Da-Ved stood and retrieved his jacket. Timothy led the way to the kitchen, pushing the double-hinged door inward. After entering, he spun about to face his visitor.

"Now what's this all about? I'm the one you want, so let's have it."

"I know, Tim. I just wanted to talk to you privately. What I have to tell you is for your ears only. It may be difficult to believe, but I have been sent to give you a message. To tell you that your prayers have been answered. James has gone home."

A puzzled look spread across Tim's face. "Look here. I don't know what your game is…Da-Ved, or whatever your name is. But if you genuinely know James, you know that he's been living on the streets and hasn't any family. So how is it he can he go home?"

Da-Ved pulled up a kitchen chair, turned it around, and sat down, leaning his forearms on its spindled back. Carefully laying his cap and jacket on a nearby stool, he continued, "James died a few minutes ago, Timothy, but not until he accepted God's gift of salvation. He then went home to be with God and to be reunited with his family. I'm here tonight to make sure you realize you didn't fail with him. And to bring you a blessing."

Tim's hands sprang to his face, and he massaged his temples in a circling motion. With eyes closed, he said, "Whoa there, pardner. You're going *way* too fast for me. You want to back up and go over that last part again?"

"I'm telling you that when morning comes, you will receive what will appear to be tragic news. I want you to know now that the man you knew as James Townsend lived the life of a fool, but his life ended in victory."

"And just how do you know all this? What's the deal? Oh! I get it. This is some kind of a scam, isn't it? What are you going to do now, channel James's spirit for me for a price? Wait. Wait. Oh, I know what it is. You want to sell me a special Bible James ordered but hasn't paid for yet, right? Something like that, I'll bet.

Ha! If you're looking for money, friend, boy, did you come to the wrong place at the wrong time.

"Look, the so-called turnaround in the economy hasn't reached us here in Job yet, and our funds have all but dried up. We're in debt up to our ears. Yesterday, the sheriff told me that our creditors won't wait any longer, and our illustrious banker wants to foreclose on us. We probably won't have this house this time next month. So take a hike."

Da-Ved hung his head and sighed. "Tim, I know this is hard to accept, but you must believe me. I don't want any money or anything that you have. And like I said, I'll be gone by morning."

Tim put up both hands in protest and backed away slowly.

"Wait a minute. I haven't seen James in over a week. So how do I know he hasn't just left town. Just who are you? And how do you know James? He's never mentioned you before."

"Look, Tim, I was specifically sent here tonight to you. I didn't know why until just a few minutes ago myself. I only met James this night, just about an hour ago, I would say. Tonight, he fought and won a tremendous spiritual battle contending against his personal demons and the forces of darkness. They were all defeated, and he finally sent them packing for good. I was there as the Good News was presented to him by one of the city's defenders. But before James accepted the message of salvation, he told us about you. Afterwards, I saw him leave with his Guardian and escort."

Tim started to laugh. "Guardian? Escort? You talk as if you're some kind of angel or something."

"I am but a simple messenger, Tim. My story may not seem plausible to you, but I assure you it's true. Have faith, and remember, things aren't always as they appear. James's body will be discovered by morning, but don't mourn for him. He wanted to go home, and you planted the seed that made it possible. That's why he made it. You prepared the way."

Reclaiming his hat and coat from the stool, Da-Ved rose to his feet. "Now, I'm sorry, but I have to leave."

"Wait! This is ridiculous. You can't waltz in here, tell me a wild tale like this, and just leave. I need some kind of proof."

Wham!

A door slammed as someone stormed noisily into the front hall. A loud commotion commenced in the outer room, spilling over into the library. Shouting down the carolers, a brazen male voice boomed, "Hey, you guys! Come see what *I* got!"

The double-hinged door leading to the kitchen abruptly exploded inward as a red blur barged into the room. "Pastor Tim! Pastor Tim! Quick, come look! Oof!"

A dark-skinned Santa Claus collided with the young pastor, knocking him to the floor. A small black kettle containing a few silver coins spilled onto the floor with a crash, and the Santa landed on top of him. The two men lay momentarily dazed, trying to regain their breath.

As Tim untangled himself from beneath the boisterous Santa, Da-Ved made his exit from the room with the outward swing of the rebounding door. The Santa caught a glimpse of him as he escaped into the library.

Slowly rising to his feet, Santa cried out, "Hey! I know you! You were there! You're the one!"

Tim pulled the black man back to the floor with one good tug on his sleeve. "Charlie! Charlie! What's your problem?"

Falling to his backside, Santa cried out, "Hey, everybody! It's him! It's him! He's the one!"

Once again, the door swung back into the kitchen, and Clara and several of the men flooded into the large room. Hands on her wide hips, Clara scolded, "Charlie Perkins! What is all this? What do you mean coming in here disrupting our party screaming like some kind of wild banshee? And look at my clean floor!"

A contrite Charlie Perkins looked up from his sprawled position. His red Santa's hat had fallen from his head, and his cottony beard lay in his sizable lap. A small puddle of water was forming on the kitchen floor from the melting snow on his boots.

Sheepishly, he muttered, "That's what I'm trying to tell ya 'all, con-sarn-it."

The men surrounded the fallen pair and pulled them to their feet. Tim asked, "Do you have something to say or not, Charlie?"

"You won't believe it! You just...won't...believe it!"

He unbuttoned his coat and reached into an inner pocket to pull out several more coins. Tim reached out and took a gold coin from Charlie's hand for closer inspection. It looked foreign...and old.

"There's silver ones, too, and there's a lot more where that came from! Look here. I kept a couple so I could show ya, but I turned most of 'em over to the police for safekeeping. Basically, they said they'd have to check 'em out, but if they're not reported stolen, they're ours. It may take a few months, and they say we may have to pay taxes on them, but we ain't broke anymore!"

The room erupted into a noisy celebration of applause and laughter. Clara wormed her way into the center of the noisy group and took Charlie by his furry white collar. The angst of impending doom seemed to rain down into the kitchen, and the room became deathly quiet. She brought her face close, her nose almost touching his. Their eyeballs locked for a few seconds.

In a no-nonsensical tone, she asked, "Charlie Perkins...*where* did you get those coins?"

"Ask...that...that...that...guy that was here. Just ask 'em."

"Who?" she questioned. "Ask who?"

"That guy. You know. He was talking to Pastor Tim when I came in."

Clara looked up, scanning the room for the missing man, but he was nowhere to be seen. The group pushed through the connecting door into the empty library. Seeing the library unoccupied Tim ran to the front hallway to intercept the fleeing visitor but found the foyer was unoccupied also.

"Where'd he go?" he asked no one in particular. "He was just here a second ago. Where'd he go?"

Charlie pushed his way through the mob and ran to the front door, opening it. "He didn't go out this way! Look!"

The men crowded out the front door and onto the porch. It had been snowing hard for the last half hour, and there in the snow, traveling up the walkway from the front gate, was a single set of footprints left by Charlie Perkins minutes earlier.

"Let's check upstairs!" Timothy cried. "Quick, everyone! Check the house! He must still be inside!"

The men scrambled back inside to search for the missing stranger. As Tim tried to press his way back into the house, Charlie caught him by the arm.

"Don't bother, Tim," he whispered. "You're wasting your time."

Tim spun around to look into Charlie's laughing eyes. "Huh? What do you mean?"

"I mean you haven't heard my whole story yet. There's some queer things going on tonight. And besides, I just noticed something."

"Oh! Look! We didn't see this before," a feminine voice cried out.

Wrapped tightly in a long woolen shawl, Clara joined them on the porch. She'd been rocking on her heels, enjoying the crisp night air and the pristine starkness of the falling snow.

Descending the steps, she knelt to look at the walkway. The two men followed, their breath coming in small puffs in the frigid air.

Adjacent to the steps was a single set of crisp footprints that ended abruptly as if someone had leaped from the porch, taken a few steps, and then simply stopped.

"It's as if he just vanished. Or as if…as if—" she pondered aloud.

"As if what, Clare?" Tim asked.

"As if…nothing. I was just thinking out loud."

"Come on, Clare. If you think you know something, spill it," Tim said.

"I was just thinking it's as if a big bird had swooped down from out of the sky and just carried him off."

"Oh, Clara, now you're talking crazy—"

"Both of you, come here!" Charlie said. "I want to show you something and tell you a story you're not going to believe!"

With a wide grin on his face, he reached down into the snow and picked up a long tapered object. Twirling the thing between forefinger and thumb, he said, "Oh yeah! Oh yeah! Look...at...this."

Clara looked closely. She gasped, and her hand sprung to her open mouth. "It can't be," she said.

Charlie was adamant. "Yes, it is. Yes, it is too!"

She reached out to take the object. Eying the slender thing in Clara's trembling hand, Tim slipped on the icy steps and grabbed the porch's railing for support. He caught himself and stared hard.

The object was a large green feather—a full eighteen inches long.

And now abideth faith, hope, charity, these
three; but the greatest of these is charity.

—1 Corinthians 13:13 (KJV)

CHAPTER FOURTEEN

Charity

DECEMBER 24 – 9:40 PM
EXITING JOB'S HOUSE

Da-Ved dashed out the front door and bounded down the porch steps, stutter-stepping as he searched for a quick exit from the property. Before he could choose an escape route, a green blur descended from out of the winter storm and snatched him skyward.

Spiraling out of an accelerating climb, Shamar plummeted headfirst towards the city's water tower. At the last second, he pulled up, tilting his body backward. The maneuver caused him to fall into a controlled stall, and he braked into a full-blown vertical hover. He then deposited Da-Ved onto the tower's elevated catwalk with a dull thud, causing a blanket of snow to cascade from the metal platform.

"Thanks, I think," Da-Ved sputtered as he clutched a handrail with one hand and held his head with the other. "As soon as my head clears, you can tell me what just happened."

The large angel laughed and gave his smaller companion a hearty slap on the back. The blow dislodged Da-Ved from his secure perch, causing him to grab for the railing with his other hand.

"Don't tell me you're earthbound, Da-Ved. I never would have guessed it," teased Shamar.

Da-Ved steadied himself, then reached inside his coat to massage his throbbing shoulder.

"I have to confess I am for now. But it's just for the duration of this mission. The humans mustn't know who I am, and my wings were a minor sacrifice for this purpose. I'm glad you were around, though. You saved me from having to make impossible explanations. I owe you one."

"Aram suggested you might need our help when you arrived, and my troops are determined to escort you throughout the city as long as you're here. You might not see us, but we'll be around."

"Thanks. You can let them know their assistance has already made a difference tonight. Within the past hour, Arioch escorted James Townsend to the celestial city."

Shamar rose from the steel decking to hover over Da-Ved's head. "What's that you say? Another of Job's citizens has been redeemed? Tonight? That's fantastic!"

Rocketing to the top of the water tower, Shamar looked out over the countryside. Cupping his hands to his mouth, he bellowed, "Do you hear that, Old Nick? You've lost another one tonight! Ha! Ha!"

He descended with deliberate slowness to stand once again upon the tower's steel walkway and gripped its handrail with a heavy crunching sound. It resisted for a few seconds, but Shamar's powerful grip pulverized it, leaving two large hand marks crushed permanently into the thick metal.

Seeing the puzzled look upon Da-Ved's face, he said, "As Sector Commander, I wanted to help Arioch so many times but couldn't because James was so poor in spirit. His entire existence was focused on using alcohol and drugs to numb himself to this world, and without an invitation from him, we were unable to interfere. Shekar and Asthenes came very close to possessing him, and we expected to hear the worst about James any day now. I can't believe he was able to overcome their influence. That's awesome!"

"I'll say," Da-Ved said. "Can you imagine the welcome James must be receiving right now? And I'd like to have seen the look on Arioch's face when he escorts James through the gate. He must be thrilled."

Shamar looked down upon the snow-covered rooftops and nodded. "Aye. It's a wondrous night tonight for sure. But, tell me, where are you going from here?"

"That's a good question," Da-Ved said with a shrug. "The blessing I have been anointed with is freely given. His Majesty has entrusted me with a great gift, and I'm sure I'll have other appointments tonight, but I don't know where to go. I need some sort of a signal or a…a sign of some kind."

Shamar slowly looked to the west as if remembering something he'd forgotten. "A sign, you say? Tell me, how was this anointing given? Did His Glory shine upon you?"

"Yes. And upon Aram also. It completely enveloped us both, becoming part of us, expanding our potentials. It's added a new dimension to us as His servants. Even as I speak, I can feel the anointing power within me, changing me still."

Stroking his prominent chin, the large Watchman asked, "And, what does it feel like?"

Da-Ved answered in a subdued voice, "It's hard to put into words, Shamar. The only way I can describe it is empathy. No, that's not exactly right either. Love? It feels like love. Oh, I don't know. Does that make any sense to you?"

"It surely does. Don't you see? His kind of love is pure and the most powerful force in the universe. It's a creative force. It grows and reproduces. It gives life. And I think I know where you should go. If you trust me, I'll take you there."

*****

DECEMBER 24 – 10:00 PM
JOB, CALIFORNIA
THE CHAMBERLAIN RESIDENCE

Edna Chamberlain scolded her husband of forty years. "Frank, what are you doing with your coat on? It's almost time for bed."

"Oh, hush yourself, woman. I'm only going out to the car. I just remembered those books in the trunk we bought Friday for the boys. I'm going to wrap them, then I'll be up to bed."

"Shhhh! Be quiet about it. Carol just got them to sleep. Don't go waking them or we'll have them up all night."

The thought of twin seven-year-old boys running about the house for the holidays brought Frank Chamberlain a sense of home and family he'd been missing for quite some time.

It was eight years ago that his son, Kenneth, and daughter-in-law, Carol, had moved to the east coast because of a job promotion for Ken. The young couple visited Ken's parents several times during annual vacation trips, but this would be the first Christmas they would be together as a family since the boys were born. As grandparents, Frank and Edna were thrilled when Ken announced their usual August vacation trip would have to be postponed until December because of plant retooling.

Frank entered the attached garage through the side entrance of the house. He fished the car keys from his coat pocket and flipped on the garage lights. Snow was beginning to blow into the garage under its main door.

I should've replaced that weather-seal in the fall, Frank thought. *I'll have to get around to that as soon as this storm blows over. But, first, I'd better take care of this mess now.*

Grabbing a shovel, he exited the garage through its exterior man-door to clean up the drifting snow. Working vigorously for a couple of minutes, he moved the snow away from in front of the large overhead door. His breathing came hard, and he stopped to rest.

Then it hit. The combination of holiday stress, cold air, and sudden heavy exercise with the shovel brought a sharp pain to Frank's chest.

Clutching at his heart, he cried out, "Oh god!" and fell heavily to the pavement. He reached inside his coat to grab the small vial of nitroglycerin pills he always carried in his shirt pocket. Popping its lid, he poured out its contents into his left hand. His hand shook as he fumbled to pick a single pill from the pile, and several pills fell into the snow. His vision blurred.

In desperation, Frank leaned over, stuck out his tongue, and deftly stuck a single tablet to the end of it. He quickly flicked the medication into his mouth, but the crushing pain would not go away. He popped another pill into his mouth, grimacing because of the pain. His chest felt tight, and he fought for breath.

But the massive heart attack would not be fought off so easily. The pain only increased, traveling down his left arm as blood vessels constricted, depriving Frank's heart of life-giving oxygen. He became nauseated and vomited. Mercifully, he quickly lost consciousness.

*****

"Nine-one-one, what is your emergency?" the female dispatcher inquired in a monotone voice.

"Help me, please, please!" a panic-stricken woman answered. "My husband has had a heart attack and is lying out in the snow!"

The dispatcher responded quickly, "Is he conscious?"

"No! No! My son is doing CPR. Please come quickly! Please!"

"Yes, ma'am. Just confirm my computer screen for me. That's the Chamberlain residence at 3033 Churchill Drive?"

"Yes! Yes!"

"Yes, ma'am. We're on our way, but don't hang up yet. I want to confirm a call back number from you. Hang on while I first start the rescue squad for you. Then I'll get right back to you. Stay on the line."

*****

DECEMBER 24 – 10:20 PM

The distant wail of a police car announced that help was finally on the way. A first-responding fire truck arrived only a minute or two behind the police car, and together, the rescuers relieved Ken from his life-sustaining duties.

Before the paramedics arrived with the ambulance, the firefighters continued with CPR and tried three times to shock Frank's heart out of its lethal arrhythmia using an AED—an automatic external defibrillator.

After what seemed an eternity, the ambulance arrived, and its crew quickly took charge. First, Frank's airway was protected by the insertion of an endotracheal tube, and he was ventilated with 100 percent oxygen. At the same time, a second paramedic started an intravenous line to administer cardiac medications. Sadly, Frank's heart didn't respond to their efforts.

Unable to convert Frank's quivering heart to a less lethal rhythm, the firefighters continued to perform chest compressions while the medics ventilated his lungs and administered a second round of cardiac drugs.

While the rescuers packaged their patient onto the ambulance stretcher, the captain from the engine crew walked over to talk to the Chamberlain family. Approaching Edna, he said, "I'm sorry Mrs. Chamberlain. We've done about all we can do for your husband right now. The paramedics will have to take him to the emergency room right away. I'm sorry, but I have to go too."

Continuing CPR, the medics rapidly loaded Frank into the ambulance and started their race against time to the hospital.

"Will they...will they be able to save him?" Edna pleaded with a young policeman.

"I'm sorry, ma'am. I don't know. Can I give you a lift to the hospital?"

With a quivering voice, she answered, "No. No. My son will drive me. But what can we do? What can we do?"

"I guess all you can do now is pray, Mrs. Chamberlain. I'm sorry."

"Oh my lord! Yes! Yes! We can pray!" Running into the garage, she called over her shoulder, "I'm going to call my church's prayer chain right now!"

A speedy ten-minute ride through the city streets brought the ambulance quickly to the city hospital. Without interrupting CPR, the medics and firefighters removed Frank from the ambulance and rapidly wheeled him into the unoccupied trauma room. The ER staff were prepared for their arrival and assisted the rescue crew in moving Frank from the cot and onto a large hospital gurney.

*****

DECEMBER 24 – 10:42 PM
LOCAL EMERGENCY DEPARTMENT

"Talk to me, Deb!" Dr. Terrence Reynolds said loudly to the senior paramedic, Deborah Parker, as he barged through the trauma room's twin doors.

She gave the doctor a quick summary of the run. "We have a seventy-one-year-old male who has a history of heart. His wife says she found him lying in the driveway, unconscious. He must have been shoveling snow because there was a shovel lying on the ground nearby. She said he went to the garage to get something from the car, and when he didn't return, she went to look for him."

Dr. Reynolds took his stethoscope from his coat pocket and placed the ear tips into his ears. "Did anyone perform CPR at the house?"

"Yes, his son started CPR on him, so when we arrived, basic life support had already started. The fire department also tried unsuccessfully to defibrillate him three times. They then continued CPR for us while we intubated and started an IV. Our monitor showed he was in V-fib, so he got one amp of epi and one amp of lidocaine right away with no results. We then continued with the usual drug and shock therapy. When he didn't respond, we rapidly transported him to the ER continuing CPR."

"Any change during transport?" Dr. Reynold's asked.

"En route, he degraded into asystole, so we gave him another milligram of epi and two milligrams of atropine without results. We didn't have much luck with this one, Doc."

Bending over his patient, Dr. Reynolds listened to Frank's lungs to assess the endotube placement.

"How long have you worked on him?" he asked.

Looking at her watch, she replied, "Oh, I'd say about twenty-two minutes in the field, including transport and another four or five minutes here."

Turning to the head nurse, Dr. Reynolds asked, "Do you have any blood gasses yet?"

"The lab is working on it right now," she answered. "They should be back in a few minutes."

"Okay. Until then, let's administer another two milligrams of atropine and try to get some sort of rhythm back. If that doesn't work, we'll have to call it."

*****

DECEMBER 24 – 11:10 PM

Fire Captain Jeremy Slater walked through the emergency room doors with purpose. His handie-talkie crackled with static, and he checked the channel he was on. He then spoke into the portable radio. "Engine One to dispatch."

"Go ahead, Engine One."

"Engine One is out at the hospital. As soon as I retrieve my two guys, we'll be in service, returning to quarters."

"Ten-four, Engine One."

Captain Slater's dirty brown turnout gear contrasted starkly against the antiseptic white walls of the ER. Looking for his two firefighters who had responded to the hospital along with the medics in the ambulance, he walked to the supply room. There he found Deborah Parker going through her squad's drug-box inventory.

"Hey, Deb, have you seen my guys? If you're done with them, I'd like to get back into service."

"Yeah, Jer. I think they went to the snack machines. They'll be back in a minute or two. Hey, thanks for helping out tonight. It's not easy working a full arrest with just my partner."

"I just hope it was worth it. How's our patient doing? Is he going to make it? It didn't look very good back there at the house."

"Sorry. Dr. Reynolds pronounced him a few minutes ago. I guess tonight was just his night to go."

"Shoot!" Hanging his head, the captain groused, "That's tough. Tonight being Christmas Eve and all. Man, it's going to be a sad holiday for that family."

"I know, it's a shame. Come on. You can help me move the body into the cast room. The family will appreciate the privacy when they get here."

*****

Shamar winged his way to the northern outskirts of the city and banked into a long graceful glide. Slowly descending to the top floor of a five-story parking garage, he deposited Da-Ved next to a small pickup truck.

"Where are we?" Da-Ved asked, looking about.

Shamar towered over the truck. "When you were telling me about your anointing, it occurred to me where to take you. Your description of that feeling within you...*love,* you called it? Take a look over that retaining wall. What do you think?"

Da-Ved walked to the rear of the small truck and peered over a short parapet wall running the perimeter of the garage roof. Across the street, a four-story hospital was perched upon a small knoll overlooking a deep ravine. It was isolated and surrounded by thick woods.

Da-Ved asked, "I don't understand. What is it I should be seeing?"

Shamar chuckled. "You said you needed a sign, didn't you?"

Da-Ved turned to take a second look at the hospital. He studied the building hard for thirty seconds, then broke into a wide grin. "Shamar! I think you may have something there!"

Together, the two angels stared at the building's front entrance. There above the doors was a sign—an actual sign declaring the name of the hospital:

Charity Community Hospital of Job

Shamar beamed. "Isn't charity an old English word for love? There's your sign."

"Ha! Ha! Thanks, Shamar. I think you've put me back on track again."

As Da-Ved moved towards the building's stairwell, Shamar unbuckled the heavy scabbard from his back to unleash the long blade hidden within. The metal resonated as he pulled it from the scabbard to position its keen edge in Da-Ved's path.

RANG!

"Hold on, small one. I can go anywhere with you in this city, except in there. Before you enter that place, I must warn you that this hospital hasn't always been purely a medical facility. The city has only had possession of it for a score of years. Before that, it was a private psychiatric hospital. A small portion of the hospital continues to treat psychiatric patients, and it is here that Lucifer maintains a bitter stranglehold."

"Why is that?" Da-Ved asked.

"Not all of the patients being treated there are truly mentally ill. At least not because of the usual biological, psychological, or environmental factors. Some of the wretched souls in there are bedeviled with some of Satan's blackest spawn and have mistakenly been diagnosed as having mental health problems. Those foul imps use the disguise of mental illness to come and go as they please, and they defiantly flaunt their authority and influence over their victims in our faces."

A look of confusion appeared in Da-Ved's eyes. "But why can't our forces just chase them away? Why does the enemy have this authority to harass these people with such impunity?"

"I don't know, but the demons only have this type of dominion over a few patients at best. Somehow, somewhere, a few of these haunted mortals have opened a doorway for evil to enter into their lives. Sometimes, the doorway is psychedelic drugs taken in a foolish search for a higher form of consciousness or some other such nonsense. And then there are times Lucifer gains a foothold through experimentation into the spiritual realm. Ultimately, if he can find an opening or an invitation into a mortal's life, he'll take it."

Da-Ved turned and walked back to the parapet wall to look at the hospital again. "But how does he veil his dominion over them? In what way does he disguise the fact that it is *he* that is afflicting these people?"

Withdrawing his sword from Da-Ved's path, Shamar neatly re-sheathed it. "Sometimes the manifestation of his power mimics psychotic delusions or worse. His ultimate control is through possession, but those cases are very rare. It usually takes prayer and fasting to deliver those wretched souls from his power."

Da-Ved couldn't hide his anger. "Who are these demonic tormentors?"

Counting on three fingers, Shamar said, "*Depression, Guilt*, and *Despair* are the ring leaders. They've teamed up with fifty others of *The Oppression*.

"But *Depression, Guilt*, and the rest aren't all that powerful," Da-Ved said. "They only have a limited authority over the humans. It doesn't seem to me that they could put up much of a defense against God's warriors."

Shaking his head Shamar said, "They can't, at least not one-on-one. But in the form of *The Oppression*, they are many, and for the Guardians, it's like fighting a will o' the wisp. There's no form to them. They aren't all that formidable by themselves, but when united, they're like a cloud of pesky mosquitoes. Lethal mosquitoes. It's not possible to pick out any one fiend and have at it with him. As soon as a Guardian turns to fight one, a dozen others swarm to attack the attacker.

"And they are relentless. They are constantly on the hunt, giving no peace to their victims. By sheer weight of numbers, they lay siege to a mind, encumbering it and harassing it until it cracks. And once a mind surrenders, it becomes enslaved. These patients are truly the downtrodden of the downtrodden."

The smaller angel vented his anger, brushing snow from a section of the parapet with a sweeping hand. "What is the situation over there at present?" Da-Ved asked through gritted teeth.

"You know, it's funny," Shamar said. "This whole city has been scoured clean, except for that hospital. We've been powerless up till now to rout the enemy from that building, and I guess it's been pretty much a bit of a standoff. For months, they haven't been able to harm anyone, and we can't get them to leave."

"I see," Da-Ved said. "But it's not going to make any difference now."

Shamar bit his lower lip and hesitated before speaking, "I'm sorry, but my orders are to escort you to your next encounter, and then I'm to return to my post. We have other watchers stationed in the hospital, but I can go no farther with you. If you walk in there alone, you'll be an inviting target. Are you still planning to go in?"

"Yes, I am."

"Be careful, friend. It's a real snake pit in there. Lucifer has concealed some pretty ravenous beasts throughout the hospital. Besides *The Oppression*, you may also run into his *lions* and *dragons*. And the spiritual climate in there is dry as a desert. It's as dangerous as any wilderness you've ever seen."

"I know. That's why I'm going. As one of His Majesty's scribes, I've had the opportunity to memorize a fair amount of scripture, and our King said much through His prophets. Isaiah said 'Strengthen the weak hands, and make firm the feeble knees. Say to those who have an anxious heart, Be strong, fear not! Behold, your God will come with vengeance, with the recompense of God. He will come and save you.'"[6]

Shamar bowed low and, in a lowered voice, said, "Peace be unto you, Da-Ved."

"And to you, Shamar."

The large watcher slowly rose above the building enveloped within a small whirlwind of roiling snow stirred up by his powerful wings. He looked down, threw a quick salute, and streaked out of sight. Da-Ved found himself alone once again.

The woeful siren of a departing ambulance caught his attention, and he turned again to the hospital's front entrance. Gazing at the shimmering stars half hidden by the moving clouds, Da-Ved bestowed the blessing. "Blessed art thou O Charity, for The Spirit of the Lord God is upon me: He has sent me to bind up the broken-hearted, to proclaim liberty to the captives, and to open the doors to those who are bound in this stronghold."[7]

A simple light fixture encased in its protective cage illuminated the doorway to the nearby stairs. Faithful to his task, Da-Ved descended towards street level, but with each step, he could sense the growing presence of something insidiously evil below. Cautiously, he stopped between the third and second-floor landings and turned an attentive ear. A delicate hissing sound caught his attention, and the tell-tale scent of fresh blood assaulted his nostrils with its sweet sticky odor.

Leaning forward, he looked over the railing to the first-floor threshold where a thin reddish mist started to gather at floor level. In front of the large door leading into the street-level parking lot, a specter grew as it slowly poured from under the door into the enclosed stair shaft.

As the fog grew, it started to take on a physical form. The foul thing slowly doubled and redoubled in size, increasing in volume and density until it towered above the floor. Dark leathery wings spilled from its upper back.

The obscene spirit's underlying skin tone was the pale color of leprosy, but its body wore a scarlet mantle of putrid festering sores, bloody pustules, and hanging flesh.

The creature's pale skin seemed to ripple and bulge in various places on its body. From moment to moment, its rippling mass would part, and a small head, claw, or foot of some hideous entity would briefly protrude from the main body. Just as quickly, it was re-absorbed.

The stench of a rotting corpse became overwhelming within the stairwell, and Da-Ved's stomach churned as he gagged at the sight of the disease-covered demon.

Looking up, it spied Da-Ved, threw back its monstrous head, and growled a throaty multi-voiced greeting. "Da-Ved! At last, we meet! Come, my friend! Let's have a look at you! We have longed to gaze upon a real giant killer!"

Da-Ved descended the last remaining steps to stand before the hideous specter. "I'm sorry, but I fear you have the advantage of me. You would be...?"

185

"Why, Da-Ved," the dripping apparition mocked, "we're surprised at you. You have not heard of us, Yanah?"

Setting his jaw, Da-Ved replied in a husky voice, "Yanah? Yes, I have heard of Yanah. Is he not the stench that now fills my nostrils and terrorizes mortal men with his oppression of sickness and disease? Yanah, Yanah. Why do you rage against humanity so? Why should they deserve such treatment from you?"

The question seemed to infuriate the repulsive apparition. "Why? *Why?* Because God gave to the humans so much more than He gave us."

"*Man!*" The demon spat the word with obvious disgust. "What a waste of time and design. If God had spent a tenth of the time on us as He did on that little wretch, Adam, we would never have joined the rebellion. We hate the humans! We should kill them all and roast their bones over a never-ending fire!"

"I'm sorry you feel that way, Yanah," Da-Ved said. "Now step aside. There are patients I need to visit tonight."

Yanah stood to his full imposing height and took a step toward the small angel. "No, Da-Ved. This place is *our* dungeon, and *we* are jailer here."

With a mocking laugh, he continued his tirade. "You may prowl around the main complex, but do not try to enter our domain. If you dare enter the psychiatric wing, our pets will gorge themselves upon your celestial flesh. And be warned. We are not afraid of that little pouch around your neck, so don't try to play that game with us."

Da-Ved smirked. "You surprise me, Yanah. I never figured you to play the part of a fool. Who do you answer to these days? Wait. No, don't tell me. Negeph?"

Instant recognition shone in Yanah's yellow eyes.

"It is! It's Negeph! The *Pestilence*, isn't it?" Da-Ved said. "That prattling old fool has been stroking you again, hasn't he? Yanah, don't you realize that I have been anointed by the King Himself and have been given great power and authority while I'm here?"

Da-Ved lowered his voice to a coarse whisper. "Now stand aside."

Yanah backed away cautiously, then seemed to stiffen. Without warning, his wings unfurled violently, shrouding the dimly lighted staircase with almost complete darkness.

"Be warned!" he said with a guttural hiss. "You are not welcome here. If you defy us tonight, we shall make war against you."

Standing his ground, Da-Ved raised his eyes to meet Yanah's. Pulling out the small pouch which hung about his neck, Da-Ved removed from it a small silver key attached to a scarlet cord. Tucking the pouch back inside his shirt, he then hung the key around his neck, letting it sit exposed upon his chest. The key emitted a penetrating white light filling the narrow room with its pure incandescence.

With a tormented howl, Yanah's thrashing wings instantaneously enveloped his head, shielding his eyes from the radiance of the key.

Da-Ved met the demon's challenge with a threatening tone. "Hear me, Yanah. I'm revealing this key to you and your companions, just so there will be no misunderstanding between us tonight.

I reject your claims to dominion here. Yes, I, the Lord's anointed, His messenger, have decided to be merciful to this hospital. And I rebuke you. Tonight, I have decreed mercy to Charity and to all the patients who reside within its walls."

The stinging rebuke caught Yanah off guard, propelling the tyrant backward against the concrete wall of the stairwell. Yanah's many voices screeched in protest. The caterwauling demons retreated from out of the physical form of Yanah, shrinking and disintegrating back into the vaporous mist from which they had formed. The crimson fog then recoiled, tumbling and swirling across the floor, exiting the vestibule the way it had come.

Da-Ved pursued the fleeing devils into the main garage where he found the panicking and vaporous spirits pouring themselves into a nearby electrical outlet.

"Be gone, fallen spirits!" Da-Ved ordered.

They responded by hastily fleeing from the outlet into the inner recesses of the wall.

Bowing his head, Da-Ved praised his Creator with a prayer inspired by an ancient scripture.

"Now shall my head be lifted above my enemies who surround me, and I will offer in His tabernacle sacrifices of joy and praise to the Lord. I will save the flock, and they shall no more be a prey; and He will judge the saved and the lost. He shall feed them and be their shepherd. And the Lord will be their God and will make with them a covenant of peace. He will cause the evil beasts to cease out of the land, and they shall dwell safely in the wilderness and sleep in the woods. And He will make them and the places about this hill a blessing and will cause a shower of blessings to rain down."[8]

And I will make with them a covenant of peace, and will
cause the evil beasts to cease out of the land: and they shall
dwell safely in the wilderness, and sleep in the woods.
And I will make them and the places round about my
hill a blessing; and I will cause the shower to come down
in his season; there shall be showers of blessing.

—Ezekiel 34:25, 26 (KJV)

CHAPTER FIFTEEN

Covenant of Peace

DECEMBER 25 – 12:04 AM
THE PARKING GARAGE

"Da-Ved."

Hearing his name, Da-Ved turned to see Aram standing behind him. No longer did he carry the sword and shield of the Legion but was once again armed with his longsword, shield, and shepherd's staff. For now, his wings were held aloft behind him. Relieved of his command responsibilities, Aram's face now radiated the countenance of a warrior ready for battle.

Da-Ved scrambled to his feet. "Aram! I thought you were supposed to be in command of the Mibtsar. What are you doing here?"

"I asked to be relieved of my duties there. I needed to return here in Job."

"Why?"

Aram gently placed his large hands upon the smaller angel's shoulders. "What you are planning is extremely dangerous, Da-Ved, and I want to make sure you know what you're doing."

Aram folded his wings compactly behind him, and the two friends walked slowly towards the parking garage's main gate. At this time of night, it was locked down, and the large ticket booth was unattended.

The chirping of tires revealed a car departing from another exit at the far end of the building, and they slipped into the unoccupied attendant's booth unseen. Da-Ved peeked through the doorway to reconnoiter a quick approach to the hospital located directly across the street. Secure for the moment, Aram continued to counsel his small friend.

"Da-Ved, I'm afraid you don't realize what's going on here. I'm unable to assign you additional assets as an escort because Lucifer has asserted a prior claim to this site. Its sordid history is centuries old, but know this: the Lord has always supported his claim to dominion here. Your presence on the property will only dispute his authority, and he is not about to let you go unchallenged as you travel through its halls. He's already hunting you. Are you sure you want to make yourself such a blatant target?"

Da-Ved continued to study the building across the street. "I know Satan likes to strut about like a roaring lion, but hear me out. We—you and I—have been anointed for a special purpose this night and have received sovereign gifts from His Majesty so that we might fulfill it. You've been given a Guardian's equivalent of the strength of Samson, and I have received temporary dominion over all sickness and disease. Even Death himself must bend a knee to the authority granted to me this evening. Surely you don't mean to leave this putrid enclave intact when we have the means of destroying it."

"No, no, but there is more to this than meets the eye. Lucifer also has his spies, and I'm sure they have already reported back to him. He knows something profound is about to happen in this city and has surrounded this valley with a multitude of demonic warriors.

"Even worse, a brigade strength of his locust swarm has just arrived from Europe. They may even try to attack the Mibtsar here."

"Who is in command of the Mibtsar now?" Da-Ved asked.

Aram shrugged. "Who else? Miyka'el himself."

"Miyka'el? I didn't think he ever concerned himself with anything but the security of Israel. How did you get him to take command here?"

"Are you kidding? He knows you've been given an extraordinary gift to be delivered here tonight and that Lucifer has taken a special interest in both of us. Since Lucifer has diverted so many of his assets to Job, it's obvious that for the time being, this place is the hot spot on the planet."

"But, Aram, what about the Holy Land? Is it secure?"

"Ha! No need to worry about that. Miyka'el summoned another Mibtsar to Israel to provide for its defense in his absence. He's also stripped additional troops from other provinces to provide you with an extra layer of security around this city. For now, no entity may enter this outer defensive perimeter without Miyka'el's permission."

Sitting upon the floor, Aram positioned the highly polished blade fastened within his shepherd's crook to catch the reflection of the building across the street. Using the blade as a mirror, he scanned the hospital property without revealing his presence to possible sentries.

Satisfied, he lowered his staff. "Look, Da-Ved, I only mean to say if you need assistance from the Guardians assembled here, we may have to destroy this place to get to you. Sometimes spiritual battles have a way of manifesting themselves as a material force, and an intense conflict tonight could breach into the physical realm. Have you thought about what would happen to those mortals you have come to deliver if they should be caught up in such a struggle? They may have to pay a heavy price."

"Yes, I have, and I don't know just exactly what would happen to them. But I do know God has a plan for this city and that we've been entrusted to bring it to fruition. We just need to be obedient to His will. Aram, have a little faith."

"Sure, Da-Ved. But if you need us, just call out. We have assets throughout the hospital, so we'll be able to monitor your movements. Our authority is only limited in the psychiatric unit."

Gesturing towards the building, Aram winced. "Even in there, God maintains a watch. You possess His authority here tonight, so we can enforce any evacuations you might want to call for. Just give us a whistle, and we'll storm the place."

"Thanks, I know you mean well, but you won't be needed inside. The enemy may come after me, huffing and puffing, you know, full of bluster and all that, but they're pretty powerless tonight. We have a secret weapon they don't know about yet."

Aram peered again into the polished blade of his weapon, searching for any indication that he might have missed something.

Perceiving nothing unusual, he asked, "What weapon? I don't see anything new."

Da-Ved grinned. "The saints have an intact prayer network, and it's been up and running full speed all week. Especially tonight. And they've been fasting. Don't you feel it?"

Aram snapped his fingers. "Yeah, that's what it is! Come to think of it, that's *exactly* what it is! I knew something was different. Everyone's been feeling pretty jazzed tonight, but we thought it was just the anticipation of your coming. It's the prayers, isn't it? They're magnifying and focusing His Majesty's will and dominion right here in this mountain range."

"Yes, it's finally happened here in Job. The local saints have released the power of the Ruach HaKodesh—the Holy Spirit."

Aram scrambled to his feet. Grabbing the small angel, he roughly placed Da-Ved in a tight headlock and tousled his hair. "Ho! Ho! Da-Ved! Whatever you plan on doing tonight, I think you just might pull it off!"

"Ow! Okay! Okay! Take it easy there, big guy!"

Breaking away from the large Guardian, Da-Ved attempted to smooth out his tangled hair.

"Just remember," he said, "when the blessing is finally consummated, my mission will be completed, and I'll become vulnerable again. I may need you to get me out of there quickly, so don't go sightseeing."

Crouching low, Da-Ved opened the door and glanced out to his left. He whispered, "Does it look clear your way?"

"Clear."

"Good, then I'm going inside."

Da-Ved stood and brushed off his clothes. "From what you've been telling me, they already know I'm coming. Might as well try the direct approach."

He walked out of the booth and onto the sidewalk. Stepping off the curb, he crossed the street to the hospital entrance. At the last second, he turned momentarily to glance back towards the parking garage. The doors opened automatically, drawing his attention back to the hospital. He hesitated, then entered into Satan's lair.

*****

DECEMBER 25 – 12:25 AM
CHARITY HOSPITAL

A gray-haired custodian set out several Slippery When Wet signs as he prepared for a long night of stripping and waxing the hospital's lobby and visitor's lounge. Early Christmas morning was the perfect time for this chore as the number of visitors at night would be negligible, and the hospital would be staffed with a small skeleton crew for the day.

The job needed to be done. The tiled floor had lost its luster months ago, and a heavy traffic pattern was worn into the center of the hallway and lounge. Since the chore paid double time, it wasn't too difficult to find a volunteer to work the graveyard shift during the holiday. All the bosses would be gone for the day, the work was relatively easy, and one could still enjoy part of the Christmas holiday after a quick nap following work. And it would take just about six hours to complete the job.

Senior Custodian Wayne Johnson busied himself with the assembling of the chemicals and materials needed for the task. A young security guard razzed the older man.

"Hey, Wayne, I see you have your work cut out for ya. Looks like you ought to be finished by New Year's. Ha! Ha!"

Looking up at his youthful antagonist, the custodian replied, "Huh? Oh, hi, Bob. Yeah, I guess so. You know, I think this will be the last year I work the holidays. I'm getting too old for this stuff. By the time the sun comes up, my back will probably be screaming at me. But the extra money this time of year is hard to turn down."

At twenty-four years of age, Robert Sorenson found his security job at the hospital boring. He had scored well on civil service exams for the police departments in the county and was waiting for a position to open on one of them. He marked time by working as a security guard at the hospital. "I hear you, Wayno, but you should get a job like mine. *My* back won't be hurting tomorrow."

"No way!" Wayne lampooned. "I couldn't live on what they pay security guards these days. That's why the turnover rate for your position is so high."

Bob glanced at his watch. "Righto, but I guess I'll have to catch ya later. It's time for me to check the front lot before you-know-who finds me standing around talking to you."

The custodian made a face. "Don't tell me Rex is working tonight. What's he doing in the main part of the hospital? I thought he strictly worked security in the psychiatric wing now."

"I know. Go figure. I think Dr. Larson specifically asked him to coordinate hospital security tonight."

Wayne looked up from his work. "*The* Dr. Larson? The head of the hospital? He wanted Rex in charge tonight? What for?"

"Yeah, I don't know, but you know how it goes. After Rex transferred over to the psych unit a couple of years ago, he and Dr. Larson became close goombahs or something. After that, Rex started to distance himself from the rest of the staff."

Returning to his work, Wayne replied, "*Brother.* Those two were made for each other!"

"I'll say. I don't understand all that cutting-edge stuff they're messing with over there, but I suppose it must work. I know Rex is into it, so it makes sense that Dr. Voodoo would want him in charge of security. Birds of a feather and all that."

The older man made a face. "Dr. Voodoo? I don't believe Dr. Larson rates that moniker, do you?"

"Well, maybe not. I don't pretend to know anything about psychiatry, but I talked to Rex once about some of the weekend workshops the staff puts on for some of the locals. You know, there's that school or some kind of outreach program that is funded through the hospital. The Second Sight Institute, I think they call it."

"What kind of workshops?" Wayne asked.

"I'm not sure, but they sounded pretty far out to me. Parapsychology stuff, I think it's called. It's purely experimental research, but I suppose Dr. Larson leaves no stone unturned searching for new therapeutic techniques. Rex says they're always looking for new ways to treat their patients."

Leaning on his mop, Wayne said, "I'm not following you."

"You know, ways to reduce stress, new methods of releasing psychological traumas, getting it together, man! Becoming centered. In control. Some of Dr. Larson's patients and students have even volunteered to participate in different psychotherapeutic experiments."

Wayne pulled a rag from a rear pocket and wiped his brow. "You're a bit of an expert on the subject, aren't you?" he asked with a hint of suspicion in his voice.

Bob's tone softened. "You might not believe it, but once upon a time, a long time ago, Rex and I were friends. We used to talk about a lot of stuff. But not anymore. Hey, I gotta go. See you at break time?"

"Maybe. Depends on what I'm doing here. I have to go back to the supply room and get another clean mophead. But I can't let the stripper solution dry on the floor, so if I don't see you at break, I should be done with the stripping by lunchtime. I'll see you then."

"Yeah. Sounds good."

Making his way to the front door, the young guard turned to see Wayne straining to read the instructions on a can of stripper solution.

"Hey, Wayne!" he called out.

The custodian answered with a tinge of irritation, *"What?"*

Tapping his watch, Bob said, "Merry Christmas!"

Without looking up, Wayne answered, "Yeah, and a cool Yule to you too. Now get out of here and let me get some work done!"

Bob headed towards the hospital entrance and was met by Rex Van Damon, his supervisor for the evening.

"Mr. Sorenson, why are you loitering around here in the lobby? You should be making your rounds, not bothering the custodial staff."

The young guard was not easily intimidated. "Relax, Rex, I'm heading out to the front lot right now."

As he approached the entrance, it opened automatically, and Da-Ved walked in. Bob threw a quick greeting. "Evening."

Da-Ved returned the greeting with a curt nod of his head and let the security guard brush by as he exited the building.

Rex approached Da-Ved and inquired, "Sir, I'm afraid visiting hours have been over for some time now. May I be of assistance?"

Da-Ved eyed Rex with some suspicion. He noticed the guard was standing unnaturally close to a thick support column in the middle of the foyer. This part of the lobby was not well-lit, and the wide stone-encased column cast a deep shadow across the room. Looking hard, Da-Ved perceived something else lurking within its shadow.

Addressing the shadow, Da-Ved inquired, "And who might you be?"

"I am in charge of security," replied the shadow.

Rex's eyes seemed to glaze over. "I am in charge of security," he mimicked.

Da-Ved chuckled at the simultaneous response of the two allies. "Oh, I see. My name is Da-Ved. I have come to counsel a few patients tonight."

"Wouldn't tomorrow morning be more appropriate?" replied the shadow.

"Wouldn't tomorrow morning be more appropriate?" echoed Rex.

"I think not," Da-Ved answered. "I have received permission to enter the hospital tonight. Please step aside."

The security supervisor pulled away from the column to physically interpose himself between Da-Ved and the hallway leading to the patient area section of the hospital. As he did so, Da-Ved saw that the dark entity concealed within the shadows copied Rex's movements. The two moved into the light, and the translucent spirit now stood just behind the man he influenced. Both man and spirit stood with feet apart, hands on their hips. The demon was invisible to all except Da-Ved.

"What is your name?" Da-Ved asked.

The demon's reply was given sarcastically, "My name is Tabbach. Now unless there is some sort of emergency, I cannot let you enter beyond the lobby...Da-Ved."

Simultaneously, Rex replied. "My name is Rex Van Damon, and unless there is some sort of emergency, I cannot let you enter beyond the lobby...Sir." Rex placed extra emphasis on the word *sir*.

Ignoring Rex, Da-Ved sized up the malevolent specter obstructing his path. Tabbach was the main sentinel to this facility and was well-suited for the task.

Towering over Rex who was a mortal of normal height, he made a fearsome opponent. An obsidian-like helmet shielded his lower jaw with a type of curved cowling. The split cowling swept down and around the headpiece from each side of the demon's skull, terminating in a jagged fissure in front of its hideous mouth. It gave the appearance of a rather large and powerful mandible.

Tabbach's proficiency as a sentry was enhanced by four large compound eyes of which two were obscured behind a smoky-colored helmet visor. Its remaining eyes were perched at the ends of twin stalk-like appendages which protruded through holes at the top of the jet-black helmet. Moving independently of each other, these eyes could see in all directions at the same time. Very little would escape this guard's watchful gaze.

An outer layer of lightweight armor covered the demon's body, not unlike that of the exoskeleton of an insect. In fact, Tabbach resembled a rather large beetle with six membranous wings to carry him aloft. The edges of its armor were razor-sharp and full of spikes. Attired thusly, Tabbach needed no weapons to deter unwelcome visitors.

Sizing up the sentry that stood before him, Da-Ved thought, *I'm going to have to deal with Tabbach in a way that will set the tone of my authority here. Otherwise, I'll face a never-ending line of challenges from every fallen spirit within the hospital.*

He reached down to touch the small key hanging upon his chest. Seeing it for the first time, Tabbach flinched.

Mistaking the key for a cross, Rex asked, "Are you clergy?"

"You could say I have come on a spiritual matter," Da-Ved replied. "I am to be admitted."

"Yes... I see," replied the security chief.

"Yes... I see," mimicked Tabbach.

Mirroring each other's movements, man and demon backed away from Da-Ved, powerless to block his advance into the hospital.

As Da-Ved proceeded into the lobby, he smiled at the pretty clerk sitting behind the admitting desk. He caught the glint of a gold cross hanging from a necklace around her neck, and she smiled back. So did the veiled Guardian standing unseen behind her.

Moving quickly down the corridor, Da-Ved found that the floor was partly covered with a soapy solution. He smiled deviously. *I guess I might as well start right here.*

*****

Five minutes later, Wayne returned to the unoccupied lobby carrying buckets, mops, and a five-gallon container of floor wax. Reaching the work area, he sensed something amiss and looked about, scratching his head.

"What the heck?" he said.

As he scanned the hallway, the hair on the back of his neck stood on end, yet he couldn't say why.

Bob Sorenson returned from his inspection of the front lot and bellowed loudly, "Hey, you old coot, how'd you do that?"

The custodian's back was turned to the front entrance and hadn't seen Bob's approach. Startled by his friend's loud query, Wayne jumped nervously.

"Do…Do what?" he stammered.

"How the Sam Hill did you finish the floor so fast? I thought you'd be working on it until the wee hours of the morning!"

Wayne's eyes grew wide, and he sat down on the large can of stripper with a loud thud. A clattering crash echoed down the hallway as the buckets and mops fell from his grasp.

*****

Da-Ved made his way to the east end of the hallway where it was intersected by another corridor via a vaulted atrium. The junction presented him with three choices. To the left was a bank of elevators leading to the upper floor levels and patient rooms. Thirty feet to his right, two doors opened to the emergency department, and outside that lay a helicopter landing pad and ambulance entrance.

The heavy door directly across from him led to a terrace level where the hospital was built into the downward slope of a wooded hill. Affixed to this door was a plaque with the bold image of a raven in bas-relief. The plaque declared that the locked doorway was the entrance to the Ravenwood Psychiatric Institute. To enter, it was necessary to first pass through a sally port protected by electronic lock, and beyond that lay the psychiatric wing of the hospital.

Not sure in which direction he should go, Da-Ved closed his eyes and prayed. *Lord, I'm at an impasse here. Please guide me to your path.*

Yanah slipped into the corridor from the emergency department unseen. His great leathery wings trailed behind him like the train of a coal-black cape, and the crimson remnants of a dark and wispy cloud vaporized in his wake.

Ding! To Da-Ved's left rang the crisp bell of an elevator as it opened to his floor level. Da-Ved opened his eyes. "Thank you," he whispered.

"You're quite welcome!" answered a raspy multitude of voices from Yanah. "But you're too late, messenger." Glancing towards the ER, he smirked. "We have just taken another one!"

Da-Ved looked to the doors of the emergency department.

The arrogant demon swaggered closer and continued to mock the small messenger. "So, you didn't take our advice. Too bad. That's your hard luck. Be warned, my angelic friend. Do not get any ideas about going beyond those doors in front of you. The psychiatric wing is our province, and Lord Lucifer has declared it to be off-limits to all intruders. We have standing orders to inform him of any attempt by Guardians to enter this facility."

The demon folded his arms across his chest and said with contempt, "Now go play god elsewhere before we send for one of the beasts from the outer woods to devour you!"

Da-Ved's voice became icy. "Tell me, Yanah, just what was it that Lucifer offered to lure you away from God's Throne? I mean, look at what you have become. You're a third-rate potentate of just one of many small unimportant sanctuaries he now controls. At least when you were in heaven, you were able to bathe in His Majesty's warm radiance and take refreshment from His River. But here? Here are only death and an unquenchable thirst."

Yanah swallowed and licked his lips.

"Before you fell, you had an amazing identity," Da-Ved said. "Now you've forfeited your individuality for an epidemic of a hundred disease-ridden entities. You were once a glorious shining singularity, one of His faithful Seraphim burning brightly with holy adoration and praise. You were Chayil, the Worthy One. But no more. Look at you now. Now you're only a dark plurality of corruption, pus, and disease. So tell me, Yanah, just what was the attraction? Or do you enjoy living here on Earth in exile?"

Clutching its head with both hands, the demon let loose the anguished wail of condemned spirits caught in Satan's web. For a few brief seconds, Yanah's pleading eyes reflected a clear individual intellect. Its diseased and undulating body ceased pulsating, and the phantom's grotesque leathery wings morphed into appendages of beautiful gossamer. Temporarily restored to his original habitation, a wretched angel wept before Da-Ved.

"I hate you, Da-Ved, almost as much as I hate Lucifer. Oh, how I curse that miserable day when I listened with the others to his lying tongue! He set a snare for us, and the fool that I am, I didn't see it. Now it's too late. I'm forever in his service. How I hate him for that...and you for reminding me of what I once was."

Da-Ved hung his head. "I...I didn't know," he said.

The light in the fallen angel's eyes started to flicker, then quickly faded away. A multitude of manic voices quickly extinguished his angelic identity with wave after wave of mocking cries.

"Da-Ved! DA-VED! Da-Ved! DA-VED! Help us! da-VED! Help us! Da-Ved! Da-Ved! DA-VED! Da-ved! DA-ved! Help us! Da-VED! Help us! Da-Ved! HELP us! HELP US! Help US! Help us! Da-VED! Help us! Da-Ved! HELP us! HELP US! Da-Ved! Help US! Help Us! Da-Ved...Ved...elp Ussssssssssss...Ved...Da-Veeeed!"

Just as quickly, the individual voices waned, and Yanah once again spoke with the harsh unified voice of the damned.

"HAHAHAHAHAHAHAHAHAHA! Hear us, messenger! Do not be fooled! There is no mutiny here! We are One! We are Hive! We warn you, Da-Ved, do as you wish in the hospital if you can. But do not enter into Ravenwood!"

The demon stood before him once again, and Da-Ved drew back as one would from the warning clatter of a rattlesnake. He set his jaw and, with quiet authority, rebuked the demon. "Yanah, I have a blessing to deliver, so I have to leave you now. But I will return, and then we will continue this conversation."

Yanah yawned as he leaned against the wall of the corridor. "We'll be waiting, little one. We'll be waiting."

*****

Da-Ved entered an unoccupied elevator. Unsure of his destination, he silently asked again, "Your Majesty, please show me where I'm needed."

At that moment, a man wearing a white lab coat approached from the emergency room and entered the elevator. The stethoscope draped around his neck and the thick prescription pad protruding from a coat pocket revealed his occupation to be a physician. He failed to notice Da-Ved's presence as his face was buried in the day's newspaper.

Peering through a pair of bifocals perched at the tip of his fleshy nose, he scanned the sports page and reached clumsily for the car's control panel. Fumbling for the buttons, he finally managed to press 4. The door closed, and the car rose to the upper floors with a shudder.

Ding! The metallic tone heralded their arrival to the fourth floor, and the car lurched, then slowed to a stop. Still concentrating on his newspaper, the doctor promptly exited the elevator to trudge dutifully down the hallway. Da-Ved followed quietly, unnoticed.

The doctor paused momentarily to press a large metal plate on the wall. Two doors swung open, and he continued into the patient ward. Da-Ved followed, only to be accosted by the charge nurse sitting at the main workstation.

"Stop right there, sir! Who are you and what are you doing on the floor at this time of night?" she inquired with a hushed voice.

Da-Ved stopped and smiled a friendly greeting. "My name is Da-Ved, and I have come to see a patient."

"Are you a physician? Just which patient did you wish to see?"

She gave Da-Ved's informal appearance a skeptical once over and said, "You don't look like a doctor to me." Reaching for a nearby phone, she started to punch its keypad. "Maybe I'd better check with secur—"

From a room down the hallway, something fell noisily to the floor with a resounding bang. Startled, the nurse scrunched her eyes into narrow slits and pursed her thin lips. Through gritted teeth, she asked, "You wouldn't be from Ravenwood, would you? We asked them to send someone up here this afternoon. Although it's somewhat late now, isn't it?"

"No, ma'am. I'm from an outside agency. But I *have* come to do a little counseling."

"No matter. Ravenwood does that sometimes. They're a peculiar bunch down there, and I've learned not to question their ways. As you might surmise, we're a little shorthanded tonight, and in my book, anyone who wants to help lighten my load is a gift sent straight from God. Go right in, Dr. David."

"Uh, sure. Which room did you say?" Da-Ved asked, looking about.

"Oh, I'm sorry. You're here to see Mr. Starkey, right? Room 427, just down the hall. Just a warning, though. He's had a tough time, and…well…you know."

Da-Ved gave her a quizzical look.

"Let's just say he has a lot of adjusting to do. You might want to go easy on him. You know, the first interview and all."

"Oh, I know, I know. I'm sure I won't give him anything he can't handle. And thanks."

As Da-Ved approached the room, he detected a repulsive odor. Standing in the doorway, he saw the last wispy remnants of a greenish mist retreating from the middle of the room. It disappeared beneath the bed and, as he entered, appeared to burrow up into the mattress.

Ah, he thought, *Despondency is working overtime tonight, I see.*

"Get out! I don't want any visitors!" said a supine figure awash in the harsh light of a muted television.

Da-Ved's gaze traveled from the floor to the individual in bed, his upper body raised to a slight incline and propped up on two pillows. He prayed for guidance, then spoke, "Mr. Starkey?"

With arms folded defiantly across his chest, the figure appeared to be staring into empty space. He answered in a tired and strained voice, "Yeah. What now? Isn't it a little late for visiting? Or did I forget to sign all the papers? Don't tell me my insurance didn't cover the operation."

Da-Ved came closer. "No, nothing like that, sir. I've come to talk with you. I'm here to see that you're taken care of tonight."

Bruce Starkey turned to confront this new interloper.

"Taken care of?" he asked in complete astonishment. "Taken care of? Man, you have some nerve! That's just about what Dr. Sanchez told me three months ago. She told me she could save the leg, but *noooo!* After all that stomach-churning chemo, the blasted cancer got into the bone, and she had to cut it off above the knee anyway!"

His hands grabbed for the bed covers and clutched them tightly. He shuddered, then yanked the covers aside to reveal the bandaged stump of his amputated left leg.

"Here! Here, look! Look at what you people have done to me!"

Skewering Da-Ved with a penetrating glare, he said in a mocking tone, "So, tell me, just how you gonna take care of me tonight?"

Placing one hand to his chin, Da-Ved said, "I'm not sure just yet. I'm only here because your friends and family have been praying for you, and—"

"What? You're here because of what? Did my mother ask you to come talk to me?"

"No, I—"

"Oh, that's just great! What are you, a holy Joe or something? Oh, I get it. You're some kind of hospital shrink, I'll bet. So what now? Are you supposed to sell me on how losing a leg isn't all that bad in the larger scheme of things or some garbage like that? Listen, bud, I'm not exactly in the buying mood, so why don't you peddle whatever you're selling somewhere else?"

Da-Ved's disposition darkened as he walked to the foot of the bed to face the despondent man squarely. "My, you have it bad, don't you? Don't be a fool, Bruce, despair doesn't exactly become you. And, tonight, you have more going for you than you might think. Besides, I'm not selling anything. I did come to give you something, though."

Bruce looked away and said in a low voice, "Oh boy. Gee whiz. What did Santa bring this year? A wheelchair? A pair of crutches?"

Da-Ved gritted his teeth and struggled to control his irritation. "Only if that's what you truly want, Bruce. I don't think that's exactly what God had in mind for you tonight, but—"

Bruce pulled the bed covers back to cover his legs. "God! What God? If God exists, what would he have to do with this? Are you saying God wants me like this?"

"Of course not, Bruce. He loves you and He wants you to know that."

"So! You *are* a holy Joe. I thought as much. All right, I'll play along. I'm not going anywhere, and this might be entertaining. God knows I need a diversion. Okay, Joe, answer me this: if God loves me like you say, then why did He let this happen to me? Why didn't He just heal me? Tell me, why take my leg?"

"I don't know. Just when *did* you ask Him to heal your cancer?"

Bruce blanched and looked away. A long silence passed before he answered.

"I-I guess I didn't."

"So what's your beef, Bruce? Is this what it takes for you to even acknowledge His existence? Maybe now you'll talk to Him."

Bruce stared at the ceiling for a few seconds in silence, then spoke, "Why would God want to talk to me? I...I haven't exactly led a sinless life."

"Is that so?" Da-Ved said. "I have a major news flash for you. Only one person has ever managed to do that, and He's the one who sent me to you tonight. Believe me, the loss of a leg is a small price to pay if it helps you to reconcile with God."

Wiping a stubborn tear from his eye, Bruce whispered, "Easy for you to say. You're not the one flat on your back, looking down at half a leg. No thanks, man, I'd rather be whole."

Da-Ved looked skeptical. "You would rather be whole and to be lost than to be disfigured and saved?"

Bruce looked up with a confused look on his face. "Saved? From what?"

"From yourself. Your sins. And from what you deserve—hell."

"Hell? Ah, come on, man. It doesn't exist. A minister told me that once. Yeah, what do you think about that? He said it was just a fable. You know, something used by hellfire preachers to scare people into being good."

"The Scriptures disagree with you, Bruce. They speak as if hell really exists. His Majesty said if your hand should cause you to sin, then you should cut it off and throw it away. Better that than you going to hell. Not that your hand could cause you to sin, but His point was that hell exists."

Bruce scoffed. "Humph! You're telling me that a God that supposedly loves me would rather send me to hell than to forgive me? Isn't that a contradiction?"

"No. No, it's not a contradiction. And, no, He won't. You see, He never intended humans to go there. Hell was made for Satan and his angels. But if you do go there, you'll be the one sending yourself there, Bruce, not Him. He doesn't want that. He's already forgiven you, but sin demands payment. That's why He sent His Son—to pay your ransom."

"I suppose you mean Jesus, huh? I'm a little too old for Bible stories, don't you think? Yeah, don't look so surprised. I remember— childlike faith and all that stuff. Right? Yeah. I'm sorry, but I lost my faith a long time ago, and I wouldn't know how to go about getting it back."

Da-Ved snapped his fingers. "Bruce! I think that's why I'm here. To help you get it back."

"Huh?"

"Trust me. As I said before, tonight? Well, let's just say tonight is very peculiar. All you need to do is ask Him. He'll take care of the rest."

"What? Me? Pray?"

"You can call it that if you want. But, yeah, go ahead. Just talk to Him like you were having a regular conversation with someone in the room."

"Now? Right here?"

"Why not? No time like the present, I always say."

Bruce shifted uncomfortably in bed. "Nah. What would I say to Him? What would He have to say to me?"

"Ask Him to restore that childlike faith you once had. And while you're at it, tell Him you're sorry for walking away from Him so long ago. Take it from there. See what happens."

"I don't know. I don't remember how. I can't."

"You have to meet Him halfway, Bruce. He requires an invitation. He won't force Himself into your life. Besides, look at where you are now. What do you have to lose?"

Bruce looked out the window to stare into the veil of darkness outside. He didn't speak. The wind pelted the window with ice crystals as the eternal struggle raged within him.

Finally, his eyes closed, and he talked with God for the first time in twenty years. His silent lips moved ever so slightly with the whisper of a prayer.

The small messenger bowed his head, touching the bed with an anointing hand. From out of the corner of his eye, Da-Ved caught sight of the green mist as it poured out from under the bed. Utterly defeated, Despondency rolled in rapid retreat across the floor to disappear into the room's nearby heating vent. Da-Ved quietly slipped out the door as Bruce Starkey reconciled with his Creator.

Around the corner and down the hallway, Nurse Maria Petrovich pushed a wheeled medical cart carrying patient medications. Hearing loud voices within Room 427, she stopped to see who could be holding such an intense conversation at this time of night. The door was half closed, and she knocked before entering.

"Mr. Starkey? Is your TV on because I can hear you all way down the hall, and the other patients need their res—Oh!"

A searing white flash filled the room for a microsecond which caught her full in the face through the partially opened door. Off-balance, she stumbled, pushing the cart into the room.

Red spots danced about the room, and she shaded her eyes with one hand as her pupils sluggishly returned to normal size.

"Mr. Starkey, are you all right? What happened? Did the TV short out?"

Bruce Starkey was sitting bolt upright in bed, holding the amputated stump of his left leg through quaking bedcovers. The end of his severed leg emitted a continuous soft radiance through the blanket and sheet. Eyes wide, he called out to her in panic.

"It feels hot!"

Confronted by the inexplicable sight, she lost her grip on the cart which bumped into the far wall with a crash. Disposable cups, a sharps container, and paperwork scattered about the floor. The color drained from her face as Bruce's bedclothes appeared to come alive in his hands. The luminescent stump shivered and then began to move as if a large serpent had crawled under the covers with him. The living thing slowly snaked its serpentine way towards the foot of the bed, only to stop when it drew even with the end of Bruce's other leg. It appeared then that the serpent lifted its head a few degrees, raising the bedcovers into position to mimic exactly the opposite shape and form of Bruce's good leg. The head locked into position, and the luminescence faded away.

Beads of perspiration poured from the frightened man's face in rivulets. With shaking hands, Bruce raised the covers slowly and halt-ingly peeked underneath. He looked to Maria and worked his mouth but could form no words.

"Wha…What is it?" she stammered.

With a quivering voice, he whispered, "Nu-Nurse. You're not going to believe this!"

Lift up your head, O ye gates; and be ye lift up, ye
everlasting doors; and the King of glory shall come in.
Who is this King of glory? The LORD strong and mighty, the LORD
mighty in battle. Lift up your heads, O ye gates; even lift them up,
ye everlasting doors; and the King of glory shall come in. Who is
this King of glory? The LORD of hosts, he is the King of glory. Selah.

—Psalm 24:7–10 (KJV)

CHAPTER SIXTEEN

Gates

DECEMBER 25 – 1:00 AM
CHARITY HOSPITAL

While Bruce Starkey reconciled with his creator, Da-Ved quietly withdrew from the room. The sound of approaching footsteps inspired his quick retreat into a stairwell directly across the hall, and he descended the interlocking return stairs to the bottom of the shaft. There, his exit was temporarily blocked by a heavy metal door. As he reached for its handle, an immense hand emerged from inside the vestibule's interior wall to encircle his wrist.

A large Guardian emerged from within the wall and greeted the smaller angel with a laugh. "Whoa there, Da-Ved!"

The Guardian tugged on Da-Ved's arm, spinning him around roughly. "By His Majesty's Glory, *it is* you!"

Da-Ved recoiled to peer into the face of the grinning Guardian towering above him. Reacting by instinct, he broke the warrior's crushing hold and, with the speed of a skilled wrestler, brought the unsuspecting giant to the floor with an earth-shattering crash.

Straddling his sprawled opponent, Da-Ved gave him a jubilant greeting. "I'm afraid you have me at a disadvantage, Guardian. Have we met before?"

The Guardian motioned Da-Ved to help him to his feet, proffering a large hand. Grunting with effort, the likable warrior answered, "Hmmph! Yes. Yes, we have, Da-Ved. I was in Jerusalem with you once. That is, you and the Legion. I'm afraid it's been a long time."

Having hauled the large angel halfway to his feet, Da-Ved let go with disastrous consequences. The warrior fell heavily to his backside, noisily losing his weapons and shield in the bargain. He gave Da-Ved a prickly look from his painfully reacquired supine position.

Ignoring the angel's keen embarrassment, Da-Ved said, "With me in Jerusalem? You were there with me in Jerusalem?"

Rubbing his backside, the Guardian grumbled, "Yes. It was a bad time, wasn't it?"

Da-Ved winced at the bitter memory. "That it was, friend. That it was. I don't know about you, but it took me some time to work through the horror of that day. But God is patient with us, isn't He?"

"Very patient!" a new voice called out as a second Guardian bounded down the stairs to join them. "Allow me to assist you in getting this big oaf back to his feet, Da-Ved. He *can* be quite a burden."

The sentries seemed to be everywhere, coming from every direction. Offering a helping hand to this fallen confederate a second time, Da-Ved set and braced his feet and pulled.

"Uggghh!"

Brushing his hands off, Da-Ved asked, "Tell me, though, what was your station in Jerusalem? Were you very close to His Majesty during that season of Passover?"

The Guardian rearranged the circular shield strapped across his shoulders. "Close enough. Like you, I was with the Legion, but my unit was assigned to the fields encircling Gethsemane. Another eleven full battle legions occupied the rest of Israel and Judea, but ours was assigned to guard the Messiah directly within the holy city."

Two enormous wings resembling a white feathery cape spilled out from his broad back, and Da-Ved could see the pain reflected in the angel's eyes as he relived the searing two-thousand-year-old memory.

The Guardian fought to control his emotions, and he paused to adjust a set of studded leather gauntlets upon his wrists.

"If you recall," he said, "Lucifer had assembled almost his entire army in Jerusalem for the spring feast days, and our patrols suspected an impending ambush. We were prepared to bring the whole rotten rebellion to an end at Gethsemane that very night, but Miyka'el would have none of it.

"We were completely devastated by Miyka'el's apparent ludicrous decision to let the Messiah fall into enemy's hands, and I can tell you, there was almost another rebellion in the ranks that next morning. Thank God cooler heads prevailed. If we'd only understood His plan from the beginning."

Da-Ved flashed a sympathetic grin. "Yes, if we'd only known."

The Guardian momentarily looked away, and there was an awkward pause.

Eying his new friends more closely, Da-Ved saw that the other Guardian was not quite six feet in height and was slightly built, not unlike himself. This newcomer was armed with a small defensive dagger sheathed in a leather belt around his thin waist and wore a twelve-inch buckler on one arm. A double-edged battle-axe hung from his shoulder on a short leather thong.

Upon his feet were leather sandals, and he wore the simple knee-length tunic of a battle-tested warrior. Except for a difference in weapons, the larger Guardian was similarly attired.

Da-Ved asked, "What are your names, Guardians?"

The larger angel cleared his throat. "My name is Iyr, Da-Ved."

Slapping his smaller companion on the back and almost knocking him off his feet, he added, "And this chirping bird here is my good friend, Gedeón. Please excuse us, but I hope we haven't offended you in approaching you this way. We only wanted to thank you for including Charity in His Majesty's plans for tonight."

Da-Ved seemed baffled. "Huh?"

"Oh, we knew a special emissary was going to make an appearance in Job all right," said Iyr, "but we had no idea that you would visit us here at the hospital. You honor us with your presence."

"Thanks, Iyr, but I'm only a messenger. Your gratitude is misplaced. It should be reserved for He who sent me."

"We know, Da-Ved, and we do reserve our praise for Him, but it has been explained that He has given you a free hand in this mission. If He trusts you with such freedom, why shouldn't we recognize it?"

Da-Ved quickly changed the subject. "Are there very many Guardians in the hospital tonight?"

"Tonight, no, but we come and go," Gedeón said. "As you can guess, angelic presence in the hospital is always changing as the patient load changes, but the psychiatric wing is different. It's pretty stagnant there. Most of the psychiatric patients seem to end up as residents for quite a while, and not many of them leave Ravenwood in any better condition than when they first arrived. Their Guardians do the best they can for them, but they have only limited authority over those who are truly oppressed. Lucifer has the upper hand inside the institute."

"I've heard a little about that," Da-Ved said. "But I'm still not sure I completely understand the situation there. Why does the clinic abuse the patients so? I thought the doctors were here to help people, not harm them."

Iyr leaned against an interior wall, enfolding his great wings behind him. His answer was slow and measured as he reflected upon the ways of spiritual things. "For a variety of reasons, I suppose, but for one thing, the psychiatric unit here at Ravenwood is not your everyday psychiatric facility. It's a private clinic, not exactly part of the main hospital. And unfortunately, the man in charge there has deeply immersed himself in occult practices."

Recovering from Iyr's teeth-rattling slap, Gedeón drew near enough to add, "And several New Age consciousness-raising techniques are prescribed as therapy for many of the outpatients there as well as all of the in-house residents. Over the years, the director has replaced the traditional psychiatric staff and has surrounded himself with personnel who are more supportive of these esoteric treatments."

"How is it a learned psychiatrist can base his treatment of mental health issues on a New Age belief system?" Da-Ved asked.

Gedeón exhaled loudly. "What can I say? Seeking their own glory, this group has rejected truth. I'm afraid their collective professional mindset seems to be more comfortable with ancient pagan folklore than modern psychiatric medicine. The bizarre counseling and pharmaceutical procedures they employ sometimes trap and enslave the minds of the patients who have been referred here for therapy. They open doorways that shouldn't be opened, if you know what I mean."

"But I don't see how they can—"

Iyr held up a large hand. "Wait, it gets worse. Unfortunately, the patient isn't the only victim harmed by these people. Their families are eventually reduced to a shambles also. They lose fathers and mothers and sometimes children in those dismal hallways."

"How, exactly?" Da-Ved asked.

"Oh, in all sorts of ways," Iyr said. "And each case is different. For example, one of the therapists who works there practices an old religion worshiping nature. She's had a rebellious nature since childhood and has a hard time relating to male patients. The guilt she dumps on them is tremendous and usually causes them pain, sometimes extreme pain."

Gedeón was less gracious. "We call her the widow-maker."

Giving his companion a dirty look, Iyr said, "Anyway, through these occult philosophies, the clinic just about robs them of any chance for recovery. They become increasingly poor in spirit, and I'm afraid it condemns them to a life of misery. It's been quite devastating the last few years."

A sheepish Gedeón added, "And it doesn't help that most of these patients haven't been introduced to His Majesty yet. The spiritual situation they're in allows our adversary to have a free hand with them. And as you might suspect, a few of them have allowed Lucifer into their lives before they ever arrived here. You could describe them as pretty hopeless. In those cases, the Guardians are consigned to mostly observer status and can't interfere with Lucifer's influence over them. As a Guardian, it's got to be tough duty to be assigned to a patient trapped in that web of deceit."

Da-Ved's hands became clenched fists, and he spoke in a hushed but firm voice, "Those humans who deprive the poor and withhold justice from the oppressed are going to be in big trouble. They make widows their prey and rob the fatherless. What are they going to do on the day of God's reckoning when He sends them judgment and His anger won't be quenched?"

"You've come a long way to give the oppressed a second chance," said Iyr. "I know you can't force redemption upon these patients, but you can loosen the enemy's brutal dominion over them. Hopefully, a measure of peace can then be restored to them, and their Guardians will be able to provide them proper support and guidance. They'll have a chance to hear His call and possibly respond to it."

"In any event," Da-Ved said, fingering the key on his chest, "the blessing I am going to deliver is to pull down this stronghold and rout the enemy from this hospital."

Iyr averted his eyes. "Da-Ved...we...we can't go with you. We would if we could, but Lucifer's power is too strong for us in there. All our weapons have been banished from within the borders of Ravenwood, and as we said before, the Guardians inside have been reduced to simple observers. But may we accompany you to its gates?"

"Yes," said Gedeón, "allow us to escort you to its destruction."

"All right," Da-Ved said. "Come on. It's getting late, and I have work to do."

The large chrome handle disappeared in Iyr's huge fist as he yanked the heavy metal door open. The trio then quickly exited the stairwell into the first-floor hallway and set off for Ravenwood's outer gateway.

*****

DECEMBER 25 – 1:35 AM
CHARITY HOSPITAL'S CHAPEL

Escorted by her son, Edna Chamberlain made her way from the admitting office to the small hospital chapel. Presently, they were sitting in the front pew, quietly praying while awaiting some word from the Emergency Department.

Within the confines of the chapel's softly illuminated sanctuary, Edna sought a temporary refuge. Under its high cathedral ceiling, she'd come to beseech her God for mercy and possibly, a Christmas miracle. But for all her prayers and petitions, it seemed that a dark presence was closing in, engulfing the tiny woman with overwhelming fear and fatigue. She'd never felt so utterly helpless or alone before.

Edna tried reading from a small Bible she always carried in her purse, but its words held no power to penetrate through the gloom that enveloped her. Her despair seemed to have an actual physical presence to it, weighing her down, sapping her strength. Nevertheless, she clutched the Bible tightly to her breast and prayed—and wept. Throughout the city, her church's prayer chain of over one hundred prayer warriors did likewise.

The door to the chapel opened, and Dr. Reynolds walked in. He stopped at the doorway, reluctant to invade her private thoughts. With some trepidation, he walked the center aisle to where Edna and Kenneth were sitting. Edna raised her head and, with effort, turned to look him in the eyes. He sat down in the pew behind her and took her frail hands in his.

"Mrs. Chamberlain, I apologize for not coming sooner. I had to assist a doctor on the fourth floor a little while ago because the hospital is understaffed tonight.

"I'm so sorry about your husband. There just wasn't anything I could do for him."

He allowed the bad news to sink in.

"He suffered a massive MI—that is—a massive heart attack. I'm sure he didn't suffer too long. From what I understand, your son and the rescue crews gave him a fighting chance. Unfortunately, the damage to his heart was so severe he wasn't able to respond to their efforts. I wanted you to know that every effort and procedure was made for him."

Edna nodded gratefully and looked away as tears welled up in her eyes, blurring her already dim vision. She seemed to deflate before him, shrinking in size as his words rained down upon her tiny body like sledgehammers. But her grip remained firm on the small book she so fretfully clutched, and she continued to pray.

Dr. Reynolds got up to leave. "I have to go now. I've sent for the hospital chaplain. He'll be here in a few minutes if you want someone to talk with."

Creak!

Something in the roof ironwork apparently shifted, making a creaking noise. Instinctively, Dr. Reynolds glanced up but saw nothing unusual.

"It must be getting pretty windy out there," he said. Leaning forward, he whispered into Kenneth's ear, "Don't let her stay too late, son. The roads will probably be getting bad, and tomorrow will be a tough day for her."

"Yeah, Doc, I know. Just a few minutes more. Then we'll go."

Creak! Raing!

The two men looked up towards the section of the ceiling where the source of the abnormal sounds seemed to be coming from. Dr. Reynolds spoke, "Sounds like something let loose in the roof. I'd better have maintenance take a look at it. You might want to leave here. No telling if the roof will come down in this wind. It might not be safe."

Without lifting her bowed head, Edna replied meekly, "No. No, I don't know why, but I feel that this is the one place I need to be tonight. Have someone check the roof if you need to, but I'm not leaving. Not until I've—" Her voice trailed off into a silent prayer.

*****

DECEMBER 25 – 1:45 AM
THE CHAPEL ROOFTOP

A second Guardian swooped down to the peak of the chapel to accompany the first. Braking his plunging descent, he caught as much air as he could with enormous verdant wings to pull out of a plummeting nosedive at the last possible second. The angel set down as lightly as he could, but the roof still groaned lamentably with the sudden load.

Creak!

He quickly pulled his weapon from its scabbard and signaled to other warriors as they flew to the chapel's roof.

Raing!

The sky was soon dotted with scores of angels winging their way towards the chapel, the cross adorning the squat little steeple acting as a beacon. As each Guardian landed, he unsheathed his blade.

Creak!

Raing!

Creak! Raing!

Creak! Raing!

Creak!

Shirang!

Creak! Raing!

Creak!

Sher-ang!

Creak! Raing!

The large warrior with green wings took command of the small band of Guardians assembling on the roof of the chapel. "Whoa there. guys. This roof won't take much more abuse. Some of you go on inside and make room for the others."

Looking out across the city, Shamar could see warriors streaming towards the hospital from every conceivable direction and were forming what appeared to be a dark cloud. It had the appearance of a blossoming thunderstorm. A wide smile formed on his rugged face.

"By the looks of it, we're going to need some room. A lot of room."

*****

As Edna's church prayer chain offered up supplications on behalf of her mourning family, the Guardians' weapons started to burn with holy fire. Armed with these flaming swords, a multitude of Guardians invisibly descended into the chapel directly through its peaked roof. One by one, each veiled warrior entered unseen from above and found a spot to sit amongst the grieving mortals.

Soon, the pews were packed with grinning angels, and yet more continued to descend into the sanctuary. The aisles became congested—and still more came. Finally, the only open spaces available were the exposed heavy post and beam timbers overhead. They, too, began to creak their objections as the Guardians crowded onto them.

While a hedge of providential protection formed around Edna and her son, angelic weapons purged the room with an eerie luminescence. Vaporous malevolent spirits began to scurry and skitter across the chapel floor, attempting to remain hidden within the fleeting shadows. As celestial light spilled into every corner of the sanctuary, the scampering demons withdrew, departing for gloomier climes.

Edna's grip on the little book had not loosened.

*****

DECEMBER 25 – 2:00 AM
RAVENWOOD PSYCHIATRIC
INSTITUTE – SALLY PORT

Traversing the lengthy first-floor corridor, Da-Ved soon found himself approaching the security doors to the psychiatric wing of the hospital. Gedeón tugged at Da-Ved's sleeve, stopping him in mid-stride.

"Da-Ved," he said, "this is the end of the line for us. We'll wait here at the entrance and prevent the enemy from reinforcing this stronghold. But this I promise you: the moment you strip authority from Ravenwood's present overlord, we'll deal with any of his underlings that are foolish enough to hang around the institute."

"Thanks, Gedeón. I appreciate it. And I'm sure Aram will be pleased with the efforts you've made on my behalf also."

As Da-Ved walked the last few steps to Ravenwood's outer security door, Iyr stepped into his path to stop him. "May I at least get the door for you?"

"By all means. Be my guest," Da-Ved said.

Iyr withdrew his sword and inserted it into the seam between the doors. A metallic buzzing noise was heard, and the doors unlocked. Da-Ved bid farewell to the two Guardians, pushed against the doors, and entered into Ravenwood's inner security passageway. A second later, the doors swung shut behind him with a resounding electronic click.

The empty chamber was fairly large with a tall unfinished ceiling and apparently, unoccupied. Save for some austere industrial lighting, nothing lurked above in the sally port's grid of supportive ironwork although the noxious odor of brimstone lightly permeated the room.

This section of the building had once been part of the old hospital's four-bay loading dock before a renovation project added the psychiatric wing to the rear of the property. After Ravenwood moved to its present hillside facility, the loading dock situated between the two buildings was converted into a short sally port as a secure egress for incoming psychiatric patients needing immediate crisis intervention from the Emergency Department.

The psychiatric facility was now locked down and no one could enter or exit except through these electronically controlled doors.

Da-Ved looked to the ceiling, sniffing the air. He curled his nose at the odor.

"Whoo dares enter…the lair of my master?" growled two disembodied voices from somewhere high overhead.

Da-Ved warily backed away to stand against a nearby wall, then commanded, "Show yourself, spirit!"

A murky outline slowly began to solidify before him as the entity pressed itself from the spiritual dimension into a three-dimensional physical reality. As the specter took shape, its color changed from an opaque white to a pale shade of green and then to dark green. Gradually, reptilian scales the size of dinner plates materialized before Da-Ved's eyes, and the creature took the form of a hideous two-headed dragon.

"Who are you?" Da-Ved asked. "And what have you to do with me?"

"I?" asked the huge reptile. Rising from the floor, it stretched twin serpentine necks to their full eighteen-foot height to look down upon the foolish angel who had dared to enter its lair. Thick scaly armor gave the creature an appearance of invincibility, and its brown membranous wings filled the room as they extended fully to block the small angel's path. Clearly perturbed, the dragon's huge heads now loomed above the small messenger. They hissed in protest at Da-Ved's presence.

Da-Ved quickly sized up the creature's deadly offensive weapons. A long saurian tail swept back and forth across the floor ready to lash out with its broad serrated tip. The dragon's razor-sharp talons reverberated on the tile floor with pent-up energy. Speaking in a disjointed duality, a horned head would begin a sentence, and its impatient mate would interrupt to finish it. One of the creature's heads asked, "You ask who am I?"

The other head completed the thought. "It isss I…who should ask, 'Who are you?'"

Da-Ved drew nearer to the towering beast to stare up into its angry red eyes and gaping maws.

"I am Da-Ved, a servant of God. I have come to enter Ravenwood."

In see-saw fashion, the dragon heads answered, "Oh you have, have you?" The gigantic lizard smirked. "I am Drakon Sha'ar—"

"The Keeper offf thiss gate."

"And you have made a big mizztake, little angel."

"I recognizze you—NOT!"

"NOT!" echoed its twin.

Da-Ved looked away to conceal the spreading grin on his face. With effort, he steeled himself and returned his stoic gaze upon the beast.

"Hear me, Drakon Sha'ar. I am a messenger of the Lord, His Majesty, the King of Glory. I am to enter within these gates by *His* authority."

Without warning, the dragon turned to lash out at Da-Ved with a flick of its deadly tail, and the small angel nimbly ducked under its diamond-shaped tip. As it flailed overhead, Da-Ved grabbed the tail, slamming it hard to the floor with a bone-shattering crunch.

The twin heads darted to floor level for a face-to-face encounter with the brash little angel. Its refrigerator-sized heads studied the small messenger closely.

The saurian's broad ears flattened along slender horns while its monstrous foot-long whiskers twitched nervously. The bearded dragon was livid and growled bitterly, "Who is—"

"This King of Glory?"

"You dare to ask, 'Who is this King of Glory?'" Da-Ved mocked. "He is the Lord, mighty in battle. Lift up your heads, O ye gates, even lift them up, ye everlasting doors, and the King of Glory shall come in. You ask, 'Who is this King of Glory?' The Lord of Hosts, he is the King of Glory."[9]

The glint of something shimmering on Da-Ved's chest caused the stalking beast to freeze, focusing its gaze upon the object. Unexpectedly, and with full comprehension in its eyes, the beast rose, hissing from the floor to stand upon its powerful rear legs, its flailing wings clawing the air in panic.

As the leviathan backed away from the unarmed figure before it, its twin necks writhed like unstable pillars trembling in an earthquake. Seeking a way of escape, the dragon shrieked as it tried to distance itself in the corridor's exposed metal girders.

"BE-GONE, DA-VED, SERVANT—"

"OF THE MOST HIGH!"

"DEPART FROM ME!"

"I'LL NOT STAND—"

"AGAINST YOU! BE GONE!"

"GONE!"

"Fear not, dragon. I have no quarrel with you tonight…as long as you behave yourself. As gatekeeper, though, you must open Ravenwood's gates for His Majesty's servants."

"VERY WELL! ENTER, DA-VED—"

"ENTER INTO LORD YANAH'S LAIR."

"LET HIM DEAL WITH YOU."

"YES, I'LL LET LORD YANAH DEAL WITH YOU. GO, DA-VED."

"GO TO YANAH…GO TO YANAH."

"HAHAHAHAHAHAHAHAHAHA!"

The inner security doors opened slowly, allowing Da-Ved to advance to Ravenwood's receiving desk. The doors automatically closed behind him, and he approached a rather large young man seated at a workstation. The young man's head was bowed as he concentrated upon some vain diversion. Sensing a presence, he looked up from a magazine to see Da-Ved standing in front of him. He scooted backward, almost falling off the wheeled coaster chair he was sitting on.

"Hey! Oh! Wow, man! Don't creep up on people like that. Where did you come from? I didn't buzz you in."

"Sorry," Da-Ved said. "I didn't mean to startle you, but I don't have a lot of time. Please, I am to see the patients now."

"What do you mean now?" the aide asked as he crab-walked the chair back to his workstation.

"Most of them are in bed." His bulging biceps rippling under the sleeves of his white jacket and his weightlifter's build revealed he was more than just an orderly. "And how did you say you got in here?"

"The gatekeeper let me in. He recognized my authority."

"Gatekeeper? Oh, you must mean Rex. He let you in? Oh, I get it. Dr. Larson mentioned that a new staff member would be coming out to tour the facilities soon. I didn't think you'd come tonight, though, especially at this hour.

"I can give you the fifty-cent tour now, but I think you'd better check out the courtyard and the rest of the grounds when the weather turns better. It's pretty nasty out there right now."

"What do you mean out there?" Da-Ved asked.

"You know, outside—the grounds, the woods, the mystic animal paths—the whole Magilla."

Seeing the blank look on Da-Ved's face, he asked, "Aren't you familiar with Dr. Larson's theories on restorative Earth energy sites? That's why he had his Second Sight Clinic built here in this valley. The whole hillside here at Ravenwood is supposed to be an ancient holy place according to those who have studied those types of paranormal phenomena. It's a very powerful place. The back of the hillside is oriented to the west so we can catch the last rays of the setting sun."

Da-Ved chuckled.

"Did I say something funny?"

Da-Ved placed a hand over his mouth to hide his wide grin. "Oh, no, no. I was just thinking. That would orient the security gate to the—"

"East!" the large man finished the thought. "So? Is there something special about that?" he asked.

"Why, yes," Da-Ved replied. "I believe there is some significance to a set of gates oriented to the east. It is said that someday, they will catch the first rays of the risen Son at the Mount of Olives. That's in Jerusalem, you know."

"Well, Dr. Larson hasn't told me anything about that yet. I guess I have a lot to learn. I've only worked here for a year, so I'm not an authority on the subject, but I'm learning with Dr. Larson's help. Soooo...what's your specialty, Doc?"

"My specialty?"

"Yeah. You know. Dr. Larson has recruited therapists from all over the world. He likes to have a multitude of approaches for his clinic. The counselors he's assembled here all specialize in some sort of healing power or restructuring unbalanced bodily energy-flows. Each one has a specialty or two. What's your bag?"

"I see," Da-Ved said. "I guess you might say I have a different approach. More of an authoritative one."

"How's that?"

"I've been given the power to cast out unclean spirits and to heal all manner of sickness and disease."

The young man blanched. "Oh...uh...yeah...right. Are you sure you're supposed to be here? I mean, that gag seems kind of retro."

Da-Ved grinned. "Oh yes. I'm to see the patients tonight. But don't trouble yourself. I'll just have a look around."

The orderly turned his attention back to his magazine and flopped his big feet on top of the counter. Without looking up, he continued, "Whatever you say. Uh...for the record, what did you say your name was?"

"My name is Da-Ved. I'm here on behalf of the Son."

"Oh, yeah. Now I get it, Doc. Yeah...the sun god, Ra. Right? I get it now. By the way, my name's Jeffrey. You're welcome to look around, but as you can see, we have minimum staffing tonight because of the stupid holiday. Some of the patients are probably down at the TV lounge if you want to take a peek."

"At the lounge?"

Jeffrey threw the magazine onto a small pile of periodicals he'd been working on and met Da-Ved's eyes.

"Yeah. It's crazy, too, you know?"

Sitting up straight, he placed his feet on the floor and said, "Something seems to have them all stirred up tonight. Usually, they're all asleep by now, especially after they get their evening meds. Not that I mind, mind you. That is, as long as they stay quiet. That's all I care about."

"How many patients do you have here at Ravenwood?" Da-Ved asked.

"Not very many. We're a small private facility. But we have beds for men and woman, about twenty altogether. Tonight, there's only twelve in the house. Dr. Larson likes to keep things tidy."

"Thanks," Da-Ved said. "I guess I'll take a stroll. Which way is the lounge?"

"Can't miss it. It's at the end of the hall. When you're finished, come back, and I'll show you the offices and meditation rooms."

"Thank you, but as I said, my time is short tonight."

Reaching for another magazine, Jeffrey replied with casual indifference, "No sweat, man. I'll catch ya later then."

He held the magazine vertically with a leering look.

For though we walk in the flesh, we do not war after the
flesh. For the weapons of our war-fare are not carnal, but
mighty through God to the pulling down of strong holds.

—2 Corinthians 10:3, 4 (KJV)

But if I cast out devils by the Spirit of God, then the kingdom
of God is come unto you. Or else how can one enter into
a strong man's house, and spoil his goods, except he first
bind the strong man? and then he will spoil his house.

—Matthew 12:28, 29 (KJV)

CHAPTER SEVENTEEN

The Stronghold

DECEMBER 25 – 2:25 AM
RAVENWOOD PSYCHIATRIC INSTITUTE

An azure radiance flickered from an open doorway at the opposite end of the hallway, and the drone of a television emanated from within the room. As Da-Ved walked toward the light, he became aware of a disquieting tenseness in the air. Several doors to patient rooms were open, and he perceived that more than a few of the occupants were awake.

The muffled weeping of a patient caught him off guard, disturbing his concentration. Wavering for a second, he forced himself to push on to the end of the corridor. As he approached the lounge, the uncomfortable impression of anxiety and apprehension he'd sensed in the hallway increased in intensity.

From the doorway, he saw that the lounge was occupied by three men. Two middle-aged men sat on a large sofa in the middle of the room, watching television—they seemed riveted to the seasonal Jimmy Stewart movie—while a younger bald man stood behind them, shrouded in the shadows at the rear of the room.

The three men were ready to retire for the evening, dressed neatly in pajamas, robes, and slippers. No one spoke.

Da-Ved entered the room, and as he entered, the man at the window turned away to look out into the infinity of the winter storm. A sudden shadow flitted across the television screen, and the two men sitting on the sofa looked up, noticing Da-Ved for the first time. "Who are you? You shouldn't be here!" cried one.

The man at the window spun around and said in a gruff voice, "I know who he is, and he has no right to be here." Turning to Da-Ved, he ordered, "This is our home. You must leave us—now!"

Da-Ved replied calmly, "Do you know who I am? If so, where is the tyrant—your Gibbor—for I have come to bind him?"

"Who-Who did you say?" asked the bald man.

The Gibbor, the mighty one, the Warlord of this province."

The question had the effect of a thunderclap on the three men, and they fled the room without saying another word.

Da-Ved noticed that the oppressive feeling remained within the room, even as they exited. He made his way to the television and turned it off. The room was immediately cast into a heavy and morose darkness. He waited for the fallen spirit he knew to be there to make its presence known to him. For several seconds, nothing happened.

Then, precipitously, a small sprite of light flew from across the room to dance boldly in front of him only a few feet away. This tiny floating luminary was soon followed by a second and then a third. A sudden rush of radiant energy blazed from every hidden cleft and crevice within the room, and in seconds, several hundred pinpoints of light swirled in front of the small angel to form a spinning vortex of luminescent energy.

Newspapers began to blow about the room, and the hue of the spinning vortex began to oscillate from white to yellow to orange to red and back to white again. The room filled with a low buzzing sound as if someone had stirred up a nest of angry hornets.

Steadily, the color fluctuations of this spectral tempest shifted to flame red as it started to grow in size. The whirling dervish wheeled about the room, overturning a small end table, ever-expanding until it filled the vaulted space between floor and ceiling.

At last, a bloody specter stood in front of Da-Ved, and it let loose a bloodcurdling laugh. "Ho, Da-Ved! We see that you have not listened to the advice we gave you. You've made a big mistake coming here."

The diminutive angel stood his ground. "Your words bore me, Yanah. Where is the Gibbor? I have business with him tonight."

His words seem to infuriate the unyielding demon. "You speak the ancient language, we see. The Gibbor? The strong man, you say? Ha! He was but an old fool! In any event, Pharmakos is no longer here."

Da-Ved's eyes widened, and he took a step backward as if he were pushed.

The dripping specter pondered aloud, "Yes, it *is* humorous, isn't it? We are somewhat in your debt, Da-Ved. We believe your comrades had something to do with Lord Pharmakos' sudden departure this summer. And now Lucifer has finally made *us* prince here. *We* are the Gibbor now, and you cannot overthrow us, even with a legion of Guardians."

"I don't intend to. I have been sent by His Majesty and come bearing His authority, not my own. I'm afraid you have no choice in the matter."

"No! It is you, little angel, that has no choice. We are Yanah— *The Oppression*. We are many. We are Hive, and we are enemies of your God."

"Then you are a fool, Yanah. God scatters His enemies effortlessly. The heavens and Earth are His, for He created them. He is all-powerful, and justice is the habitation of His Throne. Mercy and truth walk before him. The people rejoice in His name and in His righteousness. The Lord is their defense, and He is their King. It is He that has sent me here tonight. If you depart now without doing violence, I'll not send you to the Abyss in chains. But be warned, Yanah. If you raise your arm against me, it will be as if you raised your arm against His Majesty Himself!"

"No! You lie!" railed Yanah. "Since the time of our derision in Babylon, we have fought proudly for this position of dominion. We have finally assumed our rightful station, and we will not step down! No, Guardian. Our arm shall not be quieted against you, servant of the Most High. For this is *our* Babylon, and we are finally Lord… here!"

The loathsome spirit rose to its full height and stretched its leathery wings across the room, cutting off Da-Ved from the doorway. With Da-Ved contained, Yanah sprang against the unarmed messenger, unsheathing his razor-sharp claws with explosive fury.

As Yanah attacked, the silver key hanging from Da-Ved's neck kindled a brilliant explosion of white incandescence, and for several seconds, the acrid odor of ozone and burning sulfur occupied the room. Da-Ved temporarily lost his vision. As it returned, he saw that Yanah had vanished and the floor was covered with a fine gray powder. The room was once again cast into darkness, but the oppressive feeling was finally gone.

Da-Ved spoke in a low voice, "He is against you, O proud one, for your day is come, the time that He will visit you. And the proud shall stumble and fall, and none shall raise you up, and He will kindle a fire, and it shall devour all about you. The children of Job and the children of Ravenwood were oppressed together, and all that took them captive held them fast. They refused to let them go. But their Redeemer is strong. He shall plead their cause that He may give rest to the land and subdue the tyrant of Ravenwood."[10]

Da-Ved retreated to the doorway. From here, he could see that the three men were at the far end of the corridor, engaging the burly orderly in a heated discussion. The tall bald man was pointing in the direction of the lounge, arguing some final point of contention. Jeffrey glanced towards the lounge and, spying only Da-Ved in the doorway, waved the men away and returned to his magazines.

The bald man, on seeing Da-Ved exiting the lounge, coughed and sputtered. Springing down the hallway, he lunged for Da-Ved, bellowing, "Out! Out of here, I say! Out!"

His outburst brought the rest of the patients from their rooms into the hallway, and the orderly jumped to his feet. A low and discordant murmuring started up among them.

Da-Ved's menacing approach brought the bald man to a sudden halt. Turning to his companions, the bald man asked, "Well? What are we to do with him? We can't allow his presence here. We must cast him out!"

From behind him, a sharp cry arose, waning to a whimpering moan. It caught the bully off-guard, and he pivoted to see a young woman sliding slowly to the ground against her opened door.

Sprawled across the terrazzo floor, she sobbed uncontrollably. A man and a woman rushed to her side, talking to her in hushed and quieting tones. They nervously looked to the bald man for guidance. "What are we to do?" they asked.

"What?" he demanded. "What? Do you think any of this makes any difference? He is nothing, I tell you! Nothing!"

The small group reluctantly closed in around Da-Ved and the bald man, surrounding them within a tight circle. Da-Ved raised a hand in warning.

"Wait. I have come to deliver a message. The Lord has appointed me to preach good news to you, to the poor in spirit. I've been sent to heal the brokenhearted, to recover sight to the spiritually blind, and to set at liberty those who are oppressed."

The bald man screamed, and he grabbed Da-Ved roughly by the lapels of his coat. As he did, he started to shake convulsively as if shocked by a sudden jolt of electricity. His face contorted into what appeared to be a grotesque caricature of himself and something evil that was cloaked within him.

His mouth opened, but he could form no words, and his lungs emptied in a long single breath. His darkly colored eyes seemed to plead for mercy. The man's legs lost their strength, and gradually, his grip loosened from Da-Ved's thick collar.

He, too, began a slow slide to the floor but was suddenly thrown back against the wall, repelled by some unseen force. The violent impact was hard, and he fell to the floor with a loud thud. Writhing about, he started to moan and to foam at the mouth.

The small crowd became silent and shrank away from Da-Ved. The bald man's moaning subsided to an even rhythm, languishing into gentle sobs of relief.

Da-Ved approached him and knelt to one knee, taking his hand in his. At the touch of his hand, the man's eyes opened, and Da-Ved assisted him to a sitting position. He continued to weep quietly and simply nodded to Da-Ved, his gratitude.

Da-Ved held him close, their hands clasped tightly together. The man shuddered like a small child shaking off the fading terrors of a bad nightmare.

Da-Ved whispered words of encouragement into his ear and gently patted him on his back. He then stood to face the small crowd. They retreated from him down the corridor and back toward their rooms.

"Wait!" Da-Ved cried. "Don't be afraid. I have gifts for all of you."

As he approached them, a grandmotherly woman tried to slip unnoticed into the open doorway of her room. Drawing near, Da-Ved reached inside to take her trembling hand in his. Gently pulling her back into the hallway, he reached out with his other hand to brush away a falling tear. As his hand nudged her cheek, her eyes grew wide as if she now saw him for the first time through new eyes.

"Aahh!" she gasped and pulled his hand to her lips.

Da-Ved wrapped a sheltering arm around her shoulders and walked the corridor as her escort and support. At his slightest touch, each patient in this ward received the gift of a healed mind and body made whole.

A few of them fainted as their broken hearts were warmed and restored, anointed with a soothing spiritual balm. With Lucifer's forces ravaged and scattered, their mental agitation disappeared, and clarity returned to their eyes.

During this commotion, a heavyset woman wearing a white lab coat dashed out of an office adjacent to the admitting area. Her pudgy legs propelled her towards the disturbance, and her reading glasses hanging from a silver chain bounced upon her ample bosom with each pounding step. She seemed tense and wired with a short fuse.

Addressing the large orderly, she demanded, "Jeffrey! What's got all these people so stirred up? Why aren't they in their rooms, sleeping?"

Jeffrey swore under his breath, put on a pleasant face, and turned to face his ruffled supervisor.

"Ma'am?"

Eyeing Da-Ved in the hallway, she added, "And who is this man?"

"Him? His name is David something. Dr. Davidson, I think he said. Uh, he's the new staff member Dr. Larson was expecting. And I don't know why the patients are up. They seemed a bit restless earlier tonight, but not at all like this."

Returning to her office, she said, "Go and find out what's going on and get these people back to their rooms, or I'll have to call Rex. Do it now, Jeffrey!"

The confused orderly made his way toward Da-Ved. In near panic, he asked, "Doc! Doc! I don't get it. What's happening? What did you do?"

Looking about the now tranquil corridor, Jeffrey stopped and rubbed the back of his neck. "What the? They're all...all...different now."

Da-Ved looked from face to face. "Yes, they are, aren't they?"

"I don't understand. One minute, they're yelling and crying and carrying on, and the next minute, they're quiet as church mice. What's wrong with them?"

"Nothing," Da-Ved said. "They're fine. They can all go home now."

Jeffrey took a step backward. "Home? How can they go home?" As the patients returned quietly to their rooms, he added, "Dr. Larson will have to sign off on that. I don't think he'll—"

A deafening crash from within the sally port shook the building, staggering Jeffrey. He took two steps backwards, then skittered head-long to the small observation windows located in the middle of the security doors. Colliding solidly with the heavy wood, he rebounded and scrambled back to the viewing portals. Through the wired glass, he saw that the middle section of the ceiling in the security corridor had been torn loose.

The eerie illumination of a handful of swinging light fixtures revealed the sag of twisted metal-support beams and strands of colored wiring dangling about like spun spaghetti. A loud zap accompanied by a white flash occurred every time a hot wire swung against exposed metal, and the hallway appeared to swing back and forth in the disorienting illumination. Jeffrey shaded his eyes and looked away.

Several heating ducts drooped precariously from the web of overhead ironwork, and the open sky was visible through a large opening in the roof. Strangely, there was no wind.

As Jeffrey ran for a nearby phone, Ravenwood's lights dimmed and went out. The meager emergency lighting came on and a wave of obscene curses billowed from between his gritted teeth as he clumsily felt his way through the darkened hallway.

And the great dragon was cast out, that old serpent, called the Devil, and Satan, which deceiveth the whole world: he was cast out into the earth, and his angels were cast out with him.

—Revelation 12:9 (KJV)

CHAPTER EIGHTEEN

Dragon's Lair

DECEMBER 25 – 2:40 AM
RAVENWOOD PSYCHIATRIC INSTITUTE –
THE SALLY PORT ROOFTOP

Da-Ved knelt upon the shattered roof to inspect the damage around the large hole caused by its collapse. Iyr squatted next to him.

"Thanks, Iyr. I appreciate your help in getting me out of there."

"It was easy, Da-Ved. Once Yanah was dispatched to the Abyss, it wasn't hard to persuade Drakon to leave. He was hiding in the roof's ironwork. Removing you was just part of the fun."

Gedeón and a dozen warriors soon surrounded them.

The two angels rose and backed away from the hole. "Where did your friends come from, Gedeón?" Da-Ved asked.

"These warriors are the Guardians of the patients you've just released from captivity. They've come to express their appreciation and to assure you they've routed the rest of *The Oppression* from Ravenwood."

Da-Ved turned to the group. "Well done, brothers. I have to say it's good to see so many friendly faces about."

Shaking his head, Da-Ved surveyed the shredded roof. At first glance, it appeared as if a sudden microburst had descended from above focusing its destructive energy upon a small section of the building. Upon closer examination, it was obvious that the roof had not been blown off but had been torn off from the inside out. Deep claw marks could be seen embedded in the heavy metal beams, and a four-inch tooth lay among the remains of a shattered skylight.

Da-Ved reached down to pick up the bloodied tooth and tossed it to Gedeón. "Would I be correct in surmising that this is some of your handiwork?" he asked.

"Maybe a little, and I did have a little help," Gedeón said sheepishly.

Shamar appeared above them, descending in a long lazy turn and coasted to a soft landing next to Da-Ved. Peering into the wreckage below, he gave a low whistle. "You've done it, Da-Ved! You've liberated Ravenwood!"

"Yes," Da-Ved agreed, "Ravenwood's been set free."

"But how? How did you do it? We've been trying for years to overthrow this citadel, and we couldn't make any headway."

"Our King has anointed me tonight to bind up the broken-hearted and to set the captives free. They've received God's mercy, and He's opened the prison doors to those who were bound here at Ravenwood. He's sent them a blessing."

"And what a blessing, Da-Ved! What you've done for them is awesome. These people have finally received peace—a peace they haven't known for years. You've given them the respite we've all fought for."

Looking about, Gedeón said, "Can't you feel it, Da-Ved? The spiritual realm here has been purged of the malevolent spirit that's had a stranglehold on many of the patients here. These people have a chance now."

Iyr added, "And this valley has finally been cleansed of the darkness that's infested it for centuries. Thanks to you, Da-Ved."

Da-Ved's face reddened, and he said, "We do serve an awesome God, don't we?"

Shamar agreed. "Awesome! Yes. Truly *awesome!*"

"*Wonderful!*" added Iyr with an impish smile.

"*Counselor!*" said a grinning Gedeón.

The band of Guardians took up the spontaneous chant of praise to their Creator. "*Mighty God!*" cried three of the largest warriors, their flaming swords raised high over their heads.

"*The Everlasting Father!*" shouted five more of the Host in booming voices.

Finishing their tribute, the dozen let loose with a waning shout of victory as they streaked away into the darkness. "*The Prince of Peace!*"

Da-Ved looked to Shamar. "Where are they going?"

A huge smile spread across Shamar's face. "The demons have regrouped and are attempting a counterattack at the outer edges of town. Our troops go to reinforce the defenses at the perimeter. Some of them have been here at Ravenwood for quite some time, and I'm afraid after suffering years of abuse, they may desire a little payback. They are very happily in your debt, my friend."

Da-Ved watched as the dozen soared toward the battle.

"Don't worry, Da-Ved. There's no chance for the enemy to return here. Not after tonight. But you already know that, I'm sure."

"Yes," Da-Ved agreed, "there's no chance of that. But I have a feeling my work in the hospital isn't completed yet, and if I know Lucifer, I'll encounter his most powerful Princes sometime tonight."

"It's best to be careful," Iyr said. "Lucifer would like nothing better than to turn you to his side or absorb you into his essence if you refuse to join his rebellion."

"I know. But after this final struggle is won, Aram and I will be able to return to His Majesty's court and present to Him this night of visitation as our personal gift to Him."

"And where do you think you should go next?" Gedeón asked.

A howling siren punctuated the crisp night air as a second ambulance responded from the hospital into the city. Da-Ved glanced towards the direction of the Emergency Room and pointed.

"There!" he said. "I feel it. I'm to minister a great berakah there."

"A berakah?" Iyr asked. "What kind of a berakah?"

"A blessing such as this world has not seen for a long time and I'm not sure is ready to see the likes of again. Under the circumstances, I have a simple request to make of you."

The trio answered as one, "What is it?"

"Anything, Da-Ved."

"Yes!"

"You can assist me by staying close. I would like witnesses to what will occur within the next hour."

Shamar rose into the air, stirring the snow-covered roof into a miniature whiteout. A small white cloud quickly enveloped them.

"Say no more, Da-Ved. Truly, it will be a day to remember to be able to say we were there with Da-Ved, the Messenger to Job. Let's go."

*****

THE CORRIDOR

Frank Chamberlain awoke in a dimly lighted cool dry place. The crushing chest pain rendering him unconscious was mercifully gone. He sat up upon the hard floor and tried to get his bearings. *Where in the blue blazes am I? And how did I get here?* he thought.

Getting to his feet, he gingerly moved each arm and leg, checking for injuries. "Nope. I feel fine," he said aloud. "Now how do I get out of here?"

Checking his surroundings, he saw that behind him stretched a long dark tunnel of sorts. A fuzzy light beckoned to him in the opposite direction.

"Well, I can't go that way," he said, peering into the darkness. Turning towards the light, he added, "So I guess I'll have to go this way."

He started to walk.

*****

DECEMBER 25 – 2:40 AM
CHARITY'S EMERGENCY DEPARTMENT

Dr. Reynolds entered the employee lunchroom and inserted two dollar bills into the beverage machine sitting next to the refrigerator. He selected a diet cola, and the can thumped loudly into the receiving tray. Three quarters chinked noisily below, and his fleshy fingers retrieved them from the machine's small change cup. The room's fluorescent lighting abruptly dimmed, then sluggishly returned to its normal brightness.

Wayne Johnson and Bob Sorenson were just starting to drink their coffees at one of the three tables in the room. Wayne looked towards the lights and asked with disdain, "Now what?"

Bob slumped in his seat to shove an empty chair toward the tired-looking physician and motioned for him to sit down. "Hey, ya old sawbones, take a load off."

Wayne glared at the security guard. "Kids! They have no manners anymore," he said aloud to no one in particular.

In a more respectful tone, Wayne asked, "How's it going, Dr. Reynolds?"

"Oh, not too bad." the aging physician answered with a smile. "I've got a good crew working with me tonight, and it's been kind of slow, I guess because of the storm and the holiday."

"I'll take it," Wayne replied. "Fast or slow, the pay's the same. But I think the paramedics left a few minutes ago. They go out on something bad?"

The doctor shook his head. "I don't believe so. Just a minor fender bender. I think the police just wanted to make sure no one was hurt too seriously. Better safe than sorry, I suppose."

"I'll say. You can't be too careful these days," Bob said as he peeled the cellophane wrapper from a package of cookies. He popped one into his mouth and took a sip of hot coffee. "I eard ou los won to-nigh," he mumbled with a full mouth.

Wayne gave the doctor a sympathetic look, and the physician chuckled under his breath. "Yes, I'm sorry to say. It's too bad too. His children are visiting from out of town for the holidays. Bad timing."

Bob snapped his fingers. "I'll say!" Then he lowered his voice. "How's the family taking it?"

Dr. Reynolds got up and peeked out the door. "That's a good question. They're still down at the chapel, I guess. I wanted to call for the hospital chaplain, but the patient's wife nixed that idea. She called her own minister."

Bob's eyes opened wide, and he coughed as he choked on a cookie. "They're...They're still down there?"

"Yep. I tried to get her son to take her home, but I think she's one of those holy rollers or something to that effect. The whole sanctuary is filled with them."

"The place is filled? How many?"

"About forty or fifty, I guess. The place is packed. Her son said they have some kind of phone network where church members call each other during emergencies. Someone was sure busy tonight."

"What are they doing down there? I better go check it out before Rex does."

"Don't bother, Bob. They're harmless. They're only praying, I suspect, for all the good it will do them. He's been dead over three hours. I don't think he's coming back...unless his name is Lazarus," he said with a nervous laugh.

Wayne placed a heavy foot on the chair across from him and leaned back, sipping his coffee slowly. "How old was he?"

"Oh, not too old. About seventy, I think. His son said he's had a bad ticker for years. Tonight was just his night to go, that's all."

Bob grimaced. "Too bad. I mean, today being Christmas and all."

Bob Sorenson's portable radio squawked harshly. Rex's agitated voice filled the room, "Security to portable one, come in!"

Bob reluctantly picked up the radio and answered, "Go ahead, Rex."

"Bob! The roof just caved in at Ravenwood's sally port. Get down there quick and check it out. I'll call the police and fire departments and meet you there. If you see Wayne, tell him to get down there fast."

Bob sat upright and keyed his radio. "Is anyone hurt? The ambulance just left on a car wreck."

His radio crackled. "I'm not sure. I don't think so. No one should have been in the sally port this time of night, but we have to make sure. Get down there right away. Out!"

Dr. Reynolds started to speak, but Bob cut him off, "No sense you leaving the ER until we know for sure, Doc. Wayne and I will check it out. If we need you, I'll page you over the intercom."

"If you think that's best, Bob. I'll inform the ER staff."

"Let's go, Wayne!"

The custodian slowly got to his feet and made a sour face. "First, it's the roof on the chapel. Now it's the blankety-blank sally port. Whatever happened to my quiet holiday night?"

I am he that liveth, and was dead; and behold, I am alive for evermore, A-men; and have the keys of hell and death.

—Revelation 1: 18 (KJV)

CHAPTER NINETEEN

Death and the Grave

DECEMBER 25 – 2:45 AM
OUTSIDE CHARITY HOSPITAL'S
EMERGENCY DEPARTMENT

The small group of angels landed upon the roof of a modest one-story addition attached to the emergency department. From this elevated position, their view was unobstructed across the hospital's south parking lot, clear to the helicopter landing pad three-hundred feet away.

"Here," Da-Ved said. "We can stop here. We're very close. The final struggle in the hospital will begin here."

Shamar leaned out over the roof's parapet wall to peer at the parking lot. A solitary ambulance was parked off to the side. "Are you sure?" he asked. "I don't see any signs of enemy activity."

The smaller angel was adamant. "I'm positive, Shamar. We're at the right place. I can feel it."

"Where are we?" Iyr asked. "I don't quite recognize this place from up here."

Gedeón joined Shamar at the roof's edge. "We're right outside the ambulance entrance to the hospital. The room directly below us contains a device called a CT scanner. It's used to produce cross sectional views of the human body...any part needing an internal examination."

"Humans!" Iyr said with an air of frustration. "They are an enigma, aren't they?"

"How do you mean?" Gedeón asked.

"I mean, how can they be so clever and so completely dense at the same time?"

"I don't think I understand."

Iyr pointed to the room below. "Just look at the technological marvels they're capable of inventing, yet they stumble over the simplest of truths."

Spreading his wings, Iyr hammered home his exasperation with the human race. "Mankind's overall knowledge to this day continues to expand at an ever-increasing rate. This present generation now travels across the planet with a speed, ease, and comfort not imagined by any previous generation. While their scholars continue to unravel the hidden mysteries of creation, many humans are still blind to the very existence of the Creator of that creation. That supreme contradiction has always baffled me."

"Sometimes you have to be looking for something before you can see it," Shamar said in a subdued voice.

"Maybe a few people will find it easier to believe in a Creator after tonight," Da-Ved said. "But the night is fast disappearing, and I need to get moving."

"At your service, Da-Ved," Shamar said, picking up the smaller angel in his powerful arms. "Where to?"

Da-Ved pointed to the ground. "Just get me down to the entrance below. I'm sure Lucifer has an emissary or two awaiting my arrival."

Gedeón ducked low and took a quick look around the parking lot. "An emissary? What emissary?"

The battle-axe hanging from Gedeón's back suddenly disappeared, only to materialize a second later within his hands. His quickness with his weapon was mirrored by Iyr's. A simple swift movement unsnapped Iyr's shield from its thick shoulder strap, and the heavy armor fairly hopped into his left hand. He then readied a ten-foot javelin with his right.

"Just who do you think is waiting for you, Da-Ved?" Iyr asked.

"I don't know for sure, but Lucifer isn't stupid. He's probably anticipated my final rendezvous for the evening. He'll have a welcoming party of some sort waiting for us below. And you can put your weapons away. You won't be needing them here."

Gedeón and Iyr descended first, deploying themselves on either side of the double doors, just outside the hospital's ambulance entrance. Gedeón signaled the parking lot was secure, and Shamar descended quickly, placing Da-Ved in front of the twin doors. He then shot skyward, taking a position directly above the building.

At Da-Ved's approach, the doors automatically opened. Before he entered, the telltale stench of decay gently wafted through the open doors, revealing that something sinister was approaching from within.

A discordant scratching noise was quickly drowned out by the distinctive warning rattle of a large pit viper, and Thanatos and She'Ol emerged from the hospital. Barging through the open doorway, they confronted Da-Ved standing just outside the ambulance entrance.

"Da-Ved! We meet again!" She'Ol sneered as he slithered through the doors.

"And where is your large friend, Aram?" taunted his leggy companion. "It would be nice if he were here to be part of our little party."

Da-Ved slowly backed away to a more tenable position, then stood his ground.

"I'm not sure, but he's probably about somewhere."

"Good!" cried Thanatos. "We don't want him to miss out on the big plans we have for you two tonight."

Iyr and Gedeón approached from either side of the entrance with weapons raised, and Shamar swooped in from the roof to confront Lucifer's supreme generals face-to-face.

As they advanced, Thanatos assumed the classic scorpion attack stance with its formidable pincers held low and menacing. The demon then slowly arched its segmented tail high into a lethal striking position.

The oversized arachnid was provoked and prepared for battle. Its pectines, a pair of comb-like sensory appendages, were extended from underneath its pre-abdomen almost to the ground. The sensitivity of the pectines was such that the slightest brush of air, sound, or other vibration gave early warning to the scorpion of any approaching danger. It would be a difficult task to approach this wary prince unnoticed.

The tip of its stinger oozed a black liquid, and the hairs on the scorpion's segmented back and legs bristled as it shouted a warning, "We are willing to go to war, Guardians! But you will not ambush us!"

Shamar withdrew his double-edged weapon from its long scabbard. He took up a defensive position behind Da-Ved as She'Ol glided rhythmically to within a few feet of the small angel.

Da-Ved turned to his friends. "Stand down, Guardians. I need witnesses here, not warriors."

He then wheeled to face Lucifer's highest-ranking warlords. "You know you are finished here. Why do you still linger in this place?"

She'Ol rattled a warning and spoke with a raspy voice. "Who says we are finished here? As we speak, Lord Lucifer has dispatched two legions of his locust hoard from across the ocean. They will arrive shortly, and then we'll just see who is finished here."

"You know that is simply not going to happen," Da-Ved said. "In case you haven't noticed, Miyka'el has positioned a battle platform over this valley, and more to the point, the local saints have been fasting and are on their knees this very night. I guarantee you there is absolutely no way that Lucifer's European locust hoard will be admitted into the region. Your stronghold has been lost."

"But Lord Lucifer has azzsured usss—"

Da-Ved cut him off with a wave of his hand. "Lucifer no longer holds dominion here. I serve the risen Lord and have been given authority to wield His sovereignty in the city tonight. I've been sent to take dominion over all your minions. Over all sickness and disease. You and your underlings are subservient to me for this one day. You cannot win."

Perceiving their stunned disbelief, Da-Ved stepped closer to his two antagonists. Holding out the small silver key hanging upon his chest, he asked, "Do you see this key, Thanatos? It is I who am master here tonight, not Lucifer."

"A key! He has a key!" screeched She'Ol. "It is mine! I will have it!" He stretched out a scaly hand to receive it.

Tucking the key back under his sweatshirt, Da-Ved said, "It's only yours if you can take it. I wouldn't try it, though. It seems that every foul spirit that has tried to take this particular key ends up in the Abyss. Not a pleasant outcome, I'm sure."

She'Ol pivoted and scowled at Thanatos. "There are only four of them, Thanatos! They will be no match for you. Take them down! I must have that key!"

Da-Ved let loose an outburst of mocking laughter, stopping the cruel demon dead in its tracks.

"That will be the biggest blunder of your long and miserable existence, Thanatos! Do not think that these Guardians are with me as a defensive escort. I have no need of their protection, I assure you.

"No. Their sole purpose tonight is to bear witness through all eternity the final outcome of this Day of Visitation. And as you suspected, Thanatos, Aram is also here in Job with me. He has always been a formidable opponent, wouldn't you agree? But I must warn you, he has also received a special anointing and has a similar key in his possession. He, too, wields His Majesty's authority this night."

A look of surprise flashed across each of the scorpion's twelve eyes.

"Yes, Thanatos, Aram also holds a key you once possessed. I think it would be a mistake to cross swords with him now. But it won't come to that, will it? The keys will see to that. Now stand aside. I have an appointment to keep."

She'Ol lowered his sword, and Thanatos slowly lowered its venom-laced stinger from its striking position. For a brief moment, they looked at each other, and then at the impudent angel who dared to defy them. Their demonic powers and authority on this planet were immense, and they had always been able to fight or bully their way through any enemy encounter.

"You…you foolish angel! We…ah…want nothing of you. You are to be pitied. You could have so much more power than you now possess."

"I doubt that, She'Ol. But go ahead. I'll give you a chance to enlighten me."

She'Ol's eyes burned with contempt. "The humans are like cattle. We feast on their darkest emotions and take their souls as nourishment when they die in their sins. You could be one of this planet's gods if only you would bend your knee to Lucifer and cross over to our side."

"There is only one God," Da-Ved said softly, "and I would not be a pretender to His Throne. It is in Him whom I delight and serve. I will serve no other."

"Yes...serve no other!" mocked the enraged scorpion. "You serve...while...*we* reign!"

Da-Ved's face hardened. "Nevertheless, you are powerless tonight. You must leave."

"Never!" howled Thanatos. "Do you not understand who we are, you worm? Could it be that there is an angel that has not heard of us? We are Thanatos and She'Ol—*Death and the Grave!* The institute belongs to us, and we will not leave it! We will have this victory against the Nazarene. And you and your companions will taste the venom of my sting tonight!"

Da-Ved defiantly crossed his arms upon his chest. "O Death... where is your sting? O, Grave...where is your victory?"

She'Ol rose from the floor, towering over Da-Ved. His scaly skin transformed from its usual shimmering effect to a solid bright red. The demon pulled his sword from the jeweled scabbard on his back and brandished it towards the small angel. "The sting of Death is sin, and the strength of sin is the Law!"

Da-Ved replied calmly but firmly, "But thank God, He gives us the victory through our Lord and King. So I will be steadfast... always working...always His servant. And I know I don't labor in vain, for it's by His grace that men are saved and not by the keeping of the Law. It's a gift, so no man can boast for his own sake. You've lost, She'Ol"

The demon's tail began to vibrate, filling the air with a disorientating buzzing. He hissed a warning, "Away from us, messenger!

Away with you or we will grind your bones into dust! Unfortunately, we...uh—" He turned away looking for Thanatos.

"We've been instructed not to raise our weapons against you," Thanatos lied. "Lord Lucifer would have our heads if we deprived him of the exquisite pleasure of consuming you."

She'Ol continued the charade. "Yes! Ah, lucky for you, we are under orders...not to harm you, that is. Let's go, Thanatos, before I lose my temper and destroy the lot of them."

Da-Ved only smiled.

She'Ol quickly withdrew back into the building, dematerializing within its solid walls. "Be gone, messenger! Be gone!" the demon hissed as it faded from view.

Thanatos also made a hasty retreat toward the building and spat out a final warning, "Be warned, Guardians! We will be watching you. Do not enjoy your stay here too much. It will be a short one, I promise you."

The giant arachnid's spiny legs click-clacked on the sidewalk as it fled back to the building where it, too, dematerialized within the hospital's brown brick walls.

A heavy silence descended upon the parking lot as the angels stared at the spot where Thanatos had dissolved from their view.

"Phew!" Shamar finally exclaimed. He returned his sword to its scabbard and placed both hands on the back of his head. "Did you see what I just saw?"

"Yes. I saw it, but I still don't believe it," Iyr replied. "I never would have believed it if I hadn't seen it with my own eyes. Thanatos and She'Ol turned tail and ran. They've never done that before. Never! Da-Ved, you were fantastic!"

"No," Da-Ved said, "Sorry to say, but I'm less than nothing to them. What they ran from was the Lord's anointing power. Nothing can stand against it. Not even them."

"Lucifer sure has them deceived as to how much authority he possesses," Shamar added. "They've fallen for his web of lies completely."

"And what will you do now, Da-Ved?" Iyr asked.

"I don't know. I have a few hours before my allotted time expires. I'll just have to keep looking. I may have another appointment yet. As for She'Ol and Thanatos? Who knows? They have their own appointments to maintain, I should imagine."

Gedeón grinned. "But not here. Anyway, not tonight."

Quietly, Iyr drew close to look down upon the smaller angel. "His Majesty certainly made a wise choice in the selection of His messenger. But now you must keep your final engagement. Go ahead, we'll stand watch from here."

Da-Ved entered the hospital through the twin doors and found himself in a small vestibule just off the emergency department. A hospital gurney was parked just inside the doors piled high with assorted splints, head blocks, and cervical collars, and a collection of backboards stood in a corner, awaiting pick-up by the rescue squads that served the hospital.

Passing through this outer vestibule, he entered into the rear hallway of the Emergency Department. To his left was the long rear hallway of the ER with access to three treatment rooms. It was a slow night, and for now, they were not occupied. The corridor in front of him led directly to the main desk, and a short hallway to his right led to the small addition containing the portable X-ray machine and CT scanner.

Da-Ved recalled a fitting scripture from the Psalmist. He now used it to model a prayer.

"Hear, O Lord, when I cry with my voice, have mercy also upon me. Hide not your face from me: put not your servant away in anger. You have been my help. Do not leave me, nor forsake me, O God. Show me the way, O Lord, and lead me in a plain path because of my enemies."[11]

Once again, the vague scent of brimstone wafted to his nostrils, and he tilted his head to locate its source. The foul odor seemed to be more pronounced to his left, manifesting from somewhere within one of the rear examination rooms. He marched down the hallway, passing the lunchroom's closed door as he headed towards a room in the more remote section of the emergency department.

*****

THE CORRIDOR

"Where is this place?" Frank Chamberlain wondered aloud. He'd been walking for some time, and the light at the end of the tunnel didn't appear to be any closer. Remembering the recent bout of severe chest pain and the fumbling struggle with his nitroglycerine pills, he thought, *Was that real or only a bad dream?*

Frank's mind raced as his imagination conjured up theory after theory of what was happening to him. One thing he did know: he hadn't felt this well in years. Gone was his angina and chronic shortness of breath. He no longer needed his eyeglasses, and his painfully arthritic joints strangely felt wonderful. He felt...energized. Now he was worried.

Something extraordinary has happened, he thought. *But what? Think, man! Reason it out. No! I don't dare. I can't.*

The more he tried to not think the unthinkable, the more his mind focused upon the one belief he was trying to avoid. But then... there it was. Somehow, his worn-out body had regained its youthful spring and vigor.

How? And where was he? How did he get into this strangely illuminated corridor? Finally, he could fight the thought no more and stopped walking.

He felt prickly all over as the full weight of his situation hit him.

"I must be dead," he said. "Oh, Lord, I must have died right there in the driveway."

*****

DECEMBER 25 – 2:50 AM
CHARITY'S EMERGENCY DEPARTMENT
LUNCHROOM

Nancy Fordice worked part-time in the hospital's housekeeping department for the last three years. She liked working the graveyard shift because the hospital was less busy at that time of day, and her supervisors left her alone as long as she completed her work. Besides, the night hours paid a nice shift differential.

Her lunch break was just about over, and Nancy put away the book of poetry she'd been reading. Taking the last gulp of lukewarm coffee, she grimaced and poured the rest into the sink.

Senior Paramedic Deborah Parker and her partner entered the small room, and she plunked herself down at one of the tables. "Hi, Nance. How are you doing tonight?" she asked.

"Not too bad. Outside of the fire department, being here, it's been a little slow tonight. I'm pretty much just going through the motions."

"Want a cup?" Deborah's partner asked as he poured himself a large cup of the stale black liquid.

"No thanks. One more cup, and I'll explode."

"Better be careful, Phil," Nancy quipped. "That coffee will turn you from a paramedic into one of your patients real quick."

He sniffed the pot ruefully. "That old?" he asked.

The housekeeper made a face and ran her finger across her throat in a slow cutting motion. "Give me a sec, and I'll brew you a fresh pot."

She rinsed out the rank coffee in the sink and prepared a fresh brew. "Good thing no one was hurt when the roof blew off the sally port tonight. I heard you guys were already out on a call."

"Yeah, that was lucky," Phil said. "We were tied up on an accident scene for about fifteen minutes, and then it took us another fifteen minutes to get all the release forms signed once the patients decided they didn't want to go to the hospital. Then we went for fuel. Glad we weren't needed here."

"Yeah," Nancy said, "it looks like the sally port to the psychiatric wing will be closed for a month or so, though. We heard the patient rooms are safe, but the roof is kaput."

Nancy ran clear water through the top of the brewer, and steaming black coffee immediately started to run out into the empty carafe below.

"There you go. It'll just be a minute or two."

The tired housekeeper returned to the sink and splashed cool water on her face. Pulling a paper towel from a nearby wall dispenser, she patted her eyes dry.

"I heard you guys were busy earlier tonight too. Dr. Reynolds said he lost a patient you brought in about 11:30. That's a shame."

Phil gave her the standard reply. "Yeah, but you know you can't win them all."

Nancy frowned. "I guess. I better get back to work before I fall asleep. Tomorrow's the big day, you know."

"Tomorrow?" Deborah said. "Check the calendar, girl! This morning is the big day."

She grinned good-naturedly. "Just think, in a few short hours, you can go home, and then your teenage kids and your husband will get up and ask you to make them a hearty Christmas breakfast. What a morning!"

"If anyone is going to be served breakfast this morning, it's going to be me!" Nancy said with a twinkle in her eye. "Catch you later. I gotta scoot."

*****

THE CORRIDOR

What can I do but continue to walk toward that light? Frank thought. He trudged on, ever moving towards the ambiguous radiance in the distance.

Eventually, the source of the light grew larger, and he found he was drawing near to what appeared to be two enormous iridescent doors of alabaster.

The radiance made him somewhat snow-blind, and he found it difficult to make out much more than a detail or two of the immense doorway. Forty yards from the end of the corridor, he caught a sudden shadow of movement as if something large had passed in front of a bright light. He stopped walking.

"Is someone there?" he called out.

"Yes, I am here," resonated a deep voice from somewhere up and in front of him.

Frank dropped to a low squat, his back and hands against the wall. "Who are you?" he asked. "Where is this place?"

"I am called Ne'tsach," the rich voice boomed backed, echoing off the stone walls. "I am the keeper of this gate."

"Ne-Nez...who?"

"Ne'tsach. I am the light you have been walking towards. You have arrived just outside one of His Majesty's twelve gates. I'm sorry, but I've been instructed to detain you here."

Frank stood, shielding his eyes from the bright light with raised hands. Peeking through his spread fingers, he questioned, "Gate? That's a gate? It looks like it's made out of marble or...or...some sort of seashell. No! A huge pearl!"

"Yes. You're quite perceptive, Franklin. I'm sorry, may I call you Franklin? Or do you prefer Mr. Chamberlain?"

"You...know my name?"

"Oh, yes, I have been expecting you and your companion for some time now. I must say, it appears that His Majesty has made a change of plans concerning you."

"Where are you?" Frank asked. "Are you in a guard tower or something? You sound like you're up high. Can you turn off that light? I can't see you. And what do you mean companion?"

"All in good time, Franklin. Ah! I see your escort has arrived."

The sound of heavy footsteps thudding close behind him made Frank shudder, and his shoulders scrunched up into his scrawny neck. He pivoted stiffly at the waist to behold two of the largest feet he'd ever seen.

His eyes slowly followed the huge feet upward...up...to two colossal coal-black tree trunks...up...to two massive mahogany shoulders...up...to stare at the most genteel face he had ever seen. Frank gasped as it spoke.

"Fear not, Franklin. I am Ganan. I am your champion."

Frank fainted.

Time continued to pass slowly on Earth as Frank lay supine on the stone floor, but at the gate, there was no semblance of the passage of time.

Ganan stared at Frank lying on the floor. "Why do these feeble mortals pass out every time a Guardian reveals his presence to them? I've been with this one through thick and thin for over seventy years, and the first time he sees me, he swoons like a silly school girl."

"Maybe you should take that as a hint," Ne'tsach taunted. "You are one large ugly dude."

Ganan threw his arms overhead. "Hey! Don't blame me! I can't help it if their constitutions are so fragile. The strength of a mortal pours out like water."

Ganan's height was only half that of Ne'tsach's, but he was still a formidable looking warrior. His handsome face was the color of deep ebony as was his shortly cropped beard. A thick mane of raven-black curls was held in check by a braided cord stretched across his forehead. Tied behind his head, the cord hung low down his wide back.

A pair of monumental wings containing the seven colors of the rainbow cascaded from his back to the floor like a royal mantle, and he wore a loose knee-length blue skirt of coarse fabric fastened at his waist by a gold belt.

Ne'tsach looked sideways at his grinning friend and said, "Aren't you the sensitive one?"

"Oh sure, mock me," Ganan said. "You're twice my size, but you remain hidden within the aura that fills this holy place. No one can see *you*.

Come to think of it, Miyka'el probably won't ever let you manifest yourself physically on Earth in fear that your appearance would send everyone here prematurely."

Ne'tsach's wide grin evaporated. "I think it's about time we wake the human, don't you?"

Now it was Ganan's turn to grin. "Sure, if you say so."

Turning his attention to the unresponsive figure lying on the floor, Ganan gently took him by the arm. "Wake up, Franklin. Wake up."

As if on cue, Frank groggily rolled to one side and looked up into Ganan's gentle eyes. He tried to speak, but his lips couldn't form the words.

Ganan raised a hand and spoke compassionately. "Fear not, Franklin. Peace be unto you. Be strong. Yes, strong, for you are greatly beloved by God."

The gentle giant reached down and took the frail mortal by the hand, helping him to his feet. At the touch of the dark-skinned warrior, Frank felt strength returning to his limbs, and his lips parted, allowing him to speak.

"Wh-Wh-Why—"

"Why are you here?" Ganan said the words for him softly.

Frank nodded.

"Don't be afraid, Franklin, for I have been with you since your birth."

Discerning Frank's sudden understanding, he added, "Yes, I am an angel. I am *your* angel. And I have something wonderful to tell you."

"My...My—" Frank fell to his hands and knees once again.

Ganan looked at Ne'tsach and rolled his eyes.

"*My* angel?" Frank whispered. "Angels? Like in the Bible?"

Ganan stroked his prodigious chin. "Uh, Franklin, we need to talk. And, yes, angels, just like in the Bible. But calm yourself. Have courage, for you are in the midst of a great struggle. Be not afraid of the Evil One nor of all the multitude that is with him, for there be more with us than with him. With Lucifer are Death and the Grave, but with you is the Lord our God to help you and to fight your battles."

"What...ah...do you want of me?"

"Are you aware that you have passed over?" Ganan asked. "I mean, from mortal life into eternity?"

Frank's face was awash with bewilderment. "No. I mean—yes. I mean—oh, I don't know what I mean."

"I can assure you, Franklin. Your weak heart failed you several hours ago, and you died. Your physical body lies on a table in a small hospital far away. But you've served God well through the years, and he wishes to extend to you and those who are faithfully praying for you a special gift. I have been granted the privilege of informing you that today is a day of great blessing for you. There has not been a day like this for two millennia, and the Lord would like you to take an active part in His master plan."

Frank rose to his feet. "What does He want me to do?"

"First you need to understand the systematic destruction of humanity has been Lucifer's goal since that first day he slithered into the garden. The Prince of Darkness has come to your planet to steal, kill, and destroy. But though he meant your death as evil against you and your family, God meant it unto good. To allow it to pass, as it is this day, to save many people by your testimony. His Majesty wishes that you return to Earth to be an example and a living witness to His Power and Glory. This will be your greatest gift to Him."

"But how? How do I—"

Frank stopped in mid-sentence as the huge doors behind him opened slowly, flooding the already luminescent corridor with an impossible brightness. The swarthy warrior answered Frank's unfinished question with a curt nod of his head. With eyes fixed on the figure framed in the doorway, Ganan bent over and whispered into Frank's ear, "Why don't you...ask Him?"

Both Guardians reverently knelt to one knee, bowing their heads low. Together, they paid homage to the being that had just entered through the gate.

"My Lord!"

*****

DECEMBER 25 – 3:00 AM
CHARITY'S EMERGENCY DEPARTMENT

Pushing her laundry cart down the hallway, Nancy headed to the scrub room to pick up the soiled linen for the laundry service.

Parking the cart just outside the room, she entered and dragged a heavy bag of laundry into the hallway. She hefted it into the cart and returned to pick up a second one.

She flinched as a sudden flash of light poured through the partially opened door of the nearby cast room.

"Uhhh!"

Nancy dropped the laundry bag and walked to the doorway. Tentatively, she reached out to knock softly upon the doorjamb.

"Hello?" she called out. When no answer came, she knocked again, this time on the door and a bit harder. The door swung open a little wider.

She called out again. "Hello? Is everything all right?"

Slowly, she pushed the door completely open and noticed that the wall switch was still in the off position.

"That's strange," she murmured. "How could the bulb blow if the switch is off?"

Flipping the switch up, a fluorescent ceiling light hummed and flickered on. She peeked in to observe what appeared to be the lifeless form of someone laying supine on a gurney covered by a white sheet. Nancy shook her head and murmured a halfhearted prayer.

As if he was simply enjoying a quiet afternoon nap, Frank gasped and started to breathe with snoring respirations.

"Ooooh!" Nancy cried out, sprinting from the room, into the hallway, and headlong down the corridor to the lunchroom. The lunchroom door flew open, banging noisily into the wall.

"Criminy!" Phil cussed, dropping a cup of hot coffee into his lap. He scrambled to his feet as the ashen-faced housekeeper clawed her way into the room.

"What's wrong, Nan?" Deborah asked. "You look like you've seen a ghost."

"That's not too far from it! Quick! Where is Dr. Reynolds?"

"I don't know. The last time I saw him, he was in his office. What—"

Nancy didn't wait for her question. Proceeding to the main desk quickly, she found the physician reviewing paperwork.

"Dr. Reynolds!" she cried out. "Come quick!"

Peering over the bifocals perched at the end of his nose, he looked up to see the frantic woman motioning to him with a wave of her hand.

"What's this all about?" he asked. By now, the ER staff and paramedics had gathered around the work station to see what was causing all the commotion.

"Just follow me," Nancy pleaded. "Quickly! P-l-e-a-s-e-!"

*****

DECEMBER 25 – 3:00 AM
THE CHAPEL

The collection of mourners congregating in the chapel soon swelled to over a hundred. The chapel doors were propped open, and the emerging crowd spilled out into the hallway. Almost half of the membership of Edna Chamberlain's church had come to the hospital to observe Christmas Eve services and to pray with her at the hospital.

Even under these sad circumstances, hymns of praise and thanksgiving coursed from the chapel's sanctuary out into the hallway where the music drifted down the corridor towards the Emergency Department. One by one, curious employees began to wander down the corridor to see just what was being celebrated in the chapel at this time of night. The throng continued to grow.

Edna's pastor, Charles Deplure, took the opportunity to preach a sermon on the birth of the Christ child and the eventual defeat of death and the grave. Under the circumstances, there wasn't a dry eye in the house.

Finally, Kenneth whispered into his mother's ear, "Time to go say goodbye to Dad, Mother. Carol and the boys are waiting for us at home."

The frail woman looked up into her son's eyes. Her weary face was etched with deep lines of fatigue, but strangely, it also possessed a mark of peace and contentment. Never ceasing, the saints continued with the last stanza of a Christmas hymn they were singing as she departed.

> Saints before the altar bending, Watching long in hope
> and fear, Suddenly the Lord, descending,
> in his temple shall ap-pear: Come and worship,
> come and worship, Worship Christ, the newborn King![12]

*****

DECEMBER 25 – 3:10 AM
CHARITY HOSPITAL'S EMERGENCY
DEPARTMENT

"Will everyone please go back to work while I see what is troubling Nancy?" Dr. Reynolds entreated the gathering ER staff. As they dispersed, Dr. Reynolds caught up to Nancy and took her firmly by the arm.

"Now what is this all about, Nance?" he asked.

"You know that man you pronounced earlier tonight?" she asked, wringing her hands.

"Yeah, so?" Dr. Reynolds asked.

Pulling him towards the cast room, she said, "You're not going to believe this, but...well...he's breathing again!"

*****

Pastor Deplure wrapped his arms around Edna, holding her close as he reluctantly escorted her and her son to the emergency room. He cautioned them to remain in the outer waiting room while he went to the desk to inquire as to where Frank's body lay.

It troubled him to see that Edna seemed to be taking things in stride so well. He hoped that she wasn't in a state of denial. His experience in these matters was that it was important for the family to visit a brief time with the deceased, if possible, in order for them to ease into the grieving process.

There would be hard days ahead for Edna, but he knew that she could get through them with the help of her family. The church would be there for her also, but there would be a time when she would have to eventually walk this dark and painful path alone. This opportunity to say goodbye to her husband would be of immeasurable value to her in the months ahead. He was sure of that.

Pastor Deplure approached the main desk and addressed the recordkeeper sitting at her workstation.

"Excuse me, Miss. I have the Chamberlain family out in the waiting room. Would it be all right to bring them back to visit Mr. Chamberlain's body now?"

The young woman looked up, biting her quivering lower lip. "Just a second. I'll check," she said, reaching for the phone. She hit the intercom button and, with a faltering voice, spoke into the phone's receiver.

"D-Dr. Reynolds? The Chamberlain family is here."

The lowered tone of someone talking buzzed in her ear.

"Yes. Yes, they're right outside. Right away." She looked up. "You can go in now, Pastor."

The clergyman walked to the ER's entrance doors to motion to the Chamberlain family to enter.

Ken escorted his mother through the doors to the main desk. The recordkeeper stood and said, "Dr. Reynolds will be with you shortly." Her eyes were moist, and she dabbed at them with a tissue.

As if they'd been expecting the Chamberlain family's arrival, several nurses stopped working and came to the main desk where they whispered together in hushed tones. The secretary at the admitting desk also seemed to find the need to leave her desk to walk into the emergency department. Everyone seemed to be staring at the grieving trio. Someone sobbed and started to weep quietly.

Sensing something amiss, Pastor Deplure's eyes darted about the hallway. Catching Ken's eyes, it was obvious that he too sensed something unnatural.

Dr. Reynolds walked out of the cast room at the far end of the hallway, followed closely by Nancy and the two paramedics. Removing his spectacles, the physician swiped at his eyes with a coat sleeve and walked briskly to the front desk where the Chamberlains waited.

Unsure of their role in this situation, Nancy motioned for Phil and Deborah not to follow. Obediently, they remained with her just outside the cast room doorway.

"Mrs. Chamberlain. Mrs. Chamberlain. I-I don't know just how to say this, so—"

The room immediately grew quiet as a solitary figure walked out of the cast room. It remained partially concealed behind Phil's rather large physique.

"Looking for me?" a familiar voice floated eerily down the hallway.

Absolute astonishment flooded across Pastor Deplure's face, and he grabbed the desk's countertop to steady himself.

Kenneth groaned and held his mother close. Edna sobbed for joy.

A tearful reunion was quickly followed by the emergency room staff mobbing the Chamberlain family. The ER wing of the hospital burst into pandemonium as the dying strains of a familiar hymn floated once again into the ER from the chapel hallway.

> Saints before the altar bending, Watching long in hope
> and fear, Suddenly the Lord, descending,
> in his temple shall appear: Come and worship,
> come and worship, Worship Christ, the newborn King![13]

All the while, Edna Chamberlain blissfully embraced the small book she had once clung to so desperately.

Strengthen the weak hands, and make firm the feeble knees.
Say to those who have an anxious heart, "Be strong; fear
not! Behold, your God will come with vengeance, with
the recompense of God. He will come and save you."
Then the eyes of the blind shall be opened, and the ears
of the deaf unstopped; then shall the lame man leap like a
deer, and the tongue of the mute sing for joy. For waters
break forth in the wilderness and streams in the desert.

—Isaiah 35:3–6 (ESV)

CHAPTER TWENTY

The Road Home

DECEMBER 25 – 3:55 AM
CHARITY HOSPITAL'S CHAPEL ROOF

Within moments of delivering the restorative blessing to Frank Chamberlain's lifeless body in the cast room, a familiar winged figure whisked Da-Ved away to the pinnacle of the hospital's chapel. The sun hadn't risen yet, and the pale streetlights revealed a changing weather pattern.

"Wow!" Da-Ved said. "You can see the whole valley from up here."

Aram furled his wings. "Yeah, I thought you'd like the view."

The heavenly Host had assembled at the eastern edge of town and were engaging the demonic forces recently encamped within the surrounding countryside. A multitude of eerie illuminations hurtled across the sky and scurried about the hillsides surrounding the small town. They seemed to chase each other as if playing a game of tag, but in fact, spiritual warfare was spilling over from a dimension of the supernatural into Earth's physical atmosphere.

The amount of power generated by these extradimensional combatants began to affect local climatic conditions, and the blinding snowstorm steadily abated as the air temperature began to climb.

Da-Ved grinned at the sight of his hulking escort. "I've come to expect the unexpected of you, Aram. But just where did you come from?"

"I've been keeping my eye on you all night, Da-Ved. But it wouldn't do to let our adversary find us together until you completed your mission. Let's just say, I've been around."

"Really? I've been a bit busy. I hadn't noticed," Da-Ved said with a wry smile.

"And for your information, my small wingless friend, it looks like we finally have the rebels on the run."

Da-Ved turned his gaze back to the city. "I'll say. This will be a day long remembered."

He unbuttoned his coat and stuffed his watch cap in a deep pocket. Flapping the coat's large lapels, he asked, "Is it just me or is it getting warmer?"

"Tsk-tsk. What's the matter, Da-Ved? Can't you take the heat of a good battle anymore?"

Striking a pose. Da-Ved laughed and said, "Not in this disguise. I can't wait to get my wings back. I'm getting tired of being earthbound. It's too confining. But where have all our friends gone?"

"If you mean Iyr and Gedeón, they've returned to their posts within the hospital."

Scanning the horizon, Da-Ved asked, "What about the others? Where's Shamar?"

The vague outline of an expanding black rain cloud at the distant edge of the city met his eyes. Within the whirling debris caught in the storm's turbulence was a swarm of angels and demons locked in immortal combat. A sudden outburst of radiant energy flared across the sky, and the rumblings of the distant battle rolled in waves across the valley sounding like thunder.

Cupping an ear, Aram said, "Do you hear that, Da-Ved? Miyka'el has finally allowed us to commit our troops here. And this is Shamar's city! You can bet he's somewhere in the middle of that swirling maelstrom."

"Why? What's happening over there?"

"Lucifer's amassed his European reinforcements and is attempting a second attack on the city. Too bad for them. It's not like you didn't warn them."

Da-Ved's face screwed into a question mark. "A *second* attack? Then what are you doing here? Shouldn't you be leading our forces?"

"No, my task is to provide security to you, not to engage with the enemy—unless you're threatened, that is. But that's not important now. You should be moving on. Do I drop you somewhere? Or should I take you to the Mibtsar?"

Da-Ved looked skyward. "The Mibtsar? No, I don't think so. Sometimes it's hard to know what to do. As angels, we've always operated strictly by obedience. I mean, His Majesty commands us to do something, and we just carry out His orders. But as His messenger, I've had to learn to rely on my knowledge of scripture and to operate more by faith and trust."

Snapping his fingers, Aram said, "Ah! I suppose that's what it must be like for the humans."

"Yeah, I guess so. And believe me, at times, it can be a little confusing. It's tough operating by faith alone."

"Your work is finished here then?"

Looking off into the distance, Da-Ved said, "I...I thought it was until just a few moments ago. I'm not so sure now. I have this feeling. Besides, I still have the key that was given to me."

"As do I," Aram said, pulling a cord from around his thick neck. The key was still attached.

Da-Ved sighed. "So I guess I'm not done with it then. No. I think I need to walk through the city one last time. It's like I've overlooked something...or somebody. I can't put my finger on it."

Aram leaned out to scan the eastern horizon. "The sun will be up in a little while. Where would you like to go?"

"Can you take me back to Job's House? I think I'll be able to find my way from there."

"Sure, no problem. But, remember, Lucifer has a score to settle with us. After this defeat tonight, he'll be madder than ever. Don't drop your guard for a moment."

*****

267

DECEMBER 25 – 6:30 AM
JOB, CALIFORNIA – THE ALLEY

Blue light from the rotating beacon of a police car bounced surreally throughout the alley as it reflected off the building's dingy windows. A white spotlight also played about as it probed the darker recesses of the narrow street.

A second patrol car pulled in behind the first. Its driver got out and approached the officer using the spotlight.

"You sure this is the right alley, Sarge?"

"Yeah. I'm sure. Dispatch said the caller was too spooked to go downstairs to look, but they said she could see a body lying in the street back here. I think her window is right over the—Yep! See her? She's waving back at us. To your left, the third window up."

"She's pointing down at something behind that dumpster."

"Move the light a little to the right, Sarge. That's it. Hold it right there a minute. Yeah. I think I see something. Looks like a body. C'mon. Let's take a look."

"Wait a minute. Let me call it in first. Car 11-21 to station."

"Go ahead, 11-21."

"Car 11-22 and I will be checking the alley at Fulton and Silver."

"Ten-four, 11-21."

*****

DECEMBER 25 – 6:45 AM
JOB, CALIFORNIA—THE KING RESIDENCE

Ruby King rolled to her side to check her alarm clock and flopped back to stare at the shadowy bedroom ceiling. Pulling a spare pillow to her chest, she savored the quiet stillness of the early morning she knew was soon to disappear. It wouldn't be long before her two boys would scurry into her bedroom to wake her for their traditional Christmas morning revelry.

She inhaled deeply. The pillow was a poor substitute for her husband, Martin, who deployed to Europe with the Army's 101st Aviation Brigade just before the Thanksgiving holiday.

This is it, she thought. *This is the last time. No more separations after this. Thank you, Lord, for retirement. It can't come soon enough!*

Her eyes started to mist over, which angered her. *No! I won't cave into emotion. Husband or not, this day is going to be a good day. I've got two boys to think about, and I'm not going to mope about the house during the holidays.*

Ruby had two sons. Thurman was almost fifteen, tall and athletic. She was sure he'd love the brand-new basketball waiting for him under the tree in the living room. Like his father, he lived and breathed the sport, and some said he was sure to win a spot on the high school team next year as a freshman. The middle-school coach tagged him with a nickname, T-man, and his teammates quickly shortened it to T. The new name stuck.

Nathan, ten, was another story. He was as smart as Thurman was athletic but born with spina bifida, struggled daily with knee-length leg braces, Lofstrand crutches, and at times, a wheelchair.

At thirty-nine, Ruby's second pregnancy had been at the practical end of her childbearing years and unexpected. She wiped her eyes as she recalled the day her obstetrician informed her that the lower end of her child's spinal canal was exposed outside of his body and the nerve-endings for his legs were compromised.

Ruby shut her eyes and prayed silently. *I know Nathan wants to be rough and tumble, Lord, but I'm afraid for him. Afraid the older boys in the neighborhood will hurt him. Not intentionally, Lord, but you know how boys are. Please let him be satisfied with the telescope and chess set and not be too disappointed. I just couldn't get him the basketball he wanted. And please see that my Marty is safe and well today. Turn not your face from him, but hold him securely in your hands and bring him back home safely to us soon.*

And thank you for my Thurman. He's such a special young man. He's so good to Nathan and me. Especially Nathan. He watches over him without babying him. Thank you for that.

Lord? If I could ask just one thing for myself today, please make this day a special day for Nathan. It would mean so much to me. I mean, it's already special, of course. I am so thankful that you sent your Son to us.

Oh, you know what I'm trying to say. But I do pray that Nathan learns to see his limitations without them destroying his spirit. He's kind and gentle. I don't want to see his feelings hurt or his spirit crushed. Please, Lord, if you could send something or someone across his path today to make this a day he won't forget. Just show him that you love him.

Thank you, Lord. As always, I love you. Amen.

*****

DECEMBER 25 – 6:45 AM
JOB, CALIFORNIA – THE WATER TOWER

A tall ungainly shape appeared below them, and Da-Ved recognized the old water tower from earlier in the evening. Seconds later, they arrived at Job's House, and Aram flew at treetop level to survey the area.

"Looks good, Aram. Pick a spot. Anywhere will do."

Aram glided earthward and deposited Da-Ved gently onto a nearby sidewalk.

"Here you go, Da-Ved. I have to check in with Miyka'el at the Mibtsar, but I'll continue to monitor your progress for the rest of the day. Trust me, you won't be alone."

"Thanks, Aram. I'm sure this is where I'm to begin my journey back home."

"All right, Da-Ved, but—"

Da-Ved threw his hands up in the air. "I know. *I know!*"

Scowling, Aram asked humorlessly, "What? What was I going to say?"

"Be careful?"

"Yeah, Da-Ved," Aram replied soberly. "Be careful. Be *very* careful."

*****

DECEMBER 25 – 07:00 AM
JOB, CALIFORNIA – THE KING RESIDENCE

A small hand tugged at Ruby King's sleeve.

"Mom! Mom! C'mon, you sleepyhead! It's Christmas morning!"

Ruby pulled the heavy comforter over her head and secretly smiled. Lowering her voice, she pretended to scold her youngest son. "Nathan! It's still dark out. Go back to bed and let me sleep."

"Aw, Mom! T's up already and checking out everything. You have to get up!"

Ruby pretended to roll away from her small tormentor, then without warning, unleashed her ambush. Reaching out from under the covers, she grabbed him by his pajama tops and pulled him briskly but gently from his wheelchair back under the blankets.

Squeals of muffled laughter spilled out from under the covers as she smothered him with kisses.

"Hahahahahaha! Stop! Stop! Mom! Stop!"

His arms flailed about as he tried to squirm his way away from her.

Thurman's adolescent voice cackled from the doorway. "Hey, you guys! What's going on in there?"

With two bounding steps, he was upon them attacking them through the heavy bed covers. He took advantage of their inability to fight back and tickled them to tears.

Throwing off the covers, Ruby finally called a truce. "Boys! Boys! Okay, you win! You win! Let me get my robe on, and then let's see what Santa brought us!"

Nathan screeched with delight, "Yeeaaaaaay!"

*****

DECEMBER 25 – 7:00 AM
JOB, CALIFORNIA – JOB'S HOUSE

Da-Ved watched Aram disappear into the early morning sky. The wind had tapered off, and the air temperature was growing warmer. He continued to travel eastward while searching for a sign or direction on where to go. An hour later, he stopped walking.

I'm lost, he thought.

He raised his eyes and spoke. "Your Majesty, you've sent your angels to this planet this day with a great anointing. I hope that what we've accomplished has been pleasing to you. But I feel I've left something undone, and I fear my time is almost gone. If you have another person who you want me to bless, could you please direct my feet to their location? Are you not Jehovah-Rophe? Jehovah who heals? Surely, you have brought healing to the bitter waters of this small community today.

"As I study the landscape, I find I am caught in a shallow valley. My escort informs me that I should be wary, that I am being hunted by the great hunter of lost souls and fallen angels, he who once was your anointed Cherub—Lucifer.

"Please be my Jehovah-Rohi now. Jehovah, my shepherd, guide my feet upon your path. Help me find my way, Lord."

As if in answer to Da-Ved's request, melting snow fell from a nearby street sign, revealing the street names. To his delight, he discovered that he was approaching the intersection of Hobb's Lane and King's Pathway.

"Not much of a choice there," he said to himself. "The King's Pathway it is."

*****

DECEMBER 25 – 8:30 AM
1343 KINGS PATHWAY – JOB, CALIFORNIA
THE KING RESIDENCE

Ping! Ping! Ping! Ping! Ping! Ping!

The echoes of Thurman dribbling his new basketball reverberated up and down the street.

"Mom! I'm going out with T and the rest of the guys. See ya later!"

"Nathan! You can't go outside until you get a hat and coat on. Do you want to catch your death of cold?"

"Aw, the other guys aren't wearing any hats, and besides, it's getting warmer now. See? The snow's all melting."

Using her sternest parental voice, Ruby chastised her youngest son, "I don't care what the other boys are wearing. You get a hat on, young man, or you don't go outside! And stay on the sidewalk. The street's no place for you."

Nathan grabbed his wool cap and coat from the closet and murmured a subdued, "Yes'm."

Ruby heard the front door open.

"Now where did you say you were going?"

"Just down the street. To Quincy's house. T said I could come down and watch. The guys are gonna play some ball."

Her voice softened. "Okay, honey, but are you sure you're just going to watch? The last time they let you play, one of your braces came apart. Those boys play too rough."

"I'll be careful this time, Mom. I promise. *Please?*"

Ruby nodded her consent, and the door closed behind him. Observing from the front window, she watched him make his way to the front gate and groaned as he wrestled with the gate's latch with one hand while holding onto his crutches with the other. After a brief struggle, it gave way, and he swung his legs through the opening. The gate swung shut behind him with a bang, and he started to hobble towards the street. Just then, a slightly built dark-haired stranger approached the boy from the west. Squatting down to Nathan's eye level, the man engaged the youngster in an animated conversation.

Instantly, Ruby's motherly instincts shifted into hyperdrive, and she bolted for the front door. Readying herself for a physical confrontation, she started outside but then remembered her early morning prayers. She hesitated, then backed into the house, closing the door behind her. She thought, *What if?*

Slowly, she opened the door again to see Nathan wave to the man as he departed. A feeling of relief flooded over her, but her instincts still sensed something out of order. Nathan seemed different... somehow.

273

"Nathan?" she called as she walked out onto the stoop. "What did he want?"

Nathan only giggled and hung his crutches on the fence.

"Nath—" She started to yell when he ducked down to disappear behind the fence and bushes.

"Nathan—David—King!" she scolded. "You had better not bang those crutches up, young man! You know that—"

He bobbed back into her sight. He was laughing.

"Young man, just what—"

Both leg braces came sailing over the fence towards her to land akimbo in the front yard. His hands steadied himself upon the fence while his legs took his full weight for the first time in his life.

"*Nathan!*" Ruby screamed. She started out the door to him.

"Stay there! I'll come get you—"

"Yippeeee!"

Ruby cupped her hands to her mouth and let out a gasp as he ran down the street.

"YIPPEEE! T! LOOK-ET ME! I CAN PLAY BALL!"

Ruby King sank slowly against the door to sit upon her front stoop. Cradling her bent legs in her arms, she rocked back and forth and laughed…and cried.

For if God spared not the angels that sinned, but cast
them down to hell, and delivered them into chains
of darkness, to be reserved unto judgment.

—2 Peter 2:4 (KJV)

And I saw an angel come down from heaven, having the
key of the bottomless pit and a great chain in his hand. And
he laid hold on the dragon, that old serpent, which is the
Devil, and Satan, and bound him for a thousand years.
And cast him into the bottomless pit and shut him up,
and set a seal upon him, that he should deceive the nations
no more till, the thousand years should be fulfilled:
and after that he must be loosed a little season.

—Revelation 20:1–3 (KJV)

CHAPTER TWENTY-ONE

Warriors

DECEMBER 25 – 08:40 AM
JOB, CALIFORNIA

A wide smile spread across Da-Ved's face when Nathan pitched his leg braces over the fence and ran down the street to join his friends. Resuming his journey through the city, Da-Ved whispered, "Thank you, Lord. You certainly revealed a taste of your power and grace to this community today. I only hope they appreciate the blessings you poured out for them. They were amazing."

He checked the cord around his neck and discovered that the key had vanished. Scratching his head, he thought, *If my mission is completed, why am I still here? Lord? Unless you have something else for me to do, I'm going to retrace my steps back to where I started yesterday.*

Following the winding road out of the valley, he came to the end of the city limits. The holiday traffic was sparse, and he walked along for another hour without seeing a single car. At last, he came to the rugged isolated section of highway where he'd first descended into Job less than twenty-four hours earlier. As he skirted the outer boundary of a sharp curve, the trees and bushes a few yards from the roadway started to whip about. Feeling no wind, he paused to assess the situation.

I'm so close. Gotta be careful. Don't want to fall into an ambush now.

Darting across the road and into the woods, he came to a clearing where a fallen tree beckoned him to sit and rest among its denuded branches. "Might as well," he said aloud. "I think I've come to the end of the trail."

"That you have, Da-Ved! That you have," boomed a loud voice from somewhere on the hillside above him.

A thicket of scrub pine and underbrush a few yards above the clearing began to glow with a ruddy radiance, and something heavy started to crash awkwardly through the brambles as it descended. Moments later, Lucifer revealed his presence by strolling through a small stand of pine trees to accompany Da-Ved who sprang nimbly to his feet.

The powerful Cherub appeared relaxed, his edged weapon safely sheathed within its scabbard. Proffering his empty hands, he tried to calm the smaller angel. "Whoa there, Da-Ved! Hang on. I just want to talk to you."

Da-Ved quickly spun about, looking for Lucifer's ever-present minions.

"Rest assured, Guardian, we'll be left alone...for now. My troops are nearby but have orders to not interfere."

Da-Ved retook his seat on the fallen tree, his back resting against a large upright branch. His tone became sarcastic. "What would the mighty Lucifer want to talk to me about?"

Lucifer smiled cagily. "Oh, I don't know. Pick a subject. How about...loyalty?"

"Loyalty?" Da-Ved asked with a pained look on his face. "What would *you* know about loyalty?"

"Don't get me wrong, Da-Ved. Loyalty is a fine quality. I admire it, but—"

"But what?" the small angel asked.

"Mmmm, how can I put this delicately? A thing like that can be taken to extremes. I mean, I hate it when I see true talent like yours going to waste. Haven't you ever wondered what it would be like to be out from under His yoke? Wouldn't you like to be your own free moral agent? For *you* to decide what's right or wrong?"

Da-Ved shifted in his seat. "And just what would that give me?" he asked.

"Why, complete freedom, of course. Free to be whatever you want to be. To obtain whatever it is you want to obtain. To be free from your god. To be your own being."

"What you really mean is to be free to work for you. Isn't that what you're driving at?"

Lucifer broke into a self-conscious grin. "Oh, sure. Sure! If you wish."

He cut through the clearing, clumsily knocking over two small trees, and sat upon the ground. Even with knees bent, he still towered over the smaller angel. Picking up a fallen limb, he casually peeled the bark from the smaller branch as he talked.

"But only if that's what you want, Da-Ved. There's no hard sell here. I only want you with me if that is what you truly wish. I just thought an angel with your natural flair for leadership could go far in my organization. You can't possibly imagine the energy—the knowledge—the wealth and power we acquire over time."

Da-Ved looked up with pity in his eyes. "But what of evil? And what of the horrible separation that happens when you no longer serve Him."

A dark cloud rolled across the fallen Cherub's face. "We serve ourselves!" he said with disgust.

Quickly recovering, Lucifer's face softened with a disarming smile. "You can still do good works serving me, Da-Ved, if that is what you truly want. And I would give you unlimited authority to do as you will. There would be no restrictions. None whatsoever. Think of it! Think of the good you could do in your name! No! Better yet, think of the good you could do in *my* name!"

Da-Ved studied Lucifer's face closely. "To what end? For what purpose?"

"For what purpose?" Lucifer scoffed. "Why, to receive the goodwill of all mankind. That's all I want. What did you think I want—"

A new tack came to the fallen Cherub's mind. "Oh, yes," he purred. "That's right. I'm afraid your boss has portrayed me in a rather bad light. You know, I'm not as bad as he says I am. I only wish to help others and to receive my due. Is that so hard to understand?"

"Don't you mean that what you desire is for all men *and* angels to worship you?"

"Would that be so bad? When I think of what I could do for humanity, it would be small compensation indeed. After all, I do rule here. And this *is…my…kingdom.*"

He waved a large hand across the horizon, and the nations of the world appeared before them in a sweeping panoramic vision.

"Look, Da-Ved. Look at the world that awaits you if you will but kneel to me. I'll give you authority over all you see here. Think of it! What you could build. If you want to help the humans, this is your chance. With your knowledge of Scripture and the key you possess, you could do anything, be anything. Together, we could rule the world…benevolently, if you like. You could wipe out sickness, hunger, poverty. The need for war would disappear. You could bring peace to this tired old planet. Why, you could finally build *his* kingdom on Earth. Isn't that what you want? Isn't that what…*he*…would want?"

"And what would you demand in return?" Da-Ved said with a scowl.

"Why, I just told you. Worship me. Bend your knee and join us. I'm told you have many old friends here. You'll be eagerly welcomed on this planet."

"The more the pity that those who were once my friends chose to align themselves with you. They made a fool's bargain. No, your price is too high. I'm not going to join you or your rebel cause. And, by the way, you need to work on your moth-eaten tactics. You've tried this ruse once before, remember? With His Majesty? In the Judean wilderness?"

"You disappoint me, Da-Ved. I thought you had more sense than this. Very well then. I only require one thing from you."

"And what would that be?"

"That key you're wearing around your neck. It's mine. Give it to me, and you can go in peace."

"Sorry," Da-Ved said with an impish smile, "it's not mine to give you. It's only a small copy of a larger key anyway. That's the one you seek. The key I had only extended His authority to me for a short time. It's gone now. I no longer have it."

Lucifer licked his lips hungrily. "Then you know where the true key is? Tell me!"

"The Redeemer has it," Da-Ved said. He suppressed the sudden urge to laugh. "Isn't He the rightful heir? Yeshua?"

Lucifer's voice became icy, but his face flushed with anger. "Rightful heir...ugh! The Nazarene is no heir! He's nothing but a gatecrasher and a grave robber! I'm so *tired* of hearing that name! Small one, do not trifle with me. If you can't give me the key, then I'll have to take my revenge upon you. Guards! Seize him!"

Several large demons immediately materialized at the edges of the clearing encircling them. Lucifer pulled his blade from its sheath and tossed the scabbard aside. As he advanced, a large shadow floated across the terrain, causing all in the clearing to look up. Lucifer used the misdirection to begin his attack and lunged at Da-Ved.

Aram swooped in to deflect the blow. His longsword cut a searing arc through the air, and a fountain of sparks cascaded from the impact of the two celestial blades. At the same time, his aerial acrobatics placed him in position to pull Da-Ved out of harm's way. The big Guardian landed hard, causing the nearby vegetation to sway, and a knee-high dust cloud floated up from the ground.

Lucifer's sword was honed to a keen edge, and he found it buried deep within the dead tree that Da-Ved was sitting on only seconds before. He extricated the blade without effort and, with a single blow, hacked the large tree in two. Effortlessly, he kicked it from the clearing.

"Good to see you, Aram. Nice of you to drop in. You've saved me the trouble of hunting for you later."

As Lucifer raised his sword, a large demon approached to whisper something to his ear. Lucifer took a step back, looking closely at Aram. A bemused expression came over his face, and he lowered his weapon.

Aram appeared to be normally attired, except for the key hanging from his neck and a heavy silver chain wrapped several times around his waist. The chain's sterling links shimmered in the late morning sunlight.

"Ha! Ha! I see something new has been added, Aram," Lucifer said in a mocking tone. "Did you lose your belt?"

Aram's voice dripped with sarcasm. "No, your worship. His Majesty has fashioned a special necklace and bracelets just for you. I've been given the responsibility to see that you wear them in style. Would you like to try them on now?"

Lucifer backed away cautiously. "Be careful, my muscular friend. Your insolence may get you into more trouble than you can possibly imagine. I can dispatch you into the pit with a simple caress of my serpentine blade or...I can absorb you right here and now. What shall it be?" He flaunted his sharpened teeth for emphasis.

"Ah! Yes, my lord!" Aram said. "Lord of the flies, that is. At one time, you may have bested me in combat, but I have recently been anointed for a special purpose. His Majesty has given me authority over all warfare on this planet, and he wishes me to pay particular attention to this town...and to you.

"Besides, the saints here have amplified our power here exponentially. I am only awaiting His Majesty's order, and when it comes, you and your minions are history. But for now, I will not allow you to harm a friend. I have come for Da-Ved. You can't have him."

"Your words intrigue me, Aram. But I'm not easily chased from my prey. Why should I believe you?"

"Because I'm not one of your toadies. I'm a servant of the true King. And you know an angel in His Majesty's service will not speak falsely."

Lucifer's cruel eyes flattened into slits, his mouth hardened, and the crystals mounted within the occult symbols on his necklace started to glow with his anger. "What's this about a chain? What chain? There's nothing in the Scriptures about any chain! You're making it up to unnerve my troops. Demons! Don't listen to this drivel!"

Aram set his jaw. "You know the Scriptures as well as anyone, Lucifer. The chain is foretold!"

A low murmur started up among the assembled bodyguards, and a small scuffle broke out within their ranks. Sensing their trepidation, Lucifer scolded them.

"Rubbish! It's all myths and lies! You can't believe this nonsense! If Jehovah had dominion here, don't you think he'd have acted upon it by now? *I* rule here, not him! If we just stick to our plan, we are invincible!"

Aram laughed, shaking his head. "By the look on your warriors' faces, Lucifer, I'm not too sure they believe you."

Unwinding the shimmering chain from his waist, he walked about, holding it out for all to see, and asked, "Does this look like a myth to you? Your Creator fashioned it Himself and placed it into my hands for safekeeping. The clock is ticking, fallen ones. It's ticking for you...and for your kingdom."

"Bah! We'll see who rules here!" Lucifer said.

He raised his serpentine blade, but a blur of wings once again interrupted his attack as two smaller demons interposed themselves between the two combatants.

"Lord Lucifer!" they cried in unison.

"Can't you see I'm busy here?" the fallen Cherub grumbled.

"Lord Lucifer! I am Tsiyr. My escort and I have been sent by the Viceroy of the Great Lakes. He sends his greetings and—"

"Yes! Yes! Out with it! What's the message?"

The demon gave Aram a scornful look. "Not here, sire. Let us not talk in front of these...these...these Guardians."

Lucifer's wings extended explosively, and his bodyguards flinched in terror. "They are of no consequence, fool! Speak freely or be prepared to join them in the Pit!"

"As...As...you wish, my Lord. There is trouble...near the northern border. We thought we had it under control, but there's been another outbreak."

"An outbreak? What kind of outbreak?"

"The...the b-boy," the sprite stammered, "that...that died in the car wreck. The one that the enemy recently stole from you."

"Steven?"

"Yes, that's the one. His death has caused unusual stirrings in his community. At first, we were on top of it. We besieged his family with grief and depression containing them nicely, as usual, but—"

"But?"

"We don't know. Something has happened to them and his friends. It's as if the void his death has left in their lives has shaken many of them to the depths of their souls."

"You fool! That's what we want to happen! You dare to bother me with this trivia?"

"Hold on, your worship. There's more. This time, it's different. The boy's death has caused many of them to return to their first love. They are starting to seek—*Him*—again. A small but significant outbreak has occurred in that city by the great lake."

Lucifer grimaced, and he massaged his left eye. "Which city?" he asked through gritted teeth.

"The large one on the south shore with the meandering river. The outbreak there has grown the last few weeks, and it shows no signs of subsiding. I'm afraid our projections show that if this outbreak continues unchecked, within a decade, it will infect the nation and much of the world. Naturally, we couldn't have foreseen this un-fortuitous situation, but—"

"Arggh! Why am I surrounded by such incompetence?"

With unpredictable fury, Satan disemboweled Tsiyr's escort with a quick flick of his blade, and its slimy innards spewed onto the ground as a putrid tarry substance. Before the fiend's body could hit the ground, it imploded, leaving a smelly black fog to settle in the air. The sticky mess on the ground festered and boiled as it worked its way into the earth, leaving a dark stain where nothing would ever grow again.

Lucifer turned to address the quaking messenger who was now hovering at treetop level. "Well?"

Tsiyr started to speak, then turned tail and rocketed into the sky without another word. He quickly vanished over the mountain.

"It never fails," the fallen Cherub said as he turned his attention back to Aram. "I've just been informed of a pressing matter that I need to attend to. Unfortunately, I will be unable to finish our contest at this time. My friends here will be willing to give you a little demonstration of *their* skill, though...if you wish."

Bowing low with exaggerated politeness, Aram said, "I am at their disposal, your worm-ship."

"Very well!" Nodding to his biggest warriors, Lucifer ordered, "Shachath! Ratsach! Maggepah! Deal with these mangy curs. The rest of you, follow me!"

Lucifer's powerful legs propelled him into the afternoon sky, his enormous wings biting harshly into the thin mountain air. Within seconds, all but three of the largest demons were gone.

Coaxing Da-Ved behind him, Aram cautioned, "This won't take long, Da-Ved. Just wait here and keep out of the way."

Before Da-Ved could protest, Ratsach strode to the center of the clearing to challenge them. Being the largest of the three demons, he boasted, "Aram! Remember me? I am Ratsach, the Manslayer! And you are correct, Guardian. This won't take long."

Ratsach bore his three-ton bulk on his sixteen-foot frame well, a formidable opponent for any number of Guardians. His only attire consisted of a skirt of knee-length chainmail clasped at his waist by a thick leather belt and two bands of brass encompassing his sixty-inch biceps.

His mane of shaggy red hair tumbled onto his massive back and was tied behind him in warrior fashion. The demon also sported a bushy red beard braided into six separate strands; each strand decorated with a small skull-shaped bell that jingled as he moved about.

Numerous battle wounds crisscrossed his chest and back, building up a thick armor of scar tissue upon his upper torso. Ratsach's great face also bore the grisly marks of combat with a plate-sized metal patch covering his right eye.

Finally, the titan's enormous weight was supported by two massive bovine-like legs culminating in a pair of cloven hooves.

His weapons of choice were a matched set of double-bladed battle-axes. Their razor-sharp profiles bore the likeness of double-headed dragons.

The burly demon taunted his two companions, "I'll take the large one. You two think you can handle the scrawny one?"

Using his forty-foot wingspan to his advantage, Ratsach cut the large clearing in half. Normally, any advantage of speed and agility would be negated when the battleground was corralled into such a small space, but no demon ever fought a Guardian such as Aram before.

"Are you sure you want to do this?" Aram asked his enormous opponent.

"No quarter! No mercy!" was Ratsach's only reply.

The large demon feinted once at Aram's legs with one axe, then proceeded to make a pivoting roundhouse chop with the other meaning to decapitate the Guardian. Not fooled by Ratsach's feint, Aram repelled the demon's savage attack, warding off the blow with the heaviest part of his sword.

Again and again, blade collided with battle-axe, and the monstrous weapons caromed off each other in a shower of celestial sparks. The enraged demon continued his withering attack, spinning the battle-axes like lethal windmills before him. In a blinding onslaught of flashing metal razors, he brutally charged Aram who once again deflected the demon's savage blows effortlessly.

Ratsach's great size and bulk were no match for Aram's agility and skill with his blade, and the merciless assault met with disastrous results for Lucifer's most boastful bodyguard.

Using his great momentum, Ratsach lunged forward, but Aram bent low and ducked his head, sidestepping the rampaging demon as he rushed by. Ratsach's explosive charge exposed his back and left flank to Aram's slashing blade who immediately capitalized upon the huge demon's miscalculation.

Without rising or turning, Aram ran his blade through the demonic gladiator in one quick backward thrust, felling Ratsach like a large tree. The brute hit hard in a thundering crash and started to writhe and twist about upon the ground. Within a few seconds, Ratsach folded in upon himself again and again until he was small enough to fall into the Abyss.

Poof! He disappeared from Earth's physical plane of existence.

Shachath and Maggepah stood slack-jawed at the edge of the clearing. Through millennia, they'd witnessed Ratsach's maniacal and devastating assaults against much worse odds and had never seen him beaten off. His opponents always retreated under the terrible onslaught of the whirling battle-axes.

Now they'd just witnessed their champion dispatched into the Abyss by a Guardian half Ratsach's size. Though neither Shachath nor Maggepah were anywhere near the size of Ratsach, they both were larger than Aram and were skillful and experienced warriors.

Aram straightened up and spoke to them in a hushed tone. "Well, my friends, what's it going to be? Shall we continue the demonstration?"

The two demons looked at each other and, without protest, threw their weapons noisily to the ground.

"No way, Aram! We have no quarrel with you. Go in peace," growled Shachath.

"And you, Maggepah? Do you agree with your friend? Or do you wish to cross blades?"

Maggepah added his large shield to the discarded weapons. "No. Let Lucifer do his own dirty work. I'll not stand against you, Guardian. Take your friend and leave this place."

With that peace offering, Maggepah and Shachath silently faded into the woods.

*****

Scanning the empty clearing Aram said, "It looks like we're alone, Da-Ved. Are you ready to go home?"

Da-Ved stood in the middle of the clearing, his mouth open with incredulity. "Whoa there, Aram! That's all you have to say? Are you ready to go home? Are you serious? That was fantastic! I've seen you in combat before, but never like this! You let Ratsach charge right by you until you were ready to take him. That was awesome!"

"Thanks, but I only did what I was pushed into."

Da-Ved looked to the spot where Maggepah and Shachath had entered the woods. "Ratsach certainly wanted your head, but the other two seemed a bit reluctant to me."

"As was I. Maggepah and Shachath were once close friends of mine before that cursed Day of Rebellion. I-I didn't want to harm them. I think they felt the same way about me."

"What will happen to them?" Da-Ved asked. "Lucifer will be sure to declare them as traitors."

"I suppose so. But I believe he has his hands pretty full for now. With a little luck, Maggepah and Shachath should be able to disappear into some unimportant backwater or deserted wilderness. He won't find them."

"Do you honestly think they'll be able to do that? Is it possible?"

"I don't see why not. There's a lot of unexplored territory on the planet. They can live in the mountains and the deserts or they can even hide on some remote island. There's plenty of places for them to hide out of Lucifer's sight. The hard part will be limiting their contact with the humans, but it's been done before. Believe me, those two aren't the first soldiers to have fallen into Lucifer's disfavor. Many a tale of giant forest creatures are based on sightings of these fallen ones. And besides, the way things are going, I don't think Lucifer will be able to spend too much time hunting for them. If they keep a low profile, they should be able to live in a modicum of peace and safety. For a while anyhow."

"But there's no real escape for them, is there?"

Aram looked away, and his voice became husky. "No, I'm afraid not."

He coughed, clearing his throat. "One day, His Majesty will return, and Satan will be bound in chains and cast into the Abyss for a thousand years. Eventually, Maggepah and Shachath will also be hunted down, bound, and cast into the everlasting fire that was prepared for the devil and his angels."

Da-Ved looked confused. "You don't seem very pleased, old friend. Won't that day be a day of great victory for us?"

With tears streaming down both cheeks, Aram replied in a subdued voice, "Yes."

Seeing the tears, Da-Ved asked, "Then why are you so heavy-hearted?"

The big Guardian didn't answer right away.

"Aram?"

Hanging his head, Aram whispered, "Because I'll be the one with the chains."

The natural person does not accept the things of the Spirit of God, for they are folly to him, and he is not able to understand them because they are spiritually discerned.

—1 Corinthians 2:14 (ESV)

EPILOGUE

DECEMBER 25 – 6:00 PM
FRESNO, CALIFORNIA

Robert Tiffin pulled into his driveway and hit the garage door opener squirreled away under his car's sun visor. The door rose slowly, and he parked the big Chevy inside.

For him, the end of his annual visit to the family homestead over the Christmas holiday came too quickly, and he had reluctantly headed home. The one-hour return trip from Porterville to Fresno would have been longer if he hadn't known about a shortcut, but even then, by the time he entered his neighborhood, the city lights were coming on, and he was glad the drive was behind him.

Shutting the car off, he pressed the trunk's release button and got out to gather his share of the assorted bags of goodies and leftovers from the Christmas feast his mother had prepared for the family.

He entered his residence through the kitchen garage door, slipped out of his coat, and cast it onto a kitchen chair. As he opened the refrigerator, he smiled at the thought of the meals he would glean from this treasure-trove of food. His mother was an excellent cook, and she always made way too much food for the Tiffin family Christmas dinner. He deposited the bags on the bottom shelf and grabbed a beer to quench his blossoming thirst.

He then made his way to the living room, kicked off his shoes, and plunked down onto his oversized couch. Taking a pull on the longneck, he plopped his big feet on the well-worn coffee table in front of him and turned on the TV remotely. The large Sony pinged to life, and he clicked through several channels looking for the evening news. He settled on channel six.

*****

EARLY EVENING TELEVISION BROADCAST

BILL SALE. Season's Greetings, everyone. I'm Bill Sale.

CHERYL WASHINGTON. And I'm Cheryl Washington, and this is *News at Six.*

ANNOUNCER. Stay tuned for local and state news and our weather forecast with Channel Six's own meteorologist, Dan Liston."

*****

Music and promotional lead-in

BILL SALE. Hey, what's with this crazy weather, Dan?

DAN LISTON. I don't know, Bill, but it's safe to say that folks in the normally quiet mountain town of Job had a holiday they won't soon forget. Snow, rain, lightning, and a reported funnel cloud had the residents there pretty nervous for a while. But we'll get into all that a little later. Bill?"

BILL SALE. Besides the bizarre weather, we also have a number of puzzling reports coming out of that part of the state. Cheryl, just what the devil is going on in Job tonight? Some of these stories are bordering on the fantastic, aren't they?

CHERYL WASHINGTON. Yes, we've received a few unbelievably bizarre stories from the residents of that secluded community today, but none more troubling than the report of a man found dead in a deserted midtown back alley.

BILL SALE. Gosh, Cheryl, that story sounds somewhat out of place for the holiday season to me.

CHERYL WASHINGTON. That's true, Bill. It's a very disturbing story, not the sort of news we'd expect during the Christmas holiday. The body of a homeless man was found in an alley early this morning near the intersection of Fulton and Silver avenues in Job. Authorities say the man expired sometime the day before, most likely during the early evening hours, and at this time, it appears he died from exposure. Police have started an investigation as to how the man may have got there and why he wasn't in a shelter. For more on this story, we're going live to our on-scene reporter, Lisa Silverton. Lisa, just how did this man fall through the public safety net last night?

LISA SILVERTON, *via split-screen TV broadcast*. Good evening, everyone. Authorities aren't saying much at this point Cheryl, but I'm sure they'll be asking some rather poignant questions in the next few days as this story continues to unfold. I think it saddens us all when something like this happens, especially during the winter holidays. All of the local shelters were open last night, but in a small community like this, I suppose their resources were stretched pretty tight."

BILL SALE. Lisa, are you saying that some people may have been turned away from the shelters last night? Were they that full?

LISA SILVERTON. We have no report of that occurring at this time, Bill, but we're continuing to look at that. I think the local church folk will be doing some real soul-searching after a tragedy such as this. I mean, it's hard to comprehend how someone could have fallen through the cracks of Social Services like this when the nation has had such a stellar economic recovery. Bill? Cheryl?

BILL SALE. Yes, a senseless tragedy, Lisa, as well as a sad ending to human life. It's a real failure by our secular and religious leaders. And this certainly cheapens the real meaning of Christmas. I hate to say it, but even the homeless Christ child was able to find lodging for that one evening in Bethlehem. It's going to be difficult to see anything good coming out of this holiday season. At least it will be for the residents in Job.

CHERYL WASHINGTON. Tsk, tsk. Yes, Bill, such a senseless loss.

BILL SALE. We'll be right back, folks, after this commercial message from one of our local sponsors.

Yet among the mature we do impart wisdom, although it is not a wisdom of this age or of the rulers of this age, who are doomed to pass away. But we impart a secret and hidden wisdom of God, which God decreed before the ages for our glory. None of the rulers of this age understood this, for if they had, they would not have crucified the Lord of glory. But, as it is written, "What no eye has seen, nor ear heard, nor the heart of man imagined, what God has prepared for those who love him"—these things God has revealed to us through the Spirit. For the Spirit searches everything, even the depths of God. For who knows a person's thoughts except the spirit of that person, which is in him? So also no one comprehends the thoughts of God except the Spirit of God. Now we have received not the spirit of the world, but the Spirit who is from God, that we might understand the things freely given us by God. And we impart this in words not taught by human wisdom but taught by the Spirit, interpreting spiritual truths to those who are spiritual. The natural person does not accept the things of the Spirit of God, for they are folly to him, and he is not able to understand them because they are spiritually discerned.

—1 Corinthians 2:6–14 (ESV)

GLOSSARY

The supernatural characters in this story are based upon the biblical belief of the reality of angels and their antagonistic counterparts—fallen angels/demons. The names of these characters as employed in this book reveal their nature and or temperament and are derived from portions of *Strong's Exhaustive Concordance of the Bible* using Hebrew, Chaldee, and Greek dictionaries.

Based on Hebrew, Chaldean, and Greek words taken from *Strong's Exhaustive Concordance of the Bible*, which is in the Public Domain.

Word Number—Definition/ Character/How it is used in this story

Aram (758)—from the highland/ Son of Shem Commander of the Heavenly Host.

Arioch (746)—captain of the king's guard in the book of Daniel/ Guardian angel of James Townsend.

Ariy'el (739)—lion of God/ Guardian angel of Steven Thorn.

Asthenes (772)—Greek: sick, weakness/ Demon of illness attacking James Townsend.

Ba'al (1168)—Hebrew: Baal, master, a Phoenician deity/ Used to call Lucifer Lord. Ba'al Lucifer.

Berakah (1293)—Hebrew: prosperity, blessing, present/The Blessing of a life restored.

Bachiyr (972)—Hebrew: chosen one, elect/ God's chosen people; the Jewish people.

Chayil (2428)—Hebrew: force, army, worthy, valiant/ Yanah's former angelic identity as one of God's angels.

Chareb (2717)—Hebrew: to parch, destroy, slayer/ A member of Lucifer's personal guard.

David (1732) loving, youngest son of Jesse/ Messenger of Blessing sent to the city of Job (spelled Da-Ved).

Drakon (1404)—Greek: serpent, dragon/ Gatekeeper of Ravenwood Psychiatric Institute.

Sha'ar (8176)—Hebrew: split, open, to act as gatekeeper/ The dragon Gatekeeper).

Iyr (5894)—Chaldean: watcher, an angel as guardian/ A guardian in Charity Hospital.

Ganan (1598)—to hedge about, protect, defend/ Frank Chamberlain's Guardian Angel.

Gath (1661)—the Philistine city where Goliath lived/ A gigantic demon named Gathen.

Gedeón (1066)—Hebrew: one of the judges of Israel/ A Guardian inside Charity Hospital.

Gibbor (1368)—Hebrew: powerful warrior, tyrant, strong (man)/ The demonic strong man in charge of Ravenwood.

Ke'phiyr (3715)—Hebrew: young lion/ The lion sentry of the angelic fortress called a Mibtsar.

Maggepah (4046)—Hebrew: pestilence, slaughter, destroy/ A member of Lucifer's personal guard.

Mal'ak (4397)—Hebrew: messenger, angel, minister/ A sentry of the Sapphire Gate leading into heaven.

Mibtsar (4013)—Hebrew: fortress, castle, defender/ An angel fortress hovering over the city of Job.

Miyka'el (4317)—Hebrew: who is like God/ Archangel of God & Guardian of Israel.

Negeph (5063)—an infection, plague, disease, stumbling/A demon Overlord.

Ne'tsach (5331)—Hebrew: the bright object at a distance traveled towards/ An angelic sentry at one of heaven's twelve gates.

Oreb (6158)—Hebrew: raven (black)/ Guardian angel assisting Ariy'el.

Pharmakos (5333)—Greek: sorcerer, witchcraft, drug, potion/ The demonic Viceroy of the stronghold of addiction.

Qadosh (6918)—Hebrew: holy ones, God/ Referring to the Holy Spirit.

Ruwach (7307)—Hebrew: wind, breath, spirit/ Spirit.

Ratsach (7523)–to dash in pieces,—kill (a human) manslayer/ A member of Lucifer's personal guard.

Se-Lah (5553) to be lofty, a craggy rock or fortress rock/An angelic sentry at one of heaven's twelve gates.

Shachath (7843)— to decay, corrupt, destroy, ruin/ A member of Lucifer's personal guard.

Shamar (8104)—watchman/ The ranking Guardian Angel of the city of Job.

Shareth (8355)—minister, servant/ The Servant Sentry of the angel fortress over Job.

Shekar (7941)—alcoholic drink, intoxicant/ Demon of alcoholism attacking James Townsend.

Sheol (7585)—Hebrew: hades, hell, the grave/ The abode of the lost dead.

She'Ol (7585)—Hebrew: hades, hell, the grave/ The personification of the grave. One of Lucifer's generals.

Tabbach (2876)—Hebrew: butcher, executioner, guard/ A guard at Ravenswood.

Thanatos (2288)—Greek: death/ The personification of Death/ One of Lucifer's generals.

Tsiyr (6735)—Hebrew: mental pressure, herald, pain/ A demonic messenger.

Yanah (3238)—Hebrew: rage, oppression, violent/ Commander of Satan's forces at Charity Hospital.

ENDNOTES

1. Lyrics—"Abide with Me" written by Henry Lyte in 1847.
2. Lyrics—"Abide with Me" written by Henry Lyte in 1847.
3. Lyrics—"Abide with Me" written by Henry Lyte in 1847.
4. Based on Romans 8:38–39 (KJV).
5. Based on Psalm 147:1–7 (ESV).
6. Based on Isaiah 35:3, 4 (ESV)
7. Loosely based on Isaiah 61:1 (ESV).
8. Loosely based on Psalm 27:6 (KJV) and Ezekiel 34:22–26 (KJV).
9. Based on Psalm 24:7–10 (KJV).
10. Based on Jeremiah 50:31–34 (KJV)
11. Based on Psalm 27:7–11 (KJV).
12. Lyrics to the hymn "Angels from the Realms of Glory" written by James Montgomery in 1816.
13. Lyrics to the hymn "Angels from the Realms of Glory" written by James Montgomery in 1816.

Printed in the USA
CPSIA information can be obtained
at www.ICGtesting.com
CBHW020030020824
12556CB00038B/355

9 781685 172718